Nietzsche and the 'Problem' of Morality

STUDIES IN THEORETICAL AND APPLIED ETHICS

Sherwin Klein
General Editor

Vol. 9

PETER LANG
New York • Washington, D.C./Baltimore • Bern
Frankfurt am Main • Berlin • Brussels • Vienna • Oxford

Frank Cameron

Nietzsche and the 'Problem' of Morality

PETER LANG
New York • Washington, D.C./Baltimore • Bern
Frankfurt am Main • Berlin • Brussels • Vienna • Oxford

Library of Congress Cataloging-in-Publication Data

Cameron, Frank.
Nietzsche and the 'problem' of morality / Frank Cameron.
p. cm. — (Studies in theoretical and applied ethics; v. 9)
Includes bibliographical references and index.
1. Nietzsche, Friedrich Wilhelm, 1844–1900—Ethics. I. Title. II. Series.
B3318.E9 C35 170'.92—dc21 2002067542
ISBN 0-8204-6202-0
ISSN 1086-6809

Die Deutsche Bibliothek-CIP-Einheitsaufnahme

Cameron, Frank:
Nietzsche and the 'problem' of morality / Frank Cameron.
–New York; Washington, D.C./Baltimore; Bern;
Frankfurt am Main; Berlin; Brussels; Vienna; Oxford: Lang.
(Studies in theoretical and applied ethics; Vol. 9)
ISBN 0-8204-6202-0

The paper in this book meets the guidelines for permanence and durability
of the Committee on Production Guidelines for Book Longevity
of the Council of Library Resources.

Printed in the United States of America

for JACKIE

Contents

Acknowledgments

I would like to express my gratitude to Professor Hilliard Aronovitch for his insightful comments. These remarks not only improved the quality of this book, but also had a sobering effect on my Nietzsche-philia. Thanks are also due to Don Dombowsky and Professors Thomas Hurka, Catherine Collobert, Denis Dumas, Daniele Letocha, and Sherwin Klein for reviewing my work at various stages. In addition, I would like to express my appreciation to Tom Bailey, Brian Leiter, Kathleen Higgins, Thomas Brobjer, and Herman Siemens for their academic generosity and encouragement. A special thanks goes out to Keith Ansell-Pearson and the Philosophy Department at the University of Warwick for inviting me to present a paper at the Second Annual Nietzsche Workshop, June 6, 2001.

On a more personal level, I am grateful to the friendships that were formed during my academic career in Ottawa. I have benefited both intellectually and socially from my experiences with Sébastien Charles, Omid Payrow-Shabani, Don Dombowsky, and Derrick Farnham. Finally, my deepest thanks and appreciation go to my family, especially to my mother, Diane Cameron. It is on account of you that I am able to say—*'how could I fail to be grateful to my whole life?'*

Key to Abbreviations

Primary sources are cited, whenever possible, parenthetically in the text by an abbreviation of the English edition (and the section number), immediately followed by an abbreviation of the German edition (the volume number, and page number) in the Giorgio Colli and Mazzino Montinari critical edition of Nietzsche's writings: Friedrich Nietzsche, *Sämtliche Werke, Kritische Studienausgabe* (Berlin: de Gruyter, 1988) in 15 volumes. One exception is Nietzsche's *Philosophy in the Tragic Age of the Greeks* where a page number (and not the section number) follows the English abbreviation. For Nietzsche's published writings, I have relied primarily on the English translations of Walter Kaufmann and R.J. Hollingdale. While privileging the published works, I have on occasion cited from Nietzsche's notebooks (KSA 7–13).

Nietzsche's Writings

KSA *Friedrich Nietzsche. Sämtliche Werke: Kritische Studienausgabe* (15 volumes). G. Colli and M. Montinari, eds. Berlin: de Gruyter, 1988.

KSB *Friedrich Nietzsche. Sämtliche Briefe: Kritische Studienausgabe* (8 volumes). G. Colli and M. Montinari, eds. Berlin: de Gruyter, 1986.

BT *The Birth of Tragedy* (1872). Walter Kaufmann, tr. New York: Random House, 1967.

PTG *Philosophy in the Tragic Age of the Greeks* (1873). Marianne Cowan, tr. Washington, D.C.: Regnery Publishing, 1962.

UADH *The Uses and Disadvantages of History for Life* (1874) in *Untimely Meditations.* R.J. Hollingdale, tr. Cambridge: Cambridge University Press, 1983.

CWFN *Complete Works of Friedrich Nietzsche*, Vol. 11, *Unpublished Writings from the Period of* Unfashionable Observations. Richard T. Gray, tr. Stanford: Stanford University Press, 1995.

SE *Schopenhauer as Educator* in Hollingdale 1983.

HH *Human, All Too Human* (vol. 1) (1878). R.J. Hollingdale, tr. Cambridge: Cambridge University Press, 1986.

AOM *Assorted Opinions and Maxims* (1879) (volume 2, first part of *Human, All Too Human*) in Hollingdale, tr. 1986.

WS *The Wanderer and his Shadow* (1880) (volume 2, second part of *Human, All Too Human*) in Hollingdale, tr. 1986.

D *Daybreak* (1881), R.J. Hollingdale, tr. Cambridge: Cambridge University Press, 1982.

GS *The Gay Science* (1882; second edition with book v and an appendix of songs, 1887). Walter Kaufmann, tr. New York: Random House, 1974.

Z *Thus Spoke Zarathustra* (1883–5) in *The Portable Nietzsche*. W. Kaufmann, tr. and ed. New York: Viking, 1954.

BGE *Beyond Good and Evil* (1886). Walter Kaufmann, tr. New York: Random House, 1966.

GM *On the Genealogy of Morals* (1887). Walter Kaufmann, tr. New York: Random House, 1967.

TI *Twilight of the Idols* (written 1888, first edition 1889). Walter Kaufmann, tr. *The Portable Nietzsche*, 1954.

A *The Antichrist* (written 1888, first edition 1895). Walter Kaufmann, tr. *The Portable Nietzsche*, 1954.

EH *Ecce Homo* (written 1888, first edition 1908). Walter Kaufmann, tr. New York: Random House, 1967.

WP *The Will to Power* (Notes from Nietzsche's *Nachlaß*—posthumously published writings—of the period 1883–88, collected under the title *Der Wille zur Macht* by Nietzsche's sister, Elisabeth Forster-Nietzsche; 1st edition published 1901, 2nd edition published 1906 containing 1 067 sections). W. Kaufmann and R.J. Hollingdale, tr. New York: Random House, 1967.

VP *La Volonté de puissance*, 2 vol. G. Bianquis, trad. Paris: Gallimard, 1947.

Introduction

> **How is it, one may ask, that philosophers today do not even try to refute Nietzsche, and seem to feel morality as firm as ever under their feet? Why do we not argue with him as we argue with other philosophers of the past? Part of the answer seems to be that a confrontation with Nietzsche is a difficult thing to arrange.**[1]

It is the task of this work to arrange such a confrontation, that is, to examine Nietzsche's views on morality in order to assess his contribution to moral philosophy. In this study, I argue that Nietzsche presents a *positive* morality based on human flourishing, and that his *attack* on the prevailing, Christian morality can only be understood within the context of his fundamental 'ethical' preoccupation with exemplary individuals. Consistent with his view that values reflect the needs and interests served for particular classes or 'types' of human beings, Nietzsche rejects 'morality' insofar as it functions within society to preserve the 'herd' at the expense of those potential 'higher types' whose flourishing resides elsewhere. At the same time, Nietzsche realizes that since the 'herd' are quite content with their morality, it is unlikely that they will be concerned with or receptive to his promotion of human excellence. Hence, Nietzsche sets out to persuade a select readership, only 'those who have ears to hear', through a reliance on *performative* justification. In other words, his power of persuasion depends not on a discursive critique but on the capacity of Zarathustra and himself (based on his *heroic* self-characterization in *Ecce Homo*) to serve as models of human greatness to be emulated by those physiological successes which have yet to bloom. My study aims to fill in the details of this general outline.

There are five major themes discussed in this work that I considered crucial for a comprehensive examination of Nietzsche as a 'moral philosopher'. These include the following:

1. Nietzsche's understanding of 'morality', including his genealogical approach to the subject.
2. Nietzsche's *critique* of morality—the '*Feldzug gegen die Moral*'.
3. Nietzsche's *positive* morality.
4. Nietzsche's *moral* influences/educators.

---

1 Philippa Foot, "Nietzsche: The Revaluation of Values" in Robert C. Solomon (ed.), *Nietzsche: A Collection of Critical Essays*. New York: Anchor Press, 1973, pp.156–57.

5. Nietzsche's relation to the moral tradition.

While it is certainly the case that within the voluminous secondary literature on Nietzsche, one can find accounts of all these themes taken individually, there has been no study until now which has incorporated all of these aspects together. Thomas Brobjer's *Nietzsche's Ethics of Character: A Study of Nietzsche's Ethics and its Place in the History of Moral Thinking*[2] has broached most of these topics, but as I will argue, Brobjer ignores two of Nietzsche's main moral influences, Arthur Schopenhauer and Paul Rée, and mistakenly situates Nietzsche's ethics within the tradition of virtue ethics. Even still, the merit of my work does not lie exclusively or primarily in its ability to pool together the numerous literature on Nietzsche's work on *rebus moralibus*. In many instances, the interpretations defended here are a response to popular readings of Nietzsche which have appeared to me misguided and inaccurate.

Before engaging Nietzsche's attack on morality, it is necessary to clarify his understanding of 'morality'. This is the task of my first chapter which begins with an account of Nietzsche's natural history of morals and its evolution into a *valuative* history expressed by means of a genealogy of morals. Nietzsche's genealogical method reveals that there are essentially two types of morality: master/noble morality and slave morality. In addition to their historical importance, Nietzsche attempts to understand moral values in general as surface values, mere symptoms or signs underlying a particular physiological condition—in short, moralities are either representative of ascending life (as in master or noble morality) or declining life (as in slave morality). Yet, Nietzsche is never to be viewed as a disinterested historian of morality. In labeling himself an 'immoralist', Nietzsche reveals the scope of his attack on morality, declaring war on Christian morality and its secular surrogates (i.e. moralities which deny God but which remain under the spell of Christianity's morality of pity and equality). My fundamental concern in the first chapter is to articulate the importance of physiology for an understanding of Nietzsche's conception of morality since it relates directly to his repudiation of morality, and to his foremost ethical concern—the production of exemplary individuals (both of which comprise the content of later chapters). I intentionally avoided discussion of my own preconceived notion of 'morality' in order to let Nietzsche explain to his readership what *he* understands by the term '*Moral*' (in addition to the other German expressions he employs). This approach was motivated by my frustration at discovering various commentators smuggling in their own conception of morality, and then evaluating Nietzsche's application of the term accordingly.

---

[2] T. Brobjer, *Nietzsche's Ethics of Character*, Uppsala: Uppsala University Press, 1995.

The second chapter is devoted to an examination of Nietzsche's critique of morality. Having identified Christian morality as the target of Nietzsche's virulent attack, I proceed to discuss the components of this morality which he finds so objectionable. The point of this chapter is to show that these various strands of morality dovetail into one major objection, an objection based on Nietzsche's anti-egalitarian belief in an order of rank among human beings: Morality, insofar as it represents the interests and needs of the herd, hinders the development of human flourishing in the rare few, with different interests and needs. Nietzsche's campaign against morality, then, is directed against Christian morality as it stifles the 'higher type's' potential for greatness.

In Chapter Three, I argue that Nietzsche's campaigning spirit extends from morality to moral philosophy (*Ethik*, *Moral-Philosophie*), where he offers a critical evaluation of moral philosophers, many of whom he derisively dubs, 'the preachers of morals' (*Moralprediger*). As part of my task to arrange a confrontation with Nietzsche, and realizing that I could not possibly discuss Nietzsche's relation to every moral philosopher with whom he engages, I decided to focus on five moral philosophers—two who inspired Nietzsche's interest in (and reaction to) ethics (Schopenhauer and Rée), and three others, (J.S. Mill, Immanuel Kant, and Aristotle), each representing one of the major moral traditions. In this way, I was able to trace Nietzsche's early influences and assess his contribution to moral philosophy.[3] While it is obvious that Nietzsche is a critic of utilitarianism and Kantian ethics, there have been recent efforts to situate his moral thinking within the virtue ethics tradition. After reviewing Nietzsche's evaluations of the prominent figures representing all three traditions, I argue that he stands before each one as a *critic*. Yet, I emphatically resist the suggestion that we must therefore conclude that Nietzsche has no positive morality. The inability to place Nietzsche within the moral tradition does not indicate that his moral legacy is restricted to being a 'critic' of morality. The remaining two chapters are intended to support this contention.

Nietzsche's absence from the moral tradition has not prevented commentators from recognizing his ethical concern with exemplary human beings. In Chapter Four, I examine the 'perfectionist' readings of Nietzsche which have been inspired by Stanley Cavell's correction of John Rawls' account of Nietzschean perfectionism. Relying on Daniel Conway's distinction between Nietzsche's *moral* and *political* perfectionism (i.e. attending to the perfection of

---

3 Although I feel justified with my selection of these five philosophers, I hope to one day pursue Nietzsche's other moral influences, most notably, the French Moralists (especially LaRochefoucauld, Chamfort, and Vauvenargues), Emerson, J.M. Guyau, W.H. Rolph, Spencer, as well as some of the historians of morals whom Nietzsche had read, e.g. W.E.H. Lecky, H.L. Martensen, and J.J. Baumann.

oneself versus a social policy based on the institutionally designed production of human excellence), I discuss the relation between Nietzsche's perfectionism and his demand for a 'revaluation of all values'. I argue that Nietzsche's *moral* perfectionism corresponds temporally to the *early* stages of the 'revaluation' indicating that Nietzsche's ethical ideal of human flourishing is attainable within (decadent) late modernity.

Having established that Nietzsche's ethic of human flourishing is applicable to modernity, I turn, in Chapter Five, to an examination of the specific affirmative ideals (i.e. '*amor fati*', 'eternal return', 'give *style* to one's character', and 'become what one is') which Nietzsche advances on behalf of his 'higher type'. While there is nothing new or astonishing about claiming that Nietzsche advances an ethic of human flourishing, what will no doubt surprise readers is the *anti-voluntaristic* model of human flourishing defended here. Specifically, I argue that Nietzsche is a *fatalist* insofar as he believes that what a person becomes is determined by natural facts about that person. Whether or not one can become a 'higher type' is decided at birth, according to one's natural endowments. The common reading of Nietzsche, which I challenge throughout the text, is that human excellence is a matter of self-creation or self-fashioning which can be accomplished by dint of an act of free will. I contend that although human excellence is not the product of choice, but based on one's natural physical constitution, this does not deprive Nietzsche of advancing his ideal of human flourishing or promoting a 'revaluation of all values'. There are external factors (e.g. education, values) which might influence a person's life, even though these external factors must yield to the limits circumscribed by the natural facts. Finally, I argue that Nietzsche aims to promote his ethical ideal by means of a *performative* justification where he presents the character of Zarathustra (*Thus Spoke Zarathustra*) as well as himself (*Ecce Homo*) as concrete exemplars of human excellence whose task it is to inspire those capable of being inspired, by convincing them that his life is a better alternative to the life that person is now living.

In conclusion, it seems to me that the success of my work is to be measured by its ability to convince readers that Nietzsche demands serious attention as a moral philosopher. It is my hope that in offering a comprehensive examination of Nietzsche's work on morality, I have succeeded in laying the groundwork for a confrontation with Nietzsche as a moral philosopher. In addition to its breadth, I also hope that my study has justified the unconventional view that Nietzsche's positive morality rests on his acceptance of fatalism, and that it will remove the longstanding prejudice that Nietzsche is a philosopher of self-creation.

1

The *'Moralities'* of an Immoralist: A Prelude to Nietzsche's *Critique* of Morality

Wandering through the many subtler and coarser moralities which have so far been prevalent on earth, or still are prevalent, I found that certain features recurred regularly together and were closely associated—until I finally discovered two basic types and one basic difference. There are *master morality* and *slave morality*...

—BGE 260, KSA 5:208

Reinigung von der Rache ist meine *Moral.*

—KSA 10:363

Problem: *was ist aber die* Moral?

—KSA 12:571

Few philosophers have written so extensively and passionately on the subject of morality as Nietzsche. In fact, he wrote that there seems to be nothing *more* worth taking seriously than the problems of morality (GM P:7, KSA 5:254). However, assessing Nietzsche's contribution to moral philosophy is no easy task. For instance, his *Nachlaß* query, "*Was ist aber die Moral?*,"[1] is answered with this rather cryptic 'definition' of morality: "morals (*Moral*)—being understood as the doctrine of the relations of supremacy (*Herrschafts-Verhältnissen*) under which the phenomenon of 'life' comes to be" (BGE 19, KSA 5:34). Far from clarifying his understanding of morality, Nietzsche's 'definition' obfuscates matters since this definition itself requires exegesis.

His status as a moral philosopher, in the constructive sense, is further compromised by several noteworthy admissions. To begin with, Nietzsche refused the title of 'moralist' in favour of 'immoralist,' which he wore "as a

1 But, what is morality?

badge of honour" (EH XIV:6, KSA 6:370). Indeed, his scathing critique of morality, sardonic remarks on the 'preachers of morals' (*Moralprediger*), reference to Zarathustra as the 'annihilator of morality' (EH III:1, KSA 6:300), a self-professed immoralism (EH XIV, KSA 6:365ff.), and his claim that he does not wish to promote any morality (GS 292, KSA 3:532), seem to support the view that Nietzsche's moral legacy is restricted to being a *critic* of morality. Alexander Nehamas, for instance, claims that Nietzsche's principal aim is to undermine the moral tradition and that his "positive morality" remains "appallingly disappointing."[2] This sentiment is shared by Alasdair MacIntyre who writes that Nietzsche's greatness does not lie in such "frivolous solutions."[3]

Nietzsche's relation to morality, however, is much more complex than the label 'immoralist' seems to warrant. For instance, he realized that before one can offer a *critique* of morality, one must first call into question the *value* of these values themselves, and this preparatory task requires an examination of the conditions which gave birth to values, as well as an account of their evolution. It is imperative, then, that we ascertain the reasons for the differences in moral climates. "Why is it", Nietzsche asks, "that the sun of one fundamental moral judgment and main standard of value shines here and another there" (GS 7, KSA 3:379)? In other words, we need to be in a position to compare many moralities (i.e. those moralities which have 'actually existed, actually been lived') and the approach best suited for such a project would be genealogical in order to arrive at an understanding of the origin (*Ursprung*) of our moral prejudices.

The problem, however, is that Nietzsche's genealogical insights lead to a relentless attack on Christian or slave morality, and consequently overshadow his affirmative views, especially his serious (ethical) concern for exemplary individuals—the purveyors of human flourishing. A comprehensive examination of Nietzsche's views on morality, then, must account for his non-pejorative, and even, positive references to morality, in addition to the more familiar critique. In this chapter, my goal is to establish the full range of Nietzsche's understanding of 'morality' by way of an analysis of his historical reflections on the subject. His natural history of morals, which considers how standards of moral valuation have varied throughout different historical periods, provides a useful framework for further discussion on moral matters. In particular, it contributes to an understanding of Nietzsche's 'definition' of morality from *Beyond Good and Evil* (*Jenseits von Gut und Böse*, 1886). Moreover, these historical insights serve as a point of reference for a related discussion of

---

2 Alexander Nehamas, *Nietzsche: Life as Literature*. Cambridge: Harvard University Press, 1985, p.221.

3 Alasdair MacIntyre, *After Virtue*. Notre Dame: Notre Dame University Press, 1981, p.114.

how he can consistently claim to be an immoralist while at the same time announce his own morality ('*meine Moral*'), and praise other moralities as 'noble,' 'healthy,' and 'higher.' Exonerating Nietzsche from this apparent inconsistency will require an examination of the nature of his 'immoralism' and his understanding of morality—only then can one be in a position to assess his celebrated 'campaign against morality.'

A Natural History of Morals

In section 32 of *Beyond Good and Evil*, Nietzsche charts the moral evolution of humankind by delineating three stages in human history: the pre-moral (*vormoralische*), moral (*moralische*), and extra-moral (*aussermoralische*). Each stage offers its own manner of evaluating human conduct. In the pre-moral period, which occupied 'the longest part of human history', the value of an action was determined by its consequences—the action itself was considered irrelevant. "It was rather the way a distinction or disgrace still reaches back today from a child to its parents, in China." Here, the concern lies in the success or failure of an act.

Life during this time was dominated by custom, and for that reason was designated by Nietzsche as a 'morality of mores' (*Sittlichkeit der Sitte*), (GM II:2, KSA 5:293).[4] The concept of the 'morality of mores' was introduced in Nietzsche's earlier reflections on the 'history of the moral sensations' from *Human, All-Too-Human* (96): "To be moral, to act in accordance with custom, to be ethical means to practise obedience towards a law or tradition established from of old." Initially, the custom functioned to maintain a community, a people: the custom has "nothing to do with good and evil or with any kind of immanent categorical imperative; it is above all directed at the preservation of a *community*, a people; every superstitious usage which has arisen on the basis of some chance event mistakenly interpreted enforces a tradition which it is in accordance with custom to follow; for to sever oneself from it is dangerous, and even more injurious to the *community* than to the individual (because the gods punish the community for misdeeds and for every violation of their privileges and only to that extent punish the individual)" (HH 96, KSA 2:93). Nietzsche explains our continued adherence to custom in terms of its capacity to inspire reverence: "every tradition now continually grows more venerable the farther away its origin lies and the more this origin is forgotten; the respect paid to it increases from generation to generation, the tradition at last becomes holy and

---

4 What is lost in the English translation is Nietzsche's playfulness with the terms *Sitte* (mores) and *Sittlichkeit* (morality). In German, the words indicate that the one is derived from the other. See also KSA 12:332: "*Die Sitte als eigentliche 'Sittlichkeit'*." ("Custom as the original 'morality'", my translation).

evokes awe and reverence" (96). Under the morality of mores, the individual views himself as a member of a community, rarely acting as an *individual*, but now "he is called 'good' who does what is customary as if by nature, as a result of a long inheritance, that is to say easily and gladly, and this is so whatever what is customary may be..." (96). This marks a transition in the consequences of obeying custom, from the preservation of the community *to* its becoming merely habitual, where the habitual has proven itself both 'pleasant' and 'useful'.[5]

Nietzsche emphasizes the power of tradition by describing "*change* as the very essence of immorality (*Unsittliche*)" (GM III:9, KSA 5:359). In fact, the free individual is considered 'immoral' (*unsittlich*) insofar as he depends upon himself rather than a tradition. Realizing that he has yet to comment on specific customs, and their subsequent effect on the development of humanity, Nietzsche offers a more detailed account of the impact that the morality of mores had on human beings. In *On the Genealogy of Morals* (*Zur Genealogie der Moral*, 1887), he explains what human beings endured in the pre-moral period.

> The tremendous labour of that which I have called 'morality of custom'...the labour performed by man upon himself during the greater part of the existence of the human race, his entire *prehistoric* labour, finds in this its meaning, its great justification, notwithstanding the severity, tyranny, and idiocy involved in it: with the aid of the morality of custom and the social straitjacket man was actually *made* calculable. (GM II:2, KSA 5:293)

The severity of this era played a significant role in making human beings 'calculable'. In order to accomplish this task, it was thought necessary to first create a memory for the human being by means of '*mnemotechnics*'—the oldest psychology on earth which embraced the principle: "If something is to stay in the memory it must be burned in: only that which never ceases to *hurt* stays in

---

5 This understanding of the morality of mores from *Human, All-Too-Human* (96, 97) and *Daybreak* (9) does not conflict with the description of the pre-moral period from *Beyond Good and Evil* (32) where the value of an act is judged according to its 'consequences'. *Prima facie*, it may appear that there is a distinction between evaluating an act according to its consequences or whether it was performed out of obedience to tradition. But, in this case, the two readings are consistent insofar as actions are evaluated according to their consequences for maintaining customs, and for continued obedience to custom. For instance, under the morality of mores, actions are evaluated according to their consequences for insinuating oneself with supernatural spirits, maintaining rituals, and removing perceived guilt or punishments from the community (i.e. 'imaginary causalities', D 10, KSA 3:24). Note, that this 'consequentialist' view is nothing like the narrow, utilitarian conception, since moral worth does not lie in numbers, but rather in obedience to tradition. It is the community, and not the individual which is the basic unit of value.

the memory" (GM II:3, KSA 5:295). This tactic was based on the view that pain is the most effective means to mnemonics. During this time, such things as 'suffering', 'cruelty', 'dissembling', 'revenge', and 'slander of reason' were considered virtues, while 'well-being', 'thirst for knowledge', 'peace', and 'pity' ranked among the dangers (GM III:9, KSA 5:359). Nietzsche's main point is that the pre-moral period was crucial for shaping the development of humanity. For instance, he claims that the morality of mores preceded 'world history', and marked "the truly decisive history that determined the character of mankind" (III:9). The morality of mores, then, is the inaugural step on the path of humanity's moral development and is a defining feature of the pre-moral period. With these fundamental insights into the origin of morality, Nietzsche wanted to bring this much 'older' and 'primitive species' of morality to the attention of his readers since it differs *toto caelo* from the present-day reigning moral ideal—the altruistic mode of evaluation.[6]

It is the next period, the moral (*moralische*), which leaves the greatest impression on Nietzsche. The moral period, spanning 'the last ten thousand years', marks the gradual transition from a morality of custom to an intention-oriented mode for evaluating actions, and represents a 'reversal of perspective'. It is the 'origin' of an act which now decides its value, and this period is characterized as "the unconscious aftereffect of the rule of aristocratic values and the faith in 'descent' ('*Herkunft*')" (BGE 32, KSA 5:50). In particular, this stage marks our first attempt at self-knowledge insofar as human beings begin to reflect on the moral motives of their actions. The 'individual' acts in accord with a free will, and hence becomes subject to moral judgment. It is this second period of human history, understood as 'moral in the narrower sense,' in which Nietzsche will reserve his criticism. He writes: "The intention (*Absicht*) as the whole origin and prehistory of an action—almost to the present day this prejudice has dominated moral praise, blame, judgment, and philosophy on earth" (BGE 32, KSA 5:51). Nietzsche maintains that the conscious antecedents of an act are unknowable (GS 335, KSA 3:563). In other words, we lack epistemological access to the real motives of our acts. Instead, he insists that they are merely signs or symptoms whose value is rooted in an unconscious source. His rejection of this fundamental aspect of the moral period led to the anticipation of a new period, the 'extra-moral' (*aussermoralische*).

Nietzsche begins by asking "Don't we stand at the threshold of a period which should be designated negatively, to begin with, as *extra-moral*?" It has

---

6 KSA 12:153: "*Es fehlt das Wissen und Bewusstsein davon, welche Umdrehungen bereits das moralische Urtheil denn durchgemacht hat, und wie wirklich mehrere Male schon im gründlichsten Sinne 'Böse' auf 'Gut' umgetauft worden ist. Auf eine dieser Verschiebungen habe ich mit dem Gegensatze 'Sittlichkeit der Sitte' und - - -.*" See also BGE 260.

again become necessary, he says, to embark on a "reversal and fundamental shift in values, owing to another self-examination of man". In direct opposition to the moral period, Nietzsche and his fellow immoralists locate the value of an action in what is '*unintentional* in it' since "everything about it that is intentional, everything about it that can be seen, known, 'conscious,' still belongs to its surface and skin." The consequence of this view that the intention is merely a sign or symptom requiring interpretation, is that 'morality in the traditional sense', the 'morality of intentions,' is considered merely a prejudice—"something on the order of astrology and alchemy—but in any case something that must be overcome" (BGE 32, KSA 5:51). What the intention 'betrays' and 'conceals' is *who one is*, i.e. the individual's character, the thoughts and drives which operate on the level of the *un*conscious. For Nietzsche, there is a strong relation between physiology and valuation.[7] He attempts to understand moral values as a sign language of the underlying physiological condition of an individual or people. As early as *Daybreak* (*Morgenröthe*, 1881), he writes, "…our moral judgments and valuations are only images and fantasies concerning physiological processes unknown to us, a kind of habitual language to describe certain nervous irritations" (D 119, KSA 3:113). And, in *Twilight of the Idols* (*Götzen-Dämmerung*, 1888), the work which summarizes his philosophy, Nietzsche states, "Morality is merely sign-language, mere symptomatology…" (TI 7:1, KSA 6:98). On this view, the value of morality can only be gauged semeiotically. As we shall later see, Nietzsche will evaluate moralities precisely according to this standard—whether their values represent physiological failure (i.e. decadence) or well-being.

Nietzsche's extra-moral standpoint aims at nothing less than an overcoming of morality, even, he says, "the self-overcoming of morality" (*die Selbstüberwindung der Moral*). It most certainly does not or cannot involve a complete detachment from the moral period. Rather, the extra-moral must grow out of the soil of the preceding period. Consequently, Nietzsche's extra-moral companions, 'the finest and most honest', will assimilate the past of the moral period in an effort to sculpt it into some new creation. The moral period, then, will not only serve as the object of his attack, but as a preparatory period for a higher humanity whose (future) existence is dependent on the moral epoch. As Wolfgang Müller-Lauter writes: "The moral epoch of mankind thus falls into a double meaning: on the one hand, it seems to be a time of decline;

---

7 For an excellent discussion of the relationship between physiology and valuation in Nietzsche's thought, see Richard Brown's "Nihilism: Thus Speaks Physiology" in T. Darby, B. Egyed, B. Jones (eds.), *Nietzsche and the Rhetoric of Nihilism*, Ottawa: Carleton University Press, 1989, pp.133–144.

on the other, a time of preparation for a richer humanity, which would be impossible without it."[8]

Nietzsche's natural history of morals, then, is not merely a prelude to his critique of morality, but is also instrumental in utilizing past experience to construct the future. A self-overcoming of morality would entail the recognition that our understanding of morality has evolved. Of course, the dominance of the values belonging to the moral period would be usurped with the introduction of an extra-moral period (much to Nietzsche's delight!). But, it should come as no surprise that this 'natural history of morals' was not intended as a strictly 'impersonal', descriptive account of the evolution of morality. That Nietzsche's preoccupation with *rebus moralibus* was not restricted to a mere 'history' is evident in his major work on morals, *On the Genealogy of Morals*, to which I now turn my attention.

The Task of the *Genealogy*

Nietzsche's Preface to *On the Genealogy of Morals*, provides an insightful account of his intentions with respect to the study of morality. He explains that his interest in *morality*, "with all that has hitherto been celebrated on earth as morality" (GM P:3, KSA 5:249), was heightened by a curiosity and a suspicion regarding the *origin* of 'good' and 'evil'. Nevertheless, Nietzsche is adamant that such 'hypothesis mongering' on the origin of morality was not his 'real concern' (GM P:5, KSA 5:251). Instead, his historical philosophizing was merely a means to his fundamental concern—questioning the *value* of our moral values (P:5). This remark has prompted Michel Foucault and others to emphasize the negative dimension of Nietzsche's genealogical approach. There is certainly support for such a reading as Nietzsche articulates the following 'new demand': "we need a *critique* of moral values, *the value of these values must first be called into question*—and for that there is needed a knowledge of the conditions and circumstances in which they grew, under which they evolved and changed" (GM P:6, KSA 5:253). Still, there is a symbiotic relation between the destruction of values and the creation of new ones. In fact, the annihilation of values is a requirement for those who desire to create values,[9] since "we can destroy only as creators" (GS 58, KSA 3:422). It is crucial, then, to situate Nietzsche's genealogical method within his critical task which entails: "...the solution of the *problem of value*, the determination of the *order of rank* (*Rangordnung*) among values" (GM I:17n, KSA 5:289). He goes on to describe the *Genealogy* as a preliminary study for a revaluation of all values (EH XI, KSA 6:353). Despite its

---

8 Wolfgang Müller-Lauter, *Nietzsche: His Philosophy of Contradictions and the Contradictions of His Philosophy*, trans. David J. Parent, Chicago: University of Illinois Press, 1997, p.40.

9 See EH XIV:2, KSA 6:366.

title, the *Genealogy* can be read as having more to do with supplying the impetus for an overcoming of Christian morality, than simply documenting the origin of moral valuation.

The motivation for publishing his views on the origin of morality came from the 'perverse' moral genealogy put forth by Paul Rée,[10] who under the influence of the *English* type of genealogical hypotheses, traced the origin of morality to an 'altruistic mode of evaluation'. For Nietzsche, Rée's effort was a meager attempt "to explore the *history of the origins* (*Entstehungsgeschichte*) of these [moral] feelings," and differed significantly from either a "*critique* of moral valuations or a "history of ethical systems" (GS 345, KSA 3:578). With the exceptions of Herbert Spencer, Thomas Buckle, and Thomas Huxley, [11] the targets of Nietzsche's anglophobia are not specified. However, identifying the specific moralists is not necessary in order to glean the English 'style' of genealogy. These 'English' historians of morality treated values as given, as not subject to questioning, and consequently did not regard morality as a *problem*. Instead, they merely reaffirmed the morality of their environment which was a (Christian) morality of selflessness. Nietzsche, on the other hand, not only recognized morality as a problem but narrowed the problem to that of the *value* of pity and of the morality of pity (GM P:6, KSA 5:252). He writes:

> What was at stake was the *value* of morality...What was especially at stake was the value of the 'unegoistic,' the instincts of pity, self-abnegation, self-sacrifice...But it was against precisely *these* instincts that there spoke from me an ever more fundamental mistrust, an ever more corrosive skepticism...I understood the ever spreading morality of pity that had seized on philosophers and made them ill, as the most sinister symptom of a European culture that had itself become sinister... (GM P:5, KSA 5:251–2)

Nietzsche's genealogical method becomes a critical tool for calling into question the value of our current morality (of pity), which he perceived as 'the *great* danger to mankind' (GM P:5, KSA 5:252). The *Genealogy* is certainly not a 'disinterested' or 'impersonal' history of morals. Rather, it demands an overcoming of the morality of pity since it thwarts the development of what man can aspire to—his '*highest power and splendor*' (GM P:6, KSA 5:253). It is worth noting that although Nietzsche is undermining selfless morality, he is certainly not abandoning an (ethical) interest in human flourishing. Of

---

10 Nietzsche is referring to Rée's *Ursprung der moralischen Empfindungen* (*On the Origin of the Moral Sentiments*, 1877) which was inspired by Darwin, Schopenhauer, the French moralists (especially LaRochefoucauld), and Comte. It contains a mixture of naturalism, evolutionism and utilitarianism.

11 Nietzsche was quite possibly thinking of Thomas Hobbes, David Hume, John Stuart Mill, and W.E.H. Lecky.

significant importance is the note which he attaches to the end of the First Essay of the *Genealogy*. Here, Nietzsche expresses the hope that Philosophy Departments might award prizes for contributions to *historical* studies *of morality*, and then points out that the decisive question concerning the *value* of morality is—the 'value *for what?*' One morality may prove valuable in preserving the greatest number, while another owes its effectiveness to producing a stronger type. Each possess value but represent opposing moral standpoints. To treat the former *a priori* as representative of a higher value is, for Nietzsche, a prejudice which he would like to see remedied by the philosophers of the future whose task is to determine the *order of rank among values*. The re-establishment of a rank-ordering of values would represent an acknowledgement of the value of the rare, exemplary beings whose flourishing would no longer be thwarted by a decadent majority. Nietzsche continually campaigned against the notion that 'numbers' determine value. For now, I would like to focus my attention on the First Essay of the *Genealogy* where Nietzsche presents his account of the origin of moral valuation.

The Optics of Value: Master/Noble versus Slave Morality

The First Essay, "'Good and Evil,' 'Good and Bad'" begins with Nietzsche expressing his dissatisfaction with previous historians of morality (most notably the aforementioned English psychologists) for tracing the origin of 'good' to unegoistic actions, where the recipients of such acts deemed them good on account of their usefulness. In contrast to his predecessors, whom he thought had 'bungled' moral genealogy due to their lack of an *historical spirit*, Nietzsche writes,

> Now it is plain to me, first of all, that in this theory the source of the concept "good" has been sought and established in the wrong place: the judgment "good" did *not* originate with those to whom "goodness" was shown! Rather it was "the good" themselves, that is to say, the noble, powerful, high-stationed and high-minded, who felt and established themselves and their actions as good, that is, of the first rank, in contradistinction to all the low, low-minded, common and plebeian. (GM I:2, KSA 5:259)

The origin of the antithesis 'good' and 'bad' can be attributed to the noble's *pathos of distance*—a total feeling of distance on the part of the ruling order in relation to a lower order. The noble type of individual experiences *itself* as determining values. He seizes the right to create and label these values. This value-legislation is fundamental to these persons' very existence, indeed it speaks out of *who* they are. As a result, the origin of the term 'good', on Nietzsche's view, had nothing at all to do with 'unegoistic' actions. In fact, the 'egoistic'/'unegoistic' dichotomy was completely foreign to the noble mode of valuation. The origin of morality is traced not to questions of selflessness, but of power. Nietzsche's point is "that moral designations were everywhere first applied to *human beings* and only later, derivatively, to actions" (BGE 260, KSA 5:209).

Further evidence to support his account of the origin of the antithesis 'good' and 'bad' was culled from his philological training. Nietzsche's genealogical insights were informed by the etymological significance of the concept 'good' in the early Greeks where the term *agathos* (from which our 'good' was derived) could be traced to 'noble' or 'aristocratic' in the social sense. This explanation not only shows that the concept 'good' developed out of nobility, but that its negative corollary, the term 'bad', corresponded to those who were 'common,' 'plebeian,' and 'low'. With this '*fundamental* insight' into moral genealogy, Nietzsche hoped to dismiss the spurious accounts offered by rival genealogists. When he adds the corrective, that moral designations were first applied to human beings, not actions, he is referring specifically to the nobility of ancient Greece (BGE 260, KSA 5:209). Indeed, this preclassical Greek application of the terms 'good' and 'bad' can be found in two thinkers who Nietzsche especially admired, Homer and Theognis, where *ἀγαθός* ('good') and *κακός* (bad) meant *noble-born* and *base-born.*

This account of the origin of moral valuation from the First Essay is an elaboration of Nietzsche's typology of master and slave morality introduced in section 260 of *Beyond Good and Evil.*[12] In the earlier work, Nietzsche delineated two moralities with distinct origins. Master morality originated among a ruling group whereas slave morality emerged from those who were ruled. The first type of morality relies on a 'good' and 'bad' distinction which is synonymous with 'noble' and 'contemptible'. The noble type of individual exhibits a feeling of fullness, of overflowing power, and delights in being severe and hard with himself (BGE 260, KSA 5:210). For Nietzsche, Homer serves as a model of nobility due to his instinctive affirmation of life, and for exuding cheerfulness and joy, what Nietzsche calls "Homeric happiness" (GS 302, KSA 3:541). Nietzsche could very well have been thinking of Homer when he listed the following characteristics of affirmation: "*The affirmative affects*: pride, joy, health, love of the sexes, enmity and war, reverence, beautiful gestures, manners and objects, strong will, the discipline of high spirituality, will to power, gratitude toward earth and life—everything that is rich and desires to bestow and that replenishes and gilds and immortalizes and deifies life…" (WP 1033, KSA 13:222–23).

---

12 See HH 45, KSA 2:67 for Nietzsche's first application of the terms 'noble' and 'base', 'master' and 'slave' to moralities derived from the ruling group, and the ruled group.

For Nietzsche, the eventual downfall of aristocratic values can be attributed to what he refers to as 'the slave revolt in morality' (*Sklavenaufstand in der Moral*). The slaves, unable to live up to the standards of the noble type, sought revenge by demanding a revaluation of their enemies' values. It was the Jews, he claims, who were responsible for the inversion of aristocratic values (good = noble = powerful = beautiful = happy = beloved of God).[13] This initial revaluation of values resulted in the view that "the wretched alone are the good; the poor, impotent, lowly alone are the good; the suffering, deprived, sick, ugly alone are pious, alone are blessed by God…and you, the powerful and noble, are on the contrary the evil, the cruel, the lustful, the insatiable, the godless to all eternity; and you shall be in all eternity the unblessed, accursed, and damned" (GM I:7, KSA 5:267)! He explains:

> The slave revolt in morality begins when *ressentiment* itself becomes creative and gives birth to values: the *ressentiment* of natures that are denied the true reaction, that of deeds, and compensate themselves with an imaginary revenge. While every noble morality (*vornehme Moral*) develops from a triumphant affirmation of itself, slave morality (*Sklaven-Moral*) from the outset says No to what is 'outside,' what is 'different,' what is 'not itself'; and *this* No is its creative deed. (GM I:10, KSA 5:270)

Whereas the noble type conceives the concept 'good' out of himself unreflectively from the outset, and only seeks its opposite so as to affirm itself more gratefully and triumphantly, the slave first requires a hostile external world, an external stimuli prompting a *re*action (GM I:10, KSA 5:271). The slaves direct their view outward instead of back to themselves. In proclaiming 'No' to what is different, they are reacting against the qualities possessed by the nobles, but which are lacking in themselves. *Ressentiment* is the key motivating factor responsible for the supplanting of noble values (EH XI, KSA 5:352). It condemns that which represents ascending life, well-being, power, beauty and self-affirmation (A 24, KSA 6:192). In this sense, *ressentiment* can be viewed as the mother of slave morality.

The inversion of aristocratic values is accompanied by a change in moral vocabulary. Replacing the nobles' 'good' and 'bad' (*schlecht*) mode of valuation is the 'good' and 'evil' (*böse*) antithesis of slave morality. The 'good' of noble origin (i.e. the powerful individual) is now branded 'evil', and the 'bad' (i.e. the lowly, and contemptible) are recognized as the 'good' according to the man of *ressentiment.* It is worth noting that although Nietzsche traced the 'good'/'bad'

---

13 Although Nietzsche claims that the Jews marked the slave revolt in morality, it is evident that he is also referring to Christianity since he adds in that same section: "…One knows *who* inherited this Jewish revaluation" (GM I:7, KSA 5:267).

dichotomy to pre-Socratic Greek society,[14] and held Socrates responsible in *The Birth of Tragedy* (1872) for orchestrating the decline of Greek culture, Nietzsche offers an alternative reading of Socrates in the later writings which explains why Homer and Socrates are not presented as the main figures in the inversion of values. Instead, Nietzsche focuses his attention on Rome, not Greece, when he claims that the symbol of this struggle between the two opposing values 'good and bad' and 'good and evil' is 'Rome against Judea, Judea against Rome'. Nietzsche not only draws the battle lines, but concedes victory to the morality of *ressentiment.* He writes, "Which of them has won *for the present*, Rome or Judea? But there can be no doubt: consider to whom one bows down in Rome itself today, as if they were the epitome of all the highest values…" (GM I:16, KSA 5:286–87).

The preclassical Greeks may be Nietzsche's paradigm of master (noble) morality, but the categories of master and slave morality are not restricted to a specific era. Rather, in singling out the opposition between Rome and Judea, Nietzsche shifts his attention to a *specific* slave revolt occurring later in history where the Greeks are *not* one of the adversaries. While it is true that Socrates, for Nietzsche, symbolizes the decadence of modernity, his writings of 1888 indicate that Socrates is not to 'blame' for undermining the best Greek instincts. On Nietzsche's revised account, Socrates is merely a symptom of decay, "The same kind of degeneration was quietly developing everywhere: old Athens was coming to an end" (TI 2:9, KSA 6:71). However, unlike his contemporaries, Socrates recognized the onset of decadence (understood as the 'anarchy of the instincts'), and played the role of physician and saviour. As an 'extreme case' of decadence, Socrates opposed the tyranny of the instincts with a counter-tyranny, a fanatical rationalism. With Socrates, the nobler Greek taste had been usurped by a commitment to dialectics and rationality. For the older Hellenes, dialectical manners "were considered bad manners…all such presentations of one's reasons were distrusted…What must first be proved is worth little" (TI 2:5, KSA 6:69–70). But, dialectics and a fanatical rationalism were not something freely chosen by Socrates. Rather, the perilous condition of old Athens rendered rationality a necessity. In this state of emergency, "there was but one choice: either to perish or to be *absurdly rational*" (TI 2:10, KSA 6:72). In short, Socrates' solution to the problem of decadence "is itself but another expression of decadence; they change its expression, but they do not get rid of decadence itself" (TI 2:11, KSA 6:72).

When it comes to analyzing and overcoming decadence, Nietzsche is rather specific as to his intended target. Socrates and Plato certainly contributed to the *moralization* of antiquity, and laid the foundation for Christianity's emergence

---

14 BGE 260, KSA 5:209; GM I:5:10, KSA 5:263, 271.

and ascendancy, but Nietzsche's primary concern is to expose the decadence of *late* modernity. Hence, it is not so much Platonism that he targets as it is the "Platonism for 'the people'" (BGE P, KSA 5:12). In fact, his task of a revaluation of values can only make sense within the context of the *current* form of decadent morality which he consistently identifies, rightly or wrongly, as Christianity's morality of pity.[15] Consider, for instance, the two occasions where Nietzsche reflects on the aim of the First Essay of the *Genealogy*. He explains, "The truth of the *first* inquiry is the birth of Christianity: the birth of Christianity out of the spirit of *ressentiment*...a countermovement by its very nature, the great rebellion against the dominion of *noble* values" (EH XI, KSA 6:352). He concludes *The Case of Wagner* (*Der Fall Wagner*, 1888) with a note reading "The opposition between '*noble* morality' and 'Christian morality' was first explained in my *Genealogy of Morals* perhaps there is no more decisive turning point in the history of our understanding of religion and morality" (CW 'E', KSA 6:52). Socrates is not mentioned in the First Essay of the *Genealogy* because he is no longer viewed as a worthy adversary. He has now been reduced to a symptom of the degeneration of a former aristocratic culture.

Returning now to Nietzsche's discussion of the non-Grecian slave revolt in morality, it is evident that despite Rome's defeat, Nietzsche recognized in the Renaissance,[16] and in the French seventeenth and eighteenth centuries, an awakening of the noble mode of evaluation. So, the master/noble versus slave dichotomy is, in principle, applicable to various historical periods. For now, the crucial point is that he expressed optimism that this struggle was far from over, and did not desire at all to mask his partiality. "...It has long since been abundantly clear what my *aim* is, what the aim of that dangerous slogan is that is inscribed at the head of my last book *Beyond Good and Evil*.—At least this does *not* mean 'Beyond Good and Bad'" (GM I:17, KSA 5:288). Nietzsche's acceptance of the 'good/bad' distinction is in keeping with his view that values are necessary conditions for life, and reflect who we are as 'types'.

On the *Physiology* of Morals: Nietzsche's Immoralism

Nietzsche's preoccupation with morality extends beyond his reconstruction of our moral past. A major component of his work on morality is critique which

---

15 As we shall see in Chapter Two, 'pity' is one of the central features of the decadent morality that Nietzsche repudiates. He views Socratic ethics as another form of slave morality, but he agrees with and even *praises* Socrates' and Plato's low valuation of pity (see GM P:5). Their *agreement* on this issue suggests that Socratic ethics could not be the focal point of Nietzsche's campaign against morality which is directed against moralities of pity such as Christian ethics and Schopenhauer's morality of compassion.

16 For Nietzsche, the Renaissance, as the "last great age" (TI 9:37, KSA 6:138), served as a model of what human beings can attain to, and he specifically praises its sense of *virtù*.

necessitates a standpoint outside of morality. Nietzsche approaches the problem of morality from the perspective of an 'immoralist'—one who speaks unmorally, extra-morally, 'beyond good and evil'. His fondness for the expression 'immoralist' is evident from a letter dating from 1888, whereby he proposed that he be characterized "as an *Immoralist*", claiming that this term signifies "the highest form, till now, of 'intellectual rectitude' (*intellektuellen Rechtschaffenheit*)."[17] Nietzsche's immoralism demands an overcoming of morality in the 'narrower sense,' thereby restricting his attack to the moral period. At the same time, he associates his immoralist perspective with the extra-moral (*aussermoralische*) insofar as he attributes the value of an act to what is *unintentional* in it, what lies below the surface (BGE 32, KSA 5:51). Traditional morality is a prejudice since the intention is merely a sign or symptom in need of interpretation.

Nietzsche attempts to understand moral values as simply surface values, mere symptoms or signs which reflect some underlying physiological condition. "In short, moralities are also merely a *sign language of the affects*" (BGE 187, KSA 5:107). The following passage is crucial for an understanding of his immoral standpoint:

> My demand upon the philosopher is known, that he take his stand *beyond* good and evil and leave the illusion of moral judgment *beneath* himself. This demand follows from an insight which I was the first to formulate: that *there are no moral facts*...Morality is merely an interpretation of certain phenomena—more precisely, a misinterpretation...Moral judgments are therefore never to be taken literally: so understood, they always contain mere absurdity. Semeiotically, however, they remain invaluable: they reveal, at least for those who know, the most valuable realities of cultures and inwardness which did not know enough to 'understand' themselves. Morality, is mere sign language, mere symptomatology: one must know what it is all about to be able to profit from it. (TI 7:1, KSA 6:98)

This passage documents the intimate relation between moral values and physiology. Moral judgements are dismissed since they cannot possess any veridical worth. Judgements relating to the value of life can "never be true" (TI 5:5, KSA 6:86). Yet, Nietzsche seems to suggest that philosophers, or 'at least those who *know*' can obtain a privileged access to what lies below these illusory moral judgements. We are certainly justified, then, in asking what credentials would belong to the expert semeiologist—the master interpreter of moralities. After all, the project of a revaluation of values depends precisely on Nietzsche's proposed solution to the problem of value. In order to salvage the normative aspect of his critical project, Nietzsche would require a standard for evaluating

---

17 Letter to Fuchs, 29 July 1888 in Christopher Middleton (ed./trans.), *Selected Letters of Friedrich Nietzsche*, Chicago: University of Chicago Press, 1969, p.305.

morality which his own theory seems to eschew. This criticism would be fatal to his critical task provided that he appeals to truth (i.e. an objective standpoint) to validate his position.

Nietzsche's standard for the evaluation of moralities reflects the relation between morality and physiology. Ultimately, he relies on a conception of 'life' based on the will to power to serve as his moral standard, and determiner of an order of rank. The principle of 'will to power' informs Nietzsche's extra-moral task of overcoming morality. He raises the following decisive question: "What, seen in the perspective of *life*, is the significance of morality" (BT SC:4, KSA 1:17)? In this sense, the value of morality depends on whether it is symptomatic of life-enhancement or the impoverishment of life (life-negation).[18] "Valuations," he writes, "are physiological demands for the preservation of a certain type of life" (BGE 3, KSA 5:17). The First Essay of the *Genealogy*, in outlining two distinct moralities, provided an excellent contrast between a morality which is life-negating and one representing life-enhancement.

An appreciation of Nietzsche's critical project, then, requires an understanding of his conception of 'life' which I will now outline. In his post-Zarathustran writings, the notion of 'life' occupies a central role. It is often discussed in relation to Nietzsche's conception of power, and is assigned both a descriptive and normative function. Although he remarks that "life itself is will to power" (BGE 13, KSA 5:27), Nietzsche's interpretive emphasis is on 'life', the specific organic ramification and development of will to power. 'Life' is defined as a "multiplicity of forces, connected by a common mode of nutrition" (WP 641, KSA 10:650). To this, he adds that 'life' is "an enduring form of processes of the establishment of force, in which the different contenders grow unequally" (WP 642, KSA 11:560). This notion of a struggle between unequal forces is described in terms of 'command' and 'obedience'. Living organisms are systems of forces organized along the lines of commanding and obeying. Simply put, some forces command and others obey. From there, Nietzsche applies his understanding of 'life' specifically to the human organism. This move to the human level marks a transition from the descriptive to the normative function of 'life'. For instance, he refers to "our entire instinctual life" as a development of the will to power (BGE 36, KSA 5:55), and goes on to define the 'good' as "Everything that heightens the feeling of power in man, the will to power, power itself" (A 2, KSA 6:170). The concept of 'life' now takes on a decisively normative role. Nietzsche writes:

---

18 Although Nietzsche does not offer principled guidelines for 'life-enhancement', in various places he emphasizes the notion of inequality. And, presumably, his higher type would possess an ascending will to power.

> I reduce a principle to a formula. Every naturalism in morality, that is, every *healthy* morality, is dominated by an instinct of life—some commandment of life is fulfilled by a determinate canon of 'shalt' and 'shalt not'; some inhibition and hostile element on the path of life is thus removed. *Anti-natural* morality, that is, almost every morality which has so far been taught, revered, and preached, turns, conversely, *against* the instincts of life: it is *condemnation* of these instincts...When it says, 'God looks at the heart,' it says No to both the lowest and highest desires of life and posits God as the *enemy of life*. The saint in whom God delights is the ideal eunuch. Life comes to an end where the 'kingdom of God' begins. (TI 5:4, KSA 6:85)

In this passage, Nietzsche emphasizes the affiliation between morality and life. A natural or healthy morality is contrasted with an anti-natural one according to whether they represent an instinct of life or a condemnation of these instincts. 'Life', according to Nietzsche, is "*essentially* appropriation, injury, overpowering of what is alien and weaker; suppression, hardness, imposition of one's forms, incorporation and...exploitation" (BGE 259, KSA 5:207). Thus, he is able to reject anti-natural morality due to its refusal to recognize these necessary elements within the general economy of life.

Nietzsche's appeal to 'life' as a criterion for evaluating moralities appears quite problematic. The normative function assigned to the concept of 'life' which Nietzsche's critique of morality seems to demand, leads to a metaphysics of the kind that he typically rejects. What follows from this treatment of morality as symptomatology is a denial of the possibility of any valuation of life from some *external* standpoint (GS 346, KSA 3:580; TI 5:5, KSA 6:86). For instance, Nietzsche explicitly denies that value judgements concerning life can have 'truth' value (TI 2:2, KSA 6:68). Moreover, one's (or a community's) values seem necessary given one's particular physiological constitution. For this reason, Nietzsche writes: "Our values...grow out of us with the necessity with which a tree bears fruit..." (GM P:2, KSA 5:248). Similarly, one's "morality bears decided and decisive witness to *who he is*—that is, in what order of rank the innermost drives of his nature stand in relation to each other" (BGE 6, KSA 5:20).

Armed with a criterion of 'life' through which moralities can be evaluated, Nietzsche's immoralism begins to take shape. By definition, an 'immoralist' is one who acts contrary to moral and social standards.[19] But, Nietzsche is not inciting others to act immorally. His immoralism is of a more complex variety. As well, he realized the potentially misleading nature of the term 'immoralist'. In order to avoid being mistaken for a 'moralistic monster,' (*Moral-Ungeheuer*) Nietzsche was careful to articulate the meaning of his 'immoralism'. He writes:

---

19 Peter Angeles, *Dictionary of Philosophy*. New York: Harper & Row, 1989, p.128.

> Fundamentally, my term *immoralist* involves two negations. For one, I negate a type of man that has so far been considered supreme: the good, the benevolent, the beneficent. And then I negate a type of morality that has become prevalent and predominant as morality itself—the morality of decadence or, more concretely, *Christian* morality. (EH XIV:4, KSA 6:367–68)

Placed under the tribunal of 'life,' neither the 'good' man nor Christian morality fares well. Both are signs of physiological degeneration. Lacking the natural instincts to grow and enhance one's power means that the individual posits values which are hostile to life, and a morality which promotes these same decadent values thwarts human flourishing. In the same chapter of *Ecce Homo*, Nietzsche goes on to define morality: "*Definition of morality*: Morality—the idiosyncrasy of decadents with the ulterior motive of revenging oneself against life—successfully. I attach value to this definition" (EH XIV:7, KSA 6:373). This 'definition' is entirely consistent with that found in section 19 of *Beyond Good and Evil* insofar as both express a link between moral valuation and physiology.

The passage cited above also helps define the scope of Nietzsche's attack on morality. He is not rejecting morality *tout court*, but only Christian morality and its secular surrogates (e.g. Schopenhauer, J.S. Mill, and Auguste Comte, to name a few)[20] which continued to dominate nineteenth century Europe. The negation of a specific morality which has 'become predominant as morality itself' indicates that there have been other moralities preceding what he calls 'the morality of decadence' or 'Christian morality'. The monopolizing effect of Christian morality causes us to lose sight that this morality is merely one of many others that have existed on earth. Hence, the need for a 'typology' of morals. At times, Nietzsche, himself, will succumb to the powerful influence of Christian morality, and will write as though he is rejecting morality itself. For instance, while commenting on *Daybreak* in *Ecce Homo*, he advocates a liberation from *all* moral values (EH VII:1, KSA 6:330). Taken out of context, it would appear that Nietzsche is aiming to transcend the entire domain of morality. That this is not the case is evident from the remainder of the passage where he again identifies the morality of decadence as 'morality itself'. He concludes this section by explaining:

---

20 Nietzsche often emphasizes that moral philosophers have a tendency to reject Christianity, but still cling tenaciously to its morality, that is, its "cult of philanthropy" (D 132, KSA 3:123). The same idea is expressed in Friedrich Lange's *History of Materialism*, trans. Ernest C. Thomas, New York: Kegan Paul, 1925, vol. 3, p.271–72, including explicit references to Mill and Comte. Having read Lange with great enthusiasm, Nietzsche was certainly influenced by the Neo-Kantian on this point. Nietzsche is critical of both Christian morality and those moral philosophies who identify 'pity', 'selflessness', or 'altruism' as the basis of morality.

> The loss of the center of gravity, resistance to the natural instincts—in one word, "selflessness"—that is what was hitherto called *morality*.—With the *Dawn* I first took up the fight against the morality that would unself man. (EH VII:2, KSA 6:332)

Nietzsche qualifies his brand of immoralism by announcing his opposition to altruistic moralities, meaning Christianity and its secular derivatives.[21] It is important then always to identify the context in which he discusses his views. Although there are places in which he appears to be repudiating morality *simpliciter*,[22] he is adamant that Christian morality is "merely *one* type of human morality, before which and after which many other types, above all *higher* moralities, are or ought to be possible" (BGE 202, KSA 5:124).

In Nietzsche's philosophical autobiography, *Ecce Homo (Ecce Homo*, written 1888), most of the chapter entitled 'Why I am a Destiny' is devoted to clarifying the nature of his immoralism. In addition to the aforementioned definition, he adds: "I am the first immoralist: that makes me the annihilator *par excellence*" (EH XIV:2, KSA 6:366). It would be a mistake, however, to construe this remark as simply a call for the repudiation of values. In echoing his formula from *Thus Spoke Zarathustra*, Nietzsche insists that being creative first demands that one annihilate (XIV:2). It would appear, then, that he views his project as both negative and affirmative despite the potentially misleading label 'immoralist'. Still, Nietzsche endeavors to avoid being misinterpreted where this term is concerned. He explains:

> There is yet another sense, however, in which I have chosen the word *immoralist* as a symbol and badge of honor for myself; I am proud of having this word which distinguishes me from the whole of humanity. Nobody yet has felt *Christian* morality to be *beneath* him...Christian morality has been the Circe of all thinkers so far—they stood in her service. (EH XIV:6, KSA 6:370-71)

The following passages leave little room for doubt that Nietzsche's immoralism involves an attack on one type of morality—Christian morality. For now, I am not interested in his arguments against Christian morality, but rather the conception of morality which is operative in his writings. My intent in describing Nietzsche's opposition to a specific morality was to indicate that according to his criterion of 'life', certain moralities could be rejected as decadent while others could be esteemed as life-enhancing. Surprisingly,

---

21 I am in agreement with Thomas Brobjer who points out that Christianity represents the most important ethical tradition for Nietzsche. (*Nietzsche's Ethics of Character*, Uppsala, 1995, p.194)

22 See for instance, GM P:6, KSA 5:253 where Nietzsche speaks of one's belief in "*all* morality" faltering. And, EH VII:1, KSA 6:330 where he describes his revaluation of all values in terms of "a liberation from *all* moral values."

however, not all commentators accept this qualified version of Nietzsche's immoralism.

The Case of Clark: "Nietzsche's Immoralism, and the Concept of Morality"

Maudemarie Clark has offered an alternative reading of Nietzsche's immoralism in an effort to determine his conception of morality. Clark aligns herself with Philippa Foot, Alexander Nehamas and Frithjof Bergmann in arguing that Nietzsche is rejecting *all* morality. She begins by questioning whether immoralism is even a plausible view.

> An immoralist does not simply ignore morality, or deny its right to our compliance, but claims that morality is a bad thing that should be rejected. Immoralism therefore seems to be defensible only from the viewpoint of a morality, which makes it appear to be as self-refuting as another notorious Nietzschean claim, that truths are illusions.[23]

This paradoxical claim, Clark points out, has been circumvented by numerous interpreters (myself included) who argue that Nietzsche qualifies his brand of immoralism by restricting it to one type of morality. Her essay examines how Nietzsche could find it plausible to reject all morality. Clark begins by considering Nietzsche's prediction that those who follow him in raising questions about the morality of pity will share a similar experience. Quoting from the *Genealogy*, she writes: "A tremendous new prospect opens up…belief in morality, in all morality, falters—finally a new demand becomes audible…we need a *critique* of moral values, *the value of these values must itself for once be called into question*."[24] Clark interprets this to mean that not only would one's belief in the morality of pity be undermined, but in 'all morality'. So, she takes Nietzsche to be drawing a distinction between 'all morality' and the specific morality which he was referring to in that section (Schopenhauer's morality of pity). It is not clear, however, what significance such a distinction would have for him. Moreover, Clark fails to show that Nietzsche rejects certain features of morality which are not subsumed under Christian morality. Yet, if his immoralism extended beyond an attack on Christian morality, then one could expect to find his critique of morality addressing such features.

On my reading of the passage cited by Clark, Nietzsche is merely emphasizing that if one's belief in the morality of pity falters, by extension so too will one's belief in all morality since he is equating here the morality of pity

---

23 Maudemarie Clark, "Nietzsche's Immoralism and the Concept of Morality," in R. Schacht (ed.), *Nietzsche, Genealogy, Morality: Essays on Nietzsche's* Genealogy of Morals, Berkeley: University of California Press, 1994, pp.15–34.

24 Ibid, p.15, quoting from GM P: 6, KSA 5:253.

with all morality.[25] He makes this equation because the morality of pity holds a monopoly on our current understanding of the term. It is for this reason that he writes: "The Christian has so far been *the* 'moral being'" (EH XIV:7, KSA 6:371). Nietzsche will sometimes carelessly speak of 'morality' instead of taking the time to make the explicit reference to a 'morality of pity'. He is not always careful to separate the two, but he trusts that his readers will be cognizant of his intended meaning. It is also important to consider the work from where this quote was lifted. And, this is precisely what Nietzsche, himself, does in reflecting on the *Genealogy* in a later work. He writes: "The opposition between '*noble* morality' (*vornehme* Moral) and '*Christian* morality' (*christliche* Moral) was first explained in my *Genealogy of Morals*: perhaps there is no more decisive turning point in the history of our understanding of religion and morality" (CW 'E', KSA 6:52 second emphasis mine). This point is entirely consistent with the emphasis placed on the slave revolt in morality from that same work. In both cases, Nietzsche focuses on the antithesis—master versus slave (i.e. noble versus Christian). There seems to be ample textual support to show that Clark had erred in reading Nietzsche as an opponent of all morality. In fairness, however, we need to consider her additional evidence.

Clark turns to section 32 of BGE, the same passage which I have been making considerable use of throughout this chapter, to support her interpretation. She states correctly that Nietzsche's 'overcoming of morality' entails the overcoming of morality in the '*narrower sense*', and then wonders why Nietzsche would insist on calling himself an immoralist if he is only rejecting morality in this narrower sense. Clark adds: "My question is how Nietzsche made it comprehensible and plausible to himself that he was rejecting precisely what we have embraced as 'morality'."[26] From there, she concludes that Nietzsche's occasional reference to 'higher moralities' means that he is using 'morality' in a non-traditional, wider-sense, equivalent to 'codes for evaluating human beings and their conduct'. I do not deny that Nietzsche makes this distinction between two senses of morality: our traditional morality, and non-traditional 'higher moralities'. However, Clark states that her task is to understand how Nietzsche could have labeled himself an immoralist, and to do this, she wants to ascertain "what he thinks moral values are, and why he did not take his own values to be moral values."[27] But, an understanding of

---

25 My reading is supported by a passage from the *Nachlaß* where Nietzsche writes: "That the history of all phenomena of morality could be simplified in the way Schopenhauer believed—namely, so that pity is to be discovered as the root of *all* moral impulse hitherto…" (WP 366, KSA 12:160, my emphasis).

26 Clark, p.17.

27 Ibid, p.17.

Nietzsche's reasons for referring to himself as an immoralist simply requires a reading of *Ecce Homo*. I attribute Clark's misreading to her complete neglect of this text. This is an astonishing oversight since Nietzsche defines his immoralism with remarkable clarity, emphasizing his declaration of war on Christian morality.

In asking what Nietzsche thinks moral values are, and why he thought his own values were not moral values, Clark considers his analysis of the concept of morality from the *Genealogy*. She claims that the First Essay does *not* involve a comparison of two moralities (one originating from a ruling class and the other originating from the oppressed), but rather two different ways of determining who is good and who isn't.[28] Clark alludes to the reading of Arthur Danto, and claims that although he does not follow her in arguing that 'good/bad' is not a *moral* distinction, she thinks he provides the basis for such a reading when he writes:

> From the masters' perspective, those unlike themselves are merely bad humans; that is to say, humans that do not come up to the mark. This is similar to the way bad eggs are low in the scale of egghood. There is nothing *morally* bad in being a bad egg, or, in this usage, a bad human. It is just the way one is. Too bad, then, for the bad. They hardly can be blamed for being what they are; but they are bad.[29]

Despite making a value judgement about commoners when one refers to them as 'bad', Clark adds that this is not a *moral* judgement. In other words, they are not being judged 'immoral' or 'morally bad'. If this is the case, then it follows that the nobles are not extolling their *moral* value or worth when they refer to themselves as 'good'. This passage appears relatively straightforward, but to claim that, "There is nothing *morally* bad in being a bad egg, or in this usage, a bad human", is to presuppose a certain conception of what it means to be 'morally' bad. In this sense, Clark is putting the cart before the horse. Of course, from our traditional moral perspective, which includes the notions of praise and blame, we could say that the masters lack a morality. But, it is not important how *we* define morality, since Clark's task is to question *Nietzsche's* understanding of morality, and she has not shown that he, himself, regarded the noble mode of valuation as a non-moral distinction.

Conversely, Clark argues that Nietzsche viewed the 'good/evil' antithesis as a moral distinction pointing out that what is decisive is that the evil are blamed for being bad, or thought to be deserving of punishment. The difficulty is that even though Nietzsche isolates two distinct modes of valuation, he offers no

---

28 Ibid, p.25.

29 Ibid, p.24 quoting from Arthur Danto's *Nietzsche as Philosopher*, New York: MacMillian, 1965, p.159.

general and universal criteria of morality within which we could classify one mode of valuation as moral or non-moral. Instead, he merely unravels the transition from one mode of valuation to the other. 'Blaming people' may be idiosyncratic to slave morality, but there is no evidence to suggest that it is a necessary ingredient of moral valuation. 'Blameworthiness' is simply a feature belonging to a particular morality while lacking in another. It is not a defining characteristic of 'morality' itself. Nietzsche certainly emphasizes this component of traditional morality throughout his writings, but in order to single out one aspect of morality, is to make the same error as Frithjof Bergmann who emphasized 'freedom' as the crucial ingredient of morality.[30] Further, the difficulty with Clark's view is in accounting for Nietzsche's specific use of the term 'morality' (*Moral*) to describe noble values. Nietzsche repeatedly uses the terms 'noble *morality*' (*vornehme Moral*) and 'master *morality*' (*Herren-Moral*), but it would be curious as to why he would do this, if he did not consider them a 'morality'.

I agree with Clark that many commentators are guilty of smuggling in their own conception of morality, and then evaluating Nietzsche's views on the subject accordingly. As well, I am sympathetic to her 'new approach' that recommends consideration of Nietzsche's own analysis of the concept of morality, but I disagree with her attempt to confine Nietzsche's understanding of morality to one text—the *Genealogy*. Clark refused to heed the warning of Arthur Danto who wrote, "to treat the *Genealogy* as though it were precocious analytic philosophy is to have swallowed the bait without having yet felt the hook."[31] Readers interested in Nietzsche's conception of morality would be well-advised to survey other texts, in particular, his 'definition' of morality from section 19 of *Beyond Good and Evil*. In outlining the object of his attack, *Ecce Homo* provides a lucid description of Nietzsche's self-professed immoralism without having to squabble over terminological distinctions. It is preoccupied with a discussion of Christian morality rather than delineating *different* moralities. As for the *Genealogy*, far from giving us an exegesis of the concept 'morality' as Clark had argued, instead leaves us with two moralities with differing origins, neither of which are 'defined'.

On the Use and Abuse of 'Morality' in Nietzsche

In light of Nietzsche's seemingly inconsistent use of the term 'morality' (which includes his pejorative *and* non-pejorative references), some commentators have

30 Frithjof Bergmann, "Nietzsche's Critique of Morality" in R.C. Solomon and K. Higgins (eds.), *Reading Nietzsche*, New York: Oxford University Press, 1988, pp.29–45.

31 Arthur Danto, "Some Remarks on *The Genealogy of Morals*" in R.C. Solomon and K. Higgins (eds.), *Reading Nietzsche*, New York: Oxford University Press, 1988, p.13.

defended him against the charge of equivocation by distinguishing between two senses of morality implicit in his writings. Lester Hunt draws a distinction between a monotheistic sense of 'Morality' which does not admit of a plural, is never preceded by an article, and is only found in the singular. On this view, 'Morality' would be analogous to the way a monotheist would speak of 'God' (always capitalized), rather than god*s*. Here, 'Morality' shares the same 'imperialistic ambitions'—to be the *only* morality. However, there is a second use of morality that admits of a plural, but requires an article when it appears in the singular—'a morality of selflessness', 'the morality of mores'. In this latter instance, morality is "a code by which one lives; one which, moreover, enables one to distinguish between good and bad or right and wrong in human conduct and ways of life."[32] Similarly, Robert C. Solomon and Kathleen Higgins, distinguish between "various moralit*ies*, that is, different 'rank orders of value'" and a form of 'Morality' (also capitalized) which "is, by contrast, quite specific and particular, even if it is sometimes described in terms of very general, even 'universal' rules or principles."[33] The Divine Command Theory of morality and Immanuel Kant's ethics are two examples of such a formal Morality, one whose demands are unconditional and universal. These commentators agree that 'Morality' refers to *specific* principles or guidelines for conduct, whereas 'moralities' are equivalent to practical guidelines, "a collection of inherited, invented, or even instinctual practices (what Hegel famously called '*Sittlichkeit*')."[34] In this sense, every society has its own set of rules, its moral do's and don'ts without going so far as to demand their universality. It would be impossible to live without having a morality, regardless of whether one lives in a community, or in solitude (e.g. alone in the mountains). "Man is before everything else an evaluating animal" (KSA 12:182).[35]

Regarding the scope of Nietzsche's attack on morality, I think that Solomon and Higgins' distinction has merit. In particular, it isolates a specific conception of Morality (e.g. Christian/Kantian) which he opposes, while at the same time, expanding the moral sphere to include an alternative conception of morality. In doing so, Nietzsche has acquired some conceptual space for the articulation of an affirmative ethics. Unlike Kant's ethics, Nietzsche's is not interested in providing universal and general principles. In fact, it specifically rules these out in acknowledging differences between types of human beings. According to Nietzsche, the value of an individual is determined by the order of

---

32 Lester Hunt, *Nietzsche and the Origin of Virtue*, New York: Routledge, 1991, p.9.

33 Robert C. Solomon and Kathleen Higgins, *What Nietzsche* Really *Said*, New York: Schocken Books, 2000, pp.103–4.

34 Ibid, p.104.

35 "*Der Mensch ist vor Allem ein urtheilendes Thier.*"

rank of his drives (BGE 228, KSA 5:165). The rich diversity in human types indicates that there is no 'Morality', only 'moralities'. Still, Nietzsche's voice is neither the first nor the last when it comes to identifying the concept of morality, and it is certainly not the loudest. His emphasis on human inequality conflicts with one of the most widely agreed upon tenets in moral philosophy—the idea of impartiality. Few moral theories would reject the view that, *ceteris paribus*, each individual's interests are to be weighted equally, and that everyone's life possesses the same value. Kant, for instance, claimed that a rational agent must not only be an agent, but reflect on himself as an agent, and this requires that he regard himself as one agent among others. As a result, he would exclude from consideration his own interests and desires, and formulate rules coinciding with the interests of all rational agents. Here, reason is the arbiter of right and wrong on the basis of whether we could will that everyone act according to a particular maxim. The criterion of impartiality can thus be used to argue for certain ethical considerations. The issue then becomes a matter of evaluating rival versions of morality, Nietzsche's 'moralities' versus Kant's 'Morality'. In addressing 'morality' in the plural, Nietzsche departs from Kant's conception of 'morality' which refers to a single, specific phenomenon. One might question a certain rule of morality, say its universality, but its form is presumed given—that morality is a single phenomenon consisting of a set of basic moral principles.[36] Nietzsche's use of the plural 'moralities' would represent a sort of philosophical heresy, an abuse of the sacred institution of 'Morality'. It remains to be seen whether Nietzsche is successful in depriving the Categorical Imperative of its special authority. I shall provide a critical assessment of their moral views in Chapter Three. For now, it is important to develop Nietzsche's position in order to set the stage for a confrontation between these two moral heavyweights.

Instead of following Hunt, and Solomon and Higgins, in distinguishing between 'Morality' and 'moralities', I have focused on Nietzsche's generic 'definition' of morality (BGE 19, KSA 5:34) which is able to accommodate both his pejorative and non-pejorative reflections on the subject, and is equally effective at ascertaining the scope of his attack on morality. However, I do not deny that their approach is valuable in situating Nietzsche's *Feldzug gegen die Moral* within a historical juxtaposition between two very distinct ethical orientations (i.e. principle/rule-based versus an ethics of practice). Their approach is preoccupied with a "way to understand Nietzsche's rejection of

[36] I owe this point to Robert C. Solomon, "A More Severe Morality: Nietzsche's Affirmative Ethics" in Y. Yovel (ed.), *Nietzsche as Affirmative Thinker*, Boston: Martinus Nijhoff Publishers, 1986, p.78.

morality."[37] The question becomes how successful is their account of 'moralities' in terms of it capturing the *full* range of Nietzsche's non-pejorative, positive references to 'morality'. In other words, how informative is it to claim that 'moralities' represent different rank orders of value? In what follows, I argue that the exegesis demanded of 'moralities' exceeds Solomon and Higgins' Hegelian identification of the term.

Nietzsche's understanding of morality owes a great deal to his typology of morals. The most fundamental typology that we have encountered is his classification of various moralities as either master or slave (BGE 260, KSA 5:208). At times, however, Nietzsche will take particular moralities such as Kant's or Schopenhauer's and reduce them to Christian morality, i.e. slave morality. These sub-groupings still reflect his most basic typology of master and slave moralities. However, this does not prevent Nietzsche from experimenting with other closely related major typologies.[38] In discussing Nietzsche's anti-essentialism, Raymond Geuss remarks, astutely, that for Nietzsche, "There isn't any 'essence of morality,' that is any set of important properties that all instances of what can correctly be called 'morality' must exhibit."[39] Instead of specifying or dictating the necessary conditions to be met in order to qualify as a 'morality,' Nietzsche is more interested in examining morality as a cultural phenomenon. He writes mockingly:

> What is the criterion of a moral action? (1) its disinterestedness, (2) its universal validity, etc. But this is armchair moralizing. One must study peoples to see what the criterion is in every case, and what is expressed by it. (WP 261, KSA 12:260)

In contrast to the 'armchair moralizing' of philosophers, Nietzsche points out that moral standards are in flux, and the most salutary approach would be to examine specific peoples. Morality, being historically-conditioned, renders futile any attempt to stipulate general or universal criteria. The significance of appealing to historical examples is that it reveals that different societies have their own criterion, a criterion which reflects their specific needs. Nietzsche explains "Wherever we encounter a morality, we also encounter valuations and an order of rank of human impulses and actions. These valuations and orders of rank are always expressions of the needs of a community and herd...The conditions for the preservation of different communities were very different; hence there were different moralities" (GS 116, KSA 3:474-75). The needs of a

---

37 Solomon and Higgins, *What Nietzsche* Really *Said*, 2000, p.106.

38 For example, Nietzsche will also rely on the following antithesis: 'anti-natural'/ 'natural', 'life-affirming'/ 'life-negating', 'descending'/ 'ascending', 'nihilistic'/ 'non-nihilistic'.

39 Raymond Geuss, "Nietzsche and Morality", *European Journal of Philosophy* 5:1, 1997, p.1.

people or age reflect their capacity for strength or vitality. As a symptomatologist, Nietzsche can evaluate cultures, including their respective exemplars, according to their measure of vitality. The verdict placed on modernity is that it represents a "general decrease in *vitality*...hence each helps the other; hence everyone is to a certain extent sick" (TI 9:37, KSA 6:138). On the other hand, the Renaissance 'as the last *great* age', possesses a high measure of 'positive strength' indicative of ascending life. Consequently, the order of rank of human impulses will vary within these conflicting ages. The valuations of an age are closely tied to physiological conditions. It is precisely for this reason that Nietzsche writes: "What is certain is that we may not place ourselves in Renaissance conditions, not even by an act of thought: our nerves would not endure that reality, not to speak of our muscles" (TI 9:37, KSA 6:136–37).

When Nietzsche speaks of 'morality' it is often accompanied by the related expressions; 'condition(s) of life' (*Lebens-bedingung*) or 'conditions of existence' (*Existenz-Bedingung*). In a note from the late 1880's, he offers this account of morality: "I understand by 'morality' a system of evaluations that partially coincides with the conditions of a creature's life" (WP 256).[40] A clarification of this expression would be important for explaining Nietzsche's understanding of morality. In section 7 of *The Gay Science* (*Die fröhliche Wissenschaft*, 1882) the phrase 'conditions of existence' appears in connection with Nietzsche's advice for those interested in pursuing moral studies. As a way of stressing the importance of understanding the various moral climates, Nietzsche questions whether philosophers have researched exhaustively the diverse 'conditions of existence'. He claims that this 'immense field of work' would include the following:

> All kinds of individual passions have to be thought through and pursued throughout different ages, peoples, and great and small individuals; all their reason and all their evaluations and perspectives on things have to be brought into the light. So far, all that has given color to existence still lacks a history. Where could you find a history of love, of avarice, of envy, of conscience, of pious respect for tradition, or of cruelty? Even a comparative history of law or at least punishment is so far lacking completely. Has anyone made a study of different ways of dividing up the day or of the consequences of a regular schedule of work, festivals, and rest? What is known of the moral effects of different foods? Is there any philosophy of nutrition?...Has anyone collected men's experiences of living together—in monasteries, for example? Has the dialectic of

---

40 This note from *The Will to Power* is marked "lost" by the editors of KSA, and for that reason is not included in the standard German edition of Nietzsche's collected writings. I have chosen to cite this passage since it reflects closely what can be found in the published writings (e.g. BGE 19) as well as the *Nachlaß* material from KSA.

> marriage and friendship ever been explicated? Have the manners of scholars, of businessmen, artists, or artisans been studied and thought through? (GS 7, KSA 3:378)

This Herculean task would require centuries of experimentation. In the meantime, morality must be considered a 'work in progress'. According to this account, Nietzsche's own *Genealogy* would represent a partial contribution to the vast realm of moral studies. This is not to say that we are ignorant of all our 'conditions of existence' since we are certainly capable of identifying enough of them to pass judgement. Nietzsche is encouraging moral philosophers to widen the scope of their study. He especially wants to convey that there are unknown factors (many of which are physiological) which are responsible for who we are. Far from lamenting the incompleteness of such detailed studies, Nietzsche simply points out that we cannot speak of morality independent of our 'conditions of existence'. However, he has a specific agenda. The more information that we obtain about these conditions, the closer we get to realizing the conditions necessary for the production of exemplary human beings.[41] In fact, Nietzsche specifically contrasts his project to that of the moral philosopher: "*Not* to make men 'better', *not* to preach morality to them in any form, as if 'morality in itself', or any ideal kind of man, were given; but to *create conditions* that *require stronger men* who for their part need, and consequently will *have*, a morality (more clearly: a physiological-spiritual discipline) *that makes them strong*" (WP 981, KSA 12:495)! In each case, it is a matter of what conditions result in the preservation of a particular people. He writes: "Analysis of individual tables of value revealed that their erection (*Aufstellung*) was the erection of the conditions—often erroneous—of existence of a limited group—for its preservation" (WP 260, KSA 13:653) It is noteworthy that Nietzsche's approach is not aimed at refutation: "Morality is the concern of those who *cannot* go beyond it; it is part of their 'living conditions'. We cannot refute living conditions—we can only *have others*" (VP II:168–69, section 543).[42] Instead, he wants to recognize the possibility that there can be other *Existenzbedingungen.* Nietzsche's understanding of morality is continually linked to physiology, and his foremost task is the creation of the conditions which would spawn exemplary human beings. Insofar as he identifies morality as a 'physiological-spiritual discipline', we can say that Nietzsche's affirmative morality relates to the body, specifically its health. And, the exemplary individual is the embodiment of human flourishing.

---

41 WP 898, KSA 12:424f.

42 *La volonté de puissance*, (VP), tr. G. Bianquis, 32nd edition, 2 vols. Paris: Gallimard, 1947, quoted in Eric Blondel's *Nietzsche: The Body and Culture*, Stanford: Stanford Univ. Press, 1991, p.316. I have been unable to locate either the German or English reference.

Instead of focusing on the intimate relation between morality and physiology, some commentators[43] rely on a different approach for understanding Nietzsche's conception of morality. They consider his dissection of morality, and proceed to catalogue the various components that are emphasized. The goal of such an approach is to reveal the conception of morality which was most influential and operative in his writings. Indeed, there are numerous features of traditional morality that Nietzsche will often highlight. On many occasions, he will describe today's morality as a morality of pity or altruism (an offshoot of Christian morality). For instance, he writes: "That men today feel the sympathetic, disinterested, generally useful social actions to be the *moral* actions—this is perhaps the most general effect and conversion which Christianity has produced in Europe" (D 132, KSA 3:123). The identification of morality with the notion of pity, selflessness, *vivre pour autrui*, or the unegoistic drives is a recurring theme throughout Nietzsche's writings.[44] At other times, he will focus on the intimate connection between free will and morality. In *Daybreak*, Nietzsche notes that according to one definition of morality, those actions are moral which are performed out of freedom of will.[45] In *Twilight of the Idols*, he explicitly states that the notion of free will is a presupposition of morality (TI 6:7, KSA 6:95). In addition, however, it seems to me that Nietzsche's greatest emphasis is on the 'universal' and 'unconditional' demand of morality. He makes reference to the fact that our unegoistic morality takes itself for unconditional and addresses itself to all.[46] An unconditional morality asserts that values are binding on all individuals, independent of the interests, desires, and circumstances which distinguish them. There is also the prescriptive or normative component of morality which Nietzsche discusses. In *Human, All-Too-Human* (*Menschliches, Allzumenschliches*, 1878) he identifies the 'ought' as a fundamental component of morality (HH 34, KSA 2:54). Not only does morality speak to everyone, but dictates through the application of general rules and principles, conduct which 'ought' to be performed or prohibited. If successful, the result will be that morality has 'improved mankind' (EH P:2, KSA 6:258). After all, what else is a moralist but one who preaches "you ought to be such and such" (TI 5:6 KSA 6:86)? I have certainly not exhausted the features of morality discussed by Nietzsche, but the ones listed above constitute those aspects which repeatedly surface throughout his works.

---

43 See Hunt, p.10.

44 Some references include: HH 37, 96, 133, KSA 2:60, 93, 127; D 148, 174, KSA 3:139, 154; GS 55, KSA 3:418; BGE 201, KSA 5:122; GM P:5, KSA 5:252; TI 9:35, KSA 6:133; EH III:5, KSA 6:305.

45 See D 148, KSA 3:139; cf. CW 7, KSA 6:27.

46 See BGE 221, KSA 5:156; D 108, KSA 3:96; BGE 198, 199, 228, KSA 5:118, 119, 165.

In addition to the emphasis placed on 'freedom', the 'unconditional' and 'universal' aspects of morality highlighted by Nietzsche have a distinctively Kantian flavour.[47] Moreover, in emphasizing that morality is not concerned with consequences, but with intentions (e.g. 'principle of volition'), it would appear that Kant could serve as the philosophical spokesman for the moral period. In an unpublished note dated the end of 1880, Nietzsche writes: "Kant: the human being is a moral being: hence he is 1) free 2) immortal 3) there exists a rewarding and punishing justice: God…" (KSA 9:321).[48] Although it appears that Nietzsche's conception of morality owes a great deal to Kant, it would be mistaken to regard his immoralism as a specific attack on Kant's ethics. Kant delighted in thinking that his moral philosophy provided the basis for Christian morality.[49] Nietzsche repeatedly associates Kant with Christianity[50] and identifies the belief in absolute and unconditional rights and duties with Christianity (WP 765, KSA 13:422–26; WS 44, KSA 2:573). As well, he will often resort to *ad hominem* attacks against Kant (and others) when he refers to Kant as "a *cunning* Christian" (TI 3:6, KSA 6:79).

The most important ethical tradition, for Nietzsche, is Christianity.[51] Regardless of their exact relation, both Kantian ethics and Christian morality are relegated to the class of decadent moralities since they are symptoms of the decline of life. The attempt to ascertain Nietzsche's understanding of 'morality' by focusing on the recurring features of morality in his writings, merely results in a description of one particular morality (whether in its Christian or Kantian

---

47 One noteworthy exception is the notion of 'pity' since Nietzsche viewed Kant as a philosophical ally in claiming that pity [*Mitleid*] did not factor into the moral worth of our actions. (see GM P:5)

48 The original German reads: "*Kant: der Mensch ist ein moralisches Wesen: folgich ist er 1) frei 2) unsterblich 3) giebt es eine belohnende und strafende Gerechtigkeit: Gott…*" (KSA 9:321).

49 I. Kant, *Critique of Practical Reason* in *The Cambridge Edition of the Works of Immanuel Kant: Practical Philosophy*, New York: Cambridge University Press, 1999, p.243.

50 See HH 25, KSA 2:46; GS 335, KSA 3:562; TI 3:6, KSA 6:79; A 10, 55, KSA 6:177, 238.

51 Similarly, Brobjer writes: "The whole deontological tradition, with its many individual movements and schools, seems by Nietzsche to be subsumed under Christianity." (p.224) This is not to deny, however, the point made by Robert C. Solomon that, "It is Kant who sets up the philosophical conditions for the Nietzschean reaction, not only by so clearly codifying the central theses to be attacked but also by conceptually undermining the traditional supports of morality. The attack on authority ('heteronomy') and the emphasis on 'autonomy' by Kant is a necessary precondition for Nietzsche's moral moves, however much the latter presents himself as providing a conception of morality which precedes, rather than, presupposes the Kantian move" ("A More Severe Morality: Nietzsche's Affirmative Ethics" in Y. Yovel (ed.), *Nietzsche as Affirmative Thinker*, Boston: Martinus Nijhoff, 1986, p.77–8). I examine the relation between Nietzsche and Kant in Chapter Three.

guise)—a morality of decadence.[52] It is no coincidence that these 'defining' features of the current morality are also the subject of his harsh criticism. But, more importantly, the limitation of this approach is that it cannot accommodate Nietzsche's positive references to 'morality'. Instead, it merely highlights the features of one type of morality.

Similarly, if we attempt to derive an understanding of Nietzsche's view of 'morality' in the generic sense through conceptual analysis (i.e. the German terms that he uses for 'morality'), it will prove unsuccessful. For instance, the list of expressions include the following: *Ethik, Sittlichkeit, Moral,* and *Moralität.* Of the four terms, the first is used the least frequently, and is not confined to any specific period.[53] '*Ethik*' seems to refer to the formal, philosophical discipline. For instance, Nietzsche writes: "Who could possibly demand from such a philosophy an ethic (*Ethik*) with its necessary imperatives…" (PTG, p.62–3, KSA 1:831). In his English translation of *The Gay Science*, Walter Kaufmann will even translate '*Ethiken*' as 'ethical systems' (GS 1, KSA 3:371). The term '*Sittlichkeit*' is used most often in the earlier period, especially in *Daybreak* when Nietzsche wants to emphasize the link between '*Sitte*' (mores) and '*Sittlichkeit*' (morality). It is used to refer to ethical life, morality as a set of customs (mores) or traditions as opposed to an abstract, theoretical concept. In the early period, Nietzsche will use the more familiar expression, '*Sittlichkeit der Sitte*'[54] or 'morality of mores,' to account for the origin of morality (HH 96, KSA 2:92; D 9, KSA 3:21). This term is important for Nietzsche since it represents one of the earliest forms of morality, and thereafter can be contrasted with later developments (hence, the shift to '*Moral*'). For this reason, Nietzsche is consistent in his use of *Sittlichkeit*, *Sitten*, and *sittlich* to represent a social morality. For the most part, the term '*Sittlichkeit*' drops out in the later writings since it is '*Moral*', the moralized form of ethical life analyzed in the *Genealogy*, which is the subject of his critique. The most common expression that Nietzsche employs for 'morality' or 'morals' is '*Moral*,' and is widely used throughout his corpus. The terms '*Moral*' and '*Moralität*' can both be translated

---

52 Nietzsche can view both Kantian ethics and Christian morality as 'one particular morality' due to his tendency to classify some moralities into subgroups, for example, Kant's ethics as essentially Christian morality, i.e. slave morality. I owe this point to Thomas Brobjer.

53 See PTG, p.63, KSA 1:831; HH 37, KSA 2:60; GS 1, KSA 3:371.

54 The earliest reference that I was able to locate where Nietzsche emphasized the connection between mores (*Sitte*) and morality (*Sittlichkeit*) comes from the *Nachlaß* (Summer 1872–Early 1873), KSA 7:431. And, David S. Thatcher has suggested that Nietzsche may have borrowed the expression '*Sittlichkeit der Sitte*' from Walter Bagehot's *Physics and Politics* (1872). See Thatcher, "*Zur Genealogie der Moral*: Some Textual Annotations", *Nietzsche-Studien*, 1989, vol. 18, pp.587–99.

into English as 'morality', although the latter term is used less often.[55] At times, Schopenhauer (Nietzsche's main philosophical influence) will make a distinction between 'morality' (*die Moralität*), which concerns practice, and 'morals' (*die Moral*), which relates to theory.[56] However, there is no evidence to suggest that Nietzsche consistently followed his former 'educator's' distinction.[57] Interestingly, of the numerous references to 'morality' in Nietzsche's *Genealogy*, the only appearance of the word '*Moralität*' comes in the Third Essay where Nietzsche quotes from his own *Gay Science* (section 357). For the most part, the term '*Moral*' is used throughout the text.[58]

The German expression '*Moral*' seems to be used to represent any number of things including "the entirety of moral norms, principles, values, or the quality of being moral, moral behavior."[59] It is usually discussed in a pejorative sense except when it is preceded by such adjectives as 'noble', 'master', 'higher', 'healthy', 'aristocratic', and as we will see later, '*my*'. For instance, in the *Antichrist(ian)*, (*Der Antichrist*, written 1888), Nietzsche writes: "*Morality* (*Die Moral*)—no longer the expression of the conditions for the life and growth of a people, no longer its most basic instinct of life, but become abstract, become the antithesis of life—morality (*Moral*) as the systematic degradation of the imagination, as the 'evil eye' for all things" (A 25, KSA 6:194). This citation indicates that the meaning of the term '*Moral*' is not necessarily pejorative. 'Morality' (*die Moral*), as the conditions for the life and growth of a people, can either be life-affirming or life-negating. Similarly, in *Twilight of the Idols*, Nietzsche explains: "Every naturalism in morality (*Moral*)—that is, every healthy

---

55 The contemporary French philosopher, Vincent Descombes defines '*Moralität*' as 'personal morality' in his essay, "Nietzsche's French Moment" in Luc Ferry and Alain Renaut (eds.), *Why We Are Not Nietzscheans*, Chicago: University of Chicago Press, 1997, p.88. However, this definition is not consistent throughout Nietzsche's writings (e.g. HH 99, KSA 2:96).

56 Schopenhauer's distinction can be found in his essay devoted to the subject of ethics, *Preisschrift über die Grundlage der Moral* (*On the Basis of Morality*), OBM, 38.

57 Nietzsche was not only aware of Schopenhauer's distinction between *Moral* and *Moralität*, but he even utilized this distinction at times (e.g. KSA 11:128, "*Die thatsächliche Moralität des Menschen in dem Leben*..."). However, it is obvious that Nietzsche did not consistently adhere to this distinction (e.g. GM P:7, KSA 5:254, where he uses the term '*Moral*' to describe the morality which has actually existed, actually been lived). In keeping with Schopenhauer's usage, Nietzsche should have used '*Moralität*' to represent the practice of morality.

58 One notable exception is GM II:2, KSA 5:293 where Nietzsche uses the term '*übersittliche*' (supra-moral) to describe the 'sovereign individual' as one who is liberated from the morality of custom (*Sittlichkeit der Sitte*).

59 See M. Clark's English translation (and notes) of Nietzsche's *On the Genealogy of Morality*, Indianapolis: Hackett, 1998, p.119.

morality (*Moral*)—is dominated by an instinct of life…" (TI 5:4, KSA 6:85). Overall, I am inclined to say that possibly with the exception of '*Sittlichkeit*,' there does not appear to be much consistency in this 'old philologist's' moral vocabulary. At best, one can distinguish '*Moral*' from '*Sittlichkeit*,' insofar as the former generally connotes '*post*-customary' morality. Richard Schacht is not entirely correct in his claim that "while Nietzsche avails himself of a considerable number of German expressions and coinages in the course of his discussions of these matters—e.g., *die Moral*, *Moralität*, *Moralismus*, *moralisch*, *moralistisch*, and also *Sittlichkeit* and *sittlich*—he neither distinguishes systematically between them nor uses them in specified ways to mark the many distinctions he wishes to draw."[60] Although Schacht fails to acknowledge the consistent application of the term '*Sittlichkeit*', he is correct in claiming that a strict reliance on conceptual analysis does not shed much insight into Nietzsche's notion of 'morality' as a whole. Conversely, it seems to cloud the issue by providing an account, not of morality, but of moralities.

Surprisingly, few philosophers consider Nietzsche's 'definition' of morality (BGE 19, KSA 5:34) when attempting to ascertain his own understanding of the term. One notable exception is Martin Heidegger who writes:

> There is more than one kind of "morality," in Nietzsche's view, and these kinds vary, even in their metaphysical significance. On the one hand, morality in its broadest formal sense means every system of evaluations and relationships of dominance; morality here is conceived so broadly that even the new valuations might be called *moral* simply because they posit conditions of life. On the other hand, and as a rule, Nietzsche means by morality the system of those evaluations that are contained in the positing of the absolutely highest values in themselves—in the sense of Platonism and Christianity.[61]

Heidegger points out correctly that Nietzsche does not use the term 'morality' in a univocal sense. The value of Heidegger's reading is that it is able to accommodate both the pejorative and non-pejorative applications of the term 'morality'. In doing so, it captures, what I take to be Nietzsche's most frequent uses of the term. The first description coincides with his moral pluralism whereby he recognizes the possibility of higher moralities (BGE 202, KSA 5:124). Here, 'morality' is used in a general and non-pejorative sense and is consistent with Nietzsche's 'definition' from *Beyond Good and Evil*: "…morals (*Moral*), being understood as the doctrine of the relations of supremacy under which the phenomenon of 'life' comes to be" (BGE 19, KSA 5:34). Moreover, when Nietzsche writes: "Every naturalism in morality—that is, every healthy

---

60 Richard Schacht, *Nietzsche*, New York: Routledge, 1983, p.418.

61 Martin Heidegger, *Nietzsche*. (Vol. IV), San Francisco: Harper and Row, 1982, p.78.

morality—is dominated by an instinct of life" (TI 5:4, KSA 6:85), he is using 'morality' in this broad and formal sense of the term. Of course, this broad definition can accommodate both the non-pejorative and pejorative references to morality.

Readers, however, are most familiar with the second application of 'morality,' whereby the term is used in an entirely derogatory sense to refer to those moralities which Nietzsche deems decadent. Interestingly, he offers another 'definition' of morality which is consistent with this latter usage. In *Ecce Homo*, he writes: "*Definition of morality*: Morality (*Moral*)—the idiosyncrasy of decadents with the ulterior motive of revenging oneself against life—successfully. I attach value to this distinction" (EH XIV:7, KSA 6:373). Although I agree with Heidegger's articulation of these two senses of 'morality,' the first is so broad and general that it demands careful consideration, since there are subtleties even within Nietzsche's positive references to morality. For instance, when he refers to healthy and higher moralities, he is usually speaking of morality as "the expression of the conditions for the life and growth of a people…its most basic instinct of life" (A 25, KSA 6:194). Yet, when he uses the term "my morality," (*meine Moral*) he is alluding to a "personalized regime"[62] by positing the conditions (of existence) of his own life. Similarly, in *Beyond Good and Evil*, he writes: "In the philosopher, there is nothing whatever that is impersonal; and above all, his morality bears decided and decisive witness to *who he is*—that is, in what order of rank the innermost drives of his nature stand in relation to each other" (BGE 6, KSA 5:20). It is this notion of '*meine Moral*' which I would now like to address.

"Meine Moral"

In 1882, shortly after the publication of *The Gay Science*, Nietzsche penned no less than three letters[63] encouraging his friends to read his latest work, in particular Book IV, entitled "Sanctus Januarius." These letters are quite telling as to the reason behind Nietzsche's enthusiasm. For instance, in a letter to Paul Rée dated August 1882, he writes: "Do read 'Sanctus Januarius' [Book IV] in context! There my private morality (*meine Privat-Moral*) will be found together, as the sum of the conditions of *my* existence which prescribe an *ought* only if I *want*

62 Leslie P. Thiele, *Friedrich Nietzsche and the Politics of the Soul*, Princeton: Princeton University Press, 1990, p.39.

63 Friedrich Nietzsche, *Sämtliche Briefe: Kritische Studiensausgabe*, ed. Giorgio Colli and Mazzino Montinari, 8 vols., Berlin: De Gruyter, 1986. Hereafter KSB followed by volume and letter number. Letters to Jacob Burckhardt, August, 1882 (KSB, VI, no.277); Franz Overbeck, September 1882 (KSB, VI, no.301); Paul Rée, End of August 1882 (KSB, VI, no.292).

myself."[64] Next, consider this fragment from the period of *The Gay Science* (the work where *amor fati*[65] is first introduced in section 276 of Book IV). Nietzsche writes: "First the necessary (*das Nöthige*)—and you have to make it [the necessary] as beautiful and perfect as you can!...Love that which is necessary—*amor fati*, that would be *my morality* (*meine Moral*)." (KSA 9:643).[66] A variant of this quotation appears in the opening section of Book IV in the published work. However, *amor fati* is not described there as a morality. This omission, however, seems to me to be insignificant, since the term 'my morality' appears elsewhere in Book IV of *The Gay Science*. In section 338, Nietzsche writes: "I do not want to remain silent about my morality (*meine Moral*)..." (GS 338, KSA 3:568). For now, the actual content of this morality is not my concern. In fact, the complexity of his 'moral philosophy' is less attributed to its content, than its form (i.e. the manner in which it is presented). I will develop Nietzsche's positive morality in Chapter Four. My intent now, rather, is to show that Nietzsche's use of the expression 'my morality' indicates that he viewed himself as an affirmative thinker—certainly not just a critic of morality.

The expression 'my morality' drops out after *The Gay Science*, only to resurface five years later in *Ecce Homo* in the section entitled "Why I Am So Clever" (*Warum ich so klug bin*). What Nietzsche calls '*meine Moral*' is, however one wants to define it, a major departure from morality understood in the traditional sense. It appears that he is using the term 'my morality' simply to describe personal preferences relating to his own lifestyle. In particular, he reflects on his diet, nutrition, climate, and physiology, among other things. For instance, Nietzsche gives us some 'hints' from his morality which include such 'small things' as:

> *"Alcohol is bad for me."*
> *"A heartier meal is easier to digest than one that is too small."*
> *"No meals between meals, no coffee...Tea is wholesome only in the morning. A little, but strong."*
> *"Sit as little as possible."*
> *"Every kind of reading belongs among my recreations."*
> *"Early in the morning...to read a book at such a time is simply depraved!"* (EH II:1–3, KSA 6:278–286)

Clearly, one can detect the irony in the expression, '*meine Moral*', especially given this list of Nietzsche's moral hints. To a large extent, he is being rather playful when he reveals his 'moral code.' He is poking fun at the misguided attempts of

---

64 KSB, VI, no.292. See Friedrich Nietzsche. *The Gay Science*, trans. Walter Kaufmann, New York: Vintage, 1974, p.20.

65 Love of fate.

66 My translation.

moral philosophers who specify rules to govern our interactions with others, those who offer a code of conduct to apply to everyone. But, would it not be more appropriate for philosophers to scoff at Nietzsche's 'moral hints'?[67] Isn't it Nietzsche who is bastardizing the moral tradition by suggesting that we take seriously our diet, climate, and recreation? Am I to be chastized for writing this book (while drinking a coffee!) in uninspiring and soporific, London, Ontario, Canada instead of Paris "where men with *esprit* are living or have lived" (EH II: 2, KSA 6:282)? Is there any reason why we should include such 'small things' in our understanding of morality?

Nietzsche's appeal to physiology is by no means a novel approach.[68] A glimpse of his cultural environment reveals that Materialism dominated the German intellectual scene in the 1850's and 1860's. In particular, studies in physiology were growing rapidly due to new and important discoveries about human beings. Nietzsche's familiarity with German Materialism was evident from his careful reading of Friedrich Lange's *History of Materialism* (*Geschichte des Materialismus*, 1865), a 'treasure-house' which he had read a year after its publication. Nietzsche's 'truly burning thirst' for such studies was not short-lived as he explains that, "henceforth I really pursued nothing *more* than physiology, medicine, and natural sciences..." (EH VI:3, KSA 6:325). These same disciplines, it should be recalled, are what Nietzsche, at the end of the First Essay of the *Genealogy*, claims are of the utmost importance for the problem of the value of existing valuations. After a brief survey of some of the ideas of the prominent figures in German Materialism, it will become apparent that Nietzsche was certainly influenced by this intellectual tradition. For example, Ludwig Büchner wrote: "The researches and discoveries of modern times can no longer allow us to doubt that man, with all he has and possesses, be it mental or corporeal, is a *natural product* like all organic beings."[69] Nietzsche expressed a similar interest in 'naturalizing' humankind, and often maligned

---

67 Dan Conway dismisses Nietzsche's equation of morality with diet rather hastily since the remarks come from *Ecce Homo*, "an exceedingly dubious source", *Nietzsche's Dangerous Game*, Cambridge: Cambridge University Press, 1997, p.247. Robert C. Solomon refers to Nietzsche's moral hints (i.e. diet, good health, etc.) as "*Californische*" in *The Joy of Philosophy*, Oxford: Oxford University Press, 1999, p.35. Only Michel Haar, (*Par-delà le nihilisme: Nouveaux essais sur Nietzsche*, Paris: Presses Universitaires de France, 1998, p.2) takes seriously the expression "*mon éthique*" or "*ma morale*" but he links it to a "*religion nouvelle*". "*Cette morale qui s'adosse à l'affirmation 'dionysiaque' du monde a (ou aura) quelque chose de* sacré."

68 I owe the following description of Nietzsche's philosophical scene to Brian Leiter's insightful discussion of the influence of German Materialism in his Introduction to Nietzsche's *Daybreak*.

69 Ludwig Büchner, *Force and Matter*, cited in editor's introduction of *Daybreak*, Cambridge: Cambridge University Press, 1997, p.xi.

values which he regarded as 'anti-natural'. In his reading of Lange's *History of Materialism*, Nietzsche would have come across this materialist position: "The nature of man is…only a special case of universal physiology, as thought is only a special case in the chain of the physical processes of life."[70] The Materialists argued that human beings were products of nature, bodily organisms whose characteristics, including *values*, could be explained by reference to their physiological facts. Or, perhaps Nietzsche was familiar with the work of Jacob Moleschott, yet another physiologist from the 1850's, who wrote a detailed study on food and human digestion which led to a further study outlining the various diets that different types of people would require to flourish. By describing this aspect of Nietzsche's cultural environment, we can appreciate why he would include such things as diet, climate, nutrition, and recreation within the realm of morality. It is interesting to note that Nietzsche still preserved the term 'morality' rather than discard it in favour of a strictly physiological vocabulary. At times, however, he did rely on certain non-moralistic terms like 'healthy' versus 'sick'.

Apart from the Materialist background, there is also textual evidence to support the view that Nietzsche's use of '*meine Moral*' goes beyond mere irony. He explains:

> One will ask me why on earth I've been relating all these small things which are generally considered matters of complete indifference…Answer: these small things—nutrition, place, climate, recreation…are inconceivably more important than everything one has taken to be important so far. Precisely here one must begin to *relearn*. (EH II:10, KSA 6:295)

Is this not an expression of Nietzsche's '*Privat-Moral*'? He is describing the conditions of his existence in the same way that he confessed his private morality in a letter to Paul Rée.[71] Further, where is the irony in his letter to Rée dated December 1882 when referring to Lou Salomé, he writes?: "She [Lou] told me herself that she had no morality (*Moral*),—and I thought she had, like myself, a more severe morality (*Moral*) than anybody…"[72] These are not isolated, arbitrary remarks, but rather reflect the close relationship that Nietzsche asserts between moral values and physiology. Specifically, 'my morality' is the embodiment of a concrete way of life which is symptomatic of human flourishing. Here, it is the 'body' that teaches us how to live, informing

---

70 Friedrich Lange, *History of Materialism*, cited in editor's introduction of *Daybreak*, Cambridge: Cambridge University Press, 1997, p.xi.

71 KSB, VI, no.292.

72 KSB, VI, no.362; Letter to Rée, December 1882, translated in Kaufmann, *Portable Nietzsche*. New York: Viking, 1964 (orig. 1954), p.102.

us of what is conducive to health.[73] Indeed, Nietzsche flatters himself in thinking that he is the incarnation of human excellence. His formula for greatness, *amor fati*, "that one wants nothing to be different, not forward, not backward, not in all eternity…" (EH II:9, KSA 6:295) is not simply an ideal, but indicative of who he is, or perhaps who he *thinks* he is.[74]

There is a crucial point to be made regarding Nietzsche's positive references to 'morality' since even these remarks are not straightforward. '*Meine Moral*' expresses the conditions of Nietzsche's own existence, as the values belonging to a certain individual in late modernity. However, when he speaks of 'higher moralities' which 'ought to be possible' (BGE 202, KSA 5:124), he is alluding to the conditions for the life and growth of a *people* (see A 25, KSA 6:194). Both represent ascending life and are philosophically significant, but the former pertains to the present, the values by which Nietzsche lived, whereas the latter is *future*-oriented, viewing 'morality' as the (aristocratic) values belonging to a community or society. Consequently, I would like to propose that Nietzsche's positive reflections on morality be approached from these two perspectives: 1. his *future* aspirations—the anticipation of the 'return' to a morality which expresses the life-affirming conditions of a *people*. And, 2. the *moral interim*—the expression of the conditions of Nietzsche's '*Moral*' as his private morality. This distinction is in keeping with his claim that before we can "construct anew the laws of life and action" it is necessary that "we live an existence which is either a *prelude* or a *postlude* and the best we can do in this *interregnum* is to be as far as possible our own *reges* and found little *experimental states*" (D 453, KSA 3:274). An experimental morality of this sort is a prelude to a philosophy of the future. This distinction, I believe, has certain advantages over Heidegger's account of Nietzsche's morality. While it is not incorrect to claim that for Nietzsche "morality in its broadest formal sense means every system of evaluations and relationships of dominance,"[75] this understanding does not make explicit the bifurcation which I have noted. As well, there are interesting possibilities which emerge due to this distinction. For instance, if Nietzsche is accusing modernity with its life-negating, Christian values, of wallowing in decadence, then what sorts of values, we might ask, make life bearable for this iconoclast living within the twilight of the idols? Should we not

---

73 It is important not to confuse this notion of a 'private morality' with a morality of self-development (or individualistic morality) since the latter suggests that one decides what values to live by through a free act of will. I am reacting specifically against such voluntaristic readings of Nietzsche. In place of personal choice, Nietzsche speaks of the rank ordering of drives which amounts to passive obedience to the dictates of one's physiology.

74 See also GS 276, KSA 3:521.

75 M. Heidegger, *Nietzsche*, p.78.

be ruthless with Nietzsche and scrutinize the values which he embraces, maybe even subject him to his own symptomatology? This may not be our immediate concern, but one certainly worth pursuing at a later point.

For now, since I take Nietzsche's primary ethical concern to be the production of exemplary human beings, there is no contradiction between the two positions outlined above. Both, the future-oriented (political) task of the restoration of a healthy aristocracy, and the experimentalism located within late modernity aim towards the production of exemplary human beings. As early as *Philosophy in the Tragic Age of the Greeks* (*Die Philosophie im tragischen Zeitalter der Griechen*, 1873), Nietzsche wrote: "The task is to bring to light what we *must ever love and honor* and what no subsequent enlightenment can take away: great individual human beings" (PTG, p.24, KSA 1:802). Nietzsche's writings display a continued fascination with the lives of exemplary human beings. For instance, in the *Untimely Meditations* (*Unzeitgemässe Betrachtungen*, 1873–76) he proclaims: "No, the *goal of humanity* cannot lie in its end but only *in its highest exemplars*" (UADH 9, KSA 1:317). Throughout his corpus, one finds scattered references to great human beings such as Thucydides, Goethe, Napoleon, and Bizet, among others.

Despite his special affinity for the exceptional type, Nietzsche did not offer any clear *a priori* criteria for being this paradigm of human flourishing. What differentiates the exceptional type is that he has enough energy to create himself as a work of art. It is this 'energy', this '*overfullness of life*', which makes it possible for them not simply to recreate themselves frequently in new forms, but also to create: to give birth to what is new and surprising. Nietzsche offers a vision of the exemplary individual which involves becoming an artist of one's life, that is, a self-creator. This means 'becoming what one is', a human being who creates his own values, thereby giving *oneself* laws to live by (see GS 335, KSA 3:563). In that same passage, he contrasts this individual with 'those who sit in moral judgment', regarding the latter as offensive to his 'taste'.

Leaving aside the difficulties associated with 'life' as a criterion for evaluating moralities, and granting that morality is a sign-language of our drives and affects, we could describe exemplary human beings as embodying a high degree of vitality. For instance, they would possess certain drives which would be classified as life-enhancing, and for that reason they would be examples of human flourishing. In other words, their value would be determined by the order of rank of their drives (BGE 228, KSA 5:165). But, this view leads Nietzsche into another serious problem. An individual's drives belong to him as a matter of natural fact, and his morality is simply an expression of this endowment. It would appear then that both types of human beings (exemplary and decadent) are products of their own particular physical constitution. In other words, one's status as a human being is determined by fate. In fact, Nietzsche presents his own greatness in fatalistic terms. He writes: "The good fortune of my existence lies...in its fatality" (EH I:1, KSA 6:264). And, "It is my fate that I have to be the first *decent* human being" (EH XIV:1, KSA 6:365). This anti-volitional model of human flourishing is expressed nicely in *Twilight of the Idols* as Nietzsche claims: "a well-turned-out human being, a 'happy one,' *must* perform certain actions and shrinks instinctively from other actions; he carries the order, which he represents physiologically..." (TI 6:2, KSA 6:89). The problem, however, lies in reconciling Nietzsche's fatalism with his rhetoric of self-creation. On many occasions he will use a distinctively voluntaristic vocabulary, often counseling others to 'create themselves,' or 'give style to one's character' (GS 335,290, KSA 3:563,530). If we are to take Nietzsche seriously as an affirmative thinker, then it will be necessary to resolve this tension. Otherwise, it would appear that his moral legacy is restricted to mere classification, i.e. cataloguing those types of individuals who exude greatness and those who do not. On this view, exemplary human beings would perhaps be deserving of our admiration, but nothing more.

*

In this chapter I have attempted to demonstrate the complexity of Nietzsche's views on morality. Although known primarily for his vitriolic attacks against morality, Nietzsche did not conclude that morality as a project was bankrupt. Rather, he wanted us to become receptive to a very different conception of morality, one that is internal—relating to the body/physiology, and not some external standpoint imposed upon us. In accord with his vitalism, Nietzsche's ethics is rooted in a notion of human flourishing. His ethical concern with the production of exemplary human beings is a persistent theme throughout his philosophical career. By outlining a 'natural history of morals' featuring three periods with different means of evaluating human conduct, Nietzsche was able to show that morality had evolved. In fact, his entire approach to morality was informed by an historical sense as he appealed to 'typology' or 'genealogy' to carve out an understanding of what has hitherto been referred to as 'morality'. Nietzsche's genealogy revealed a decisive turning point in the history of our understanding of morality: there are two basic types of morality—master ('Roman, pagan, classical, Renaissance') and slave ('Christian'), the former is the sign-language of ascending life, whereas the latter is symptomatic of the negation or decline of life. Nietzsche's *Genealogy*, then, is complemented by his symptomatology—his historical analysis reveals the different moralities which are subsequently evaluated according to his standard of 'life'. In this way,

Nietzsche has given direction to the task of questioning the *value* of our moral values.

In referring to himself as an 'immoralist', Nietzsche revealed his particular standpoint. With a criterion for evaluation, the immoralist can wage war against those moralities which are hostile to life. In doing so, the goal would be to overcome Christian morality, and inspire a revaluation of values. As well, Nietzsche's definition of his 'immoralism' identified the scope of his attack on morality by limiting his opposition to decadent moralities, his favourite target being Christian morality. I turned to Maudemarie Clark's reading of Nietzsche's immoralism in order to refute her claim that he was rejecting *all* morality. I felt this to be necessary in order to present Nietzsche as an affirmative thinker with an ethics of human flourishing. By arguing that Nietzsche was only attacking a type of morality, I could explain how his 'immoralism' is consistent with his positive references to morality.

In addition to acknowledging Nietzsche's treatment of morality as symptomatology, I wanted to show the inadequacy of searching for general and universal criteria (i.e. an external criterion) for what he would label a 'morality'. I pointed out the limitations of cataloguing the various features of morality which recurred throughout his discussion on the subject. At best, this approach only informed us of the features of one type of morality, and they were usually mentioned for the purpose of criticizing. Next, I considered the different German terms that Nietzsche used for 'morality' discovering that '*Sittlichkeit*' was generally used to represent an early phase of morality (i.e. a morality of customs) before 'morals' eventually became reduced to 'Morality' ('*Moral*'), the moralized form of ethical life analyzed in the *Genealogy*. But, since Nietzsche applied the term '*Moral*' in both a derogatory and eulogistic sense, there seemed to be no good reason to treat this term as univocal.

From there, I examined Heidegger's discussion of Nietzsche's understanding of morality. Heidegger recognized that there was not just one use of the term 'morality' in Nietzsche, and provided two definitions reflecting Nietzsche's broad and narrow use of the term. I agreed with Heidegger that morality in the broad sense would include "every system of evaluations and relationships of dominance," and his narrow rendering of the term as "the system of evaluations that are contained in the positing of the absolutely highest values in themselves—in the sense of Platonism and Christianity."[76] But, even still, I felt that we must tread carefully since this broad definition is mired in ambiguity. For instance, I alluded to a distinction between Nietzsche's positive references to morality, a distinction that would be lost if we eagerly classified them under this broad definition. Specifically, we would fail to appreciate the

76 M. Heidegger, *Nietzsche*, p.78

extent of his moral concerns if we overlooked the distinction between '*meine Moral*' and the 'higher morality' of the future, despite both being a 'system' of evaluations and relations of dominance. With these reflections on Nietzsche's work on morality, we may be denied access to general and universal criteria of morality, but we are not denied an understanding of what he means by 'morality'. Indeed, he claims to be an 'immoralist' but speaks of different 'moralities'. The lesson to be learned is that it is always crucial to consider the context of his discussion of morality. Nietzsche's extra-moral project has been well-documented, and we are now in a position to examine his attack on traditional morality.

2

The 'Campaign Against Morality'

One man is as ten thousand for me, if he is best.
—Heraclitus (fragment 113)

The task is to bring to light what we *must ever love and honor* and what no subsequent enlightenment can take away: great individual human beings.
— PTG, p.24, KSA 1:802

Whoever reflects upon the way in which the type man can be raised to his greatest splendor and power will grasp first of all that he must place himself outside morality; for morality has been essentially directed to the opposite end: to obstruct or destroy that splendid evolution wherever it has been going on…A tendency hostile to life is therefore characteristic of morality, in so far as it wants to overpower the types of life.
—WP 897, KSA 12:225–26

In his retrospective examination of *Daybreak* (1881), Nietzsche wrote: "With this book my campaign against morality (*Moral*) begins" (EH VII:1, KSA 6:329). In the preceding chapter, I discussed the scope of his *Feldzug*, arguing that Nietzsche's unabashed assault on morality is restricted to 'the morality that would unself man' in which he specifically targeted, as its greatest progenitor, Christian morality. In the works following *Daybreak*, Nietzsche's 'campaigning' efforts intensified, as he waged war on all facets of Christian morality. It is the aim of this chapter to examine Nietzsche's various reasons for rejecting morality. In doing so, I proceed by outlining the major components of morality to which his critique is directed. I argue that these various strands (e.g. the moral subject, unconditional and universal morality, altruism, anti-natural morality) function as tributaries merging into one main objection. This objection can be stated as follows: Morality, in representing the needs or interests of the masses (the lowest common denominator) thwarts the development of human flourishing.[1] In other words, Nietzsche rejects Christian morality insofar as it is harmful to those rare, exemplary individuals with different needs and interests. The onus is on Nietzsche then to explain *who* these higher types are, and in what way they are being harmed by the current morality.

One of the consequences of my reading is that Nietzsche's ethics is regarded, in one very important sense, as *entirely* affirmative insofar as his critique is motivated by his concern for the production of higher types. Hence, I deny the positive/negative dichotomy so often associated with his moral thinking since he does not regard 'negation' and 'affirmation' as opposites. In fact, for Nietzsche, negation *is* affirmation, and when applied specifically to his 'critique' of morality, he explains: "whoever wants to be a creator in good and evil, must first be an annihilator and break values" (EH XIV:2, KSA 6:366). As we can see then, 'annihilating' or 'breaking' values is a necessary *condition* for the creation of new ones. What I shall show throughout the course of this chapter is that his criticisms proceed from his ethics of human flourishing. As a result, Nietzsche's caustic indictment of morality cannot be divorced from his affirmative ethics. Note, however, that there is no contradiction in drawing a distinction, as I have done, between 'morality' as the object of his attack, and his affirmative morality of human flourishing. These are two very different forms of morality despite the fact that the latter serves as the inspiration for his critique. Likewise, it is no objection to my view, then, to point out the obvious: that Nietzsche's writings contain one of the most notorious attacks on morality found throughout the history of philosophy. In what follows, I will show that the fundamental components of morality are closely connected to his affirmative insights.

The Moral 'Subject'

The term 'subject' or 'self' is often applied to a person capable of thought and experience, and able to engage in deliberative action. In other words, one possesses the capacity to choose between alternatives and is able to do what

---

1 This reading of Nietzsche's fundamental objection to morality is one that I share with Brian Leiter ("Morality in the Pejorative Sense: On the Logic of Nietzsche's Critique of Morality", British Journal of the History of Philosophy, Vol.3/No.1, 1995, pp.113–145). However, Leiter and I disagree on the scope of Nietzsche's critique of morality. As I argued in Chapter One, Nietzsche's attack on morality is directed specifically at Christian morality, and its secular derivatives. In other words, my view is that Nietzsche subsumes these other secular moralities under 'Christian morality'. However, Leiter's position is that "it will not do to say that he [Nietzsche] simply attacks Christian or Kantian or European or utilitarian morality—though he certainly at times attacks all of these" (p.114).

one chooses.[2] According to this view, the 'subject' is regarded as a causal power. This means that the individual himself is the legislator of his acts. There are no *external* causes (i.e. physical or psychological ones) which prevent the person from choosing between two options. The moral subject is endowed with a 'will' that is free. The 'will' itself is construed as a mental faculty responsible for acts of volition (e.g. choosing, deciding, and initiating motion). There is a specific reason why we might ask whether someone acted voluntarily (i.e. whether he knew what he was doing, and whether his act was intended). It is often maintained that since a person's will is under his control, his acts are subject to moral assessment. The dependency of moral responsibility upon a free will is a major theme in moral philosophy.[3] Our moral worth as persons is derived from this freedom. Indeed, moral behaviour is an expression of that freedom. By locating the foundations of moral philosophy in the nature of persons as free 'subjects', we are able to account for the basic question of ethics 'what ought we to do?'.

It is important, however, to recognize one notable exception to the aforementioned account of the 'free' moral subject. Kant offers a metaphysical conception of the moral agent, in his words, the 'noumenal' self, which is outside time and causality, hence undermining the familiar notion of an empirically determined human being. Prior to Kant, most moral philosophers recognized the dependency of morality on freedom (of some sort), but it was Kant who revolutionized the very notion of 'freedom' by denying its experiential basis. For Kant, 'freedom' in the moral sense is a transcendental Idea of reason insofar as it refers only to that which *transcends* our sensory experience. To be a moral agent, then, means that we judge how to act morally by adhering to norms determined exclusively by our own reasoning—norms that are immune from the persuasion of practical considerations. In other words, we act according to our own causal power, rather than to any causes external to reason such as our desires and inclinations. In fact, Kant defines 'freedom', in the positive sense, as the power of absolute causal self-

2 Ted Honderich (ed.).*The Oxford Companion to Philosophy*, 'Self', Oxford: Oxford University Press, 1995, p.816.

3 David Hume, however, rejected this view arguing that the doctrine of liberty cannot yield responsibility and blameworthiness since 'free' actions proceed from random acts—i.e., nothing in a person which is constant and durable. According to Hume, an action is blamable only if it proceeds from the principles of necessity, in particular, if it proceeds from one's character or disposition (see Hume's *Treatise*, Bk.II, Part III, section II). Nietzsche never questioned that freedom was a presupposition of morality, since the practical morality he was scrutinizing relied explicitly on the notion of 'free will', regardless of philosophical theories which dispute it.

determination according to our own reasoning.[4] Moreover, Kant retains the view of ordinary moral consciousness that we are responsible for our immoral actions.[5] In this way, Kant can be understood as the supreme representative of the morality of freedom, autonomy, and self-legislation despite the fact that such concepts as free will, responsibility, blame and guilt are common in various non-Kantian accounts of morality.

In addition to these two conflicting views of moral agency (i.e. the Kantian, and let us call the first, the 'traditional' interpretation), one could list other competing philosophical theories of the 'self'. As we shall see in Chapter Three, Nietzsche certainly has an axe to grind with Kantian ethics, but when it comes to identifying the account of moral agency to which his critique is directed, his attack is focused primarily on the traditional interpretation. But, why does he insist on this one particular view to the exclusion of others? To begin with, Nietzsche is first and foremost a *cultural* moral critic which means that, despite his objections to moral theories, his fundamental concern lies in the morality that is actually lived. Since he identifies the current morality as Christian, including its secular surrogates, his critique must extend to the conception of the self that it advances. One may, however, wish to question whether Nietzsche is being faithful to the Christian understanding of the 'self'.

It may prove useful then to consider St. Thomas Aquinas' account of the moral agent. In Aquinas' *On the Virtues*, he describes the nature of human beings in terms of an embodied soul, noting that this composite includes, among other things, a will which is the immediate source of action. Actions which result from the power of the will are 'immanent actions', that is, actions which originate and end in man. For instance, the act of enjoying a sunset is immanent as is the act of wanting a glass of water. When Aquinas confidently asserts that "Without doubt it must be said that man has free choice…since without free choice one could not merit or demerit, or be justly rewarded or

---

4 Kant, *Groundwork of the Metaphysics of Morals*, ed. Mary J. Gregor, in *The Cambridge Edition of the Works of Immanuel Kant: Practical Philosophy*. Cambridge: Cambridge University Press, 1996, p.94–5.

5 Kant writes: "The action is ascribed to the agent's intelligible character; in the moment when he utters the lie, the guilt is entirely his own. Reason…is completely free, and the lie is entirely due to its default" (*Pu.R.* A555/B583). And, "all moral evil springs from freedom; otherwise it would not be *morally* evil" (*Lect.* 295/67). As well, the "subjective grounds of choice…must itself always be an expression of freedom (for otherwise the use or abuse of man's power of choice (*Willkür*) in respect of the moral law could not be imputed to him nor could the good or bad in him be called moral)" (*Rel.* 21/16–17). See also *Pr.R.* 98–100.

punished,"[6] he is referring to an immanent act which is free. Moreover, he is highlighting the correlation between free choice and responsibility. According to Aquinas, a free choice is an 'elicited act of the will'—meaning acts which flow directly and immediately from the will (e.g choosing, desiring). He claims that the will is a rational power (or 'rational appetite') whose acts are dependent upon the knowledge generated by the intellect. Although Aquinas speaks of choice as involving the combined efforts of the intellect and will, he argues that since choice pertains primarily to movement, choice is primarily of the will. It may be objected that Aquinas never refers to a 'free will', only 'free choices', but since choice arises from the will, the application of either expression is warranted.[7] In *The Principles of Nature*, Aquinas again draws attention to the capacity for deliberation that one finds in the voluntary agent.[8]

While not all philosophers subscribe to this notion of the 'subject' and its correlation to moral responsibility, Nietzsche thinks that he has identified the account which permeates the cultural scene of his day. Before discussing Nietzsche's critique of moral agency, it is worth pointing out that in relation to his overall campaign against morality, this particular *descriptive* component is of lesser significance than the *normative* content of morality examined in the remaining sections of this chapter.[9] Nevertheless, Nietzsche is quite adamant in voicing his opposition to the 'moral world order' which presupposes the existence of free subjects accountable for their actions. He proceeds to unmask the 'free' moral subject as a metaphysical fiction in an effort to undermine the very notion of human subjectivity.[10] Our tendency to posit the 'subject' or 'substratum' as the cause underlying all attributes and actions betrays an ingrained prejudice. Specifically, we have acquired the grammatical habit of assuming that there must be a subject behind the action, a doer behind the deed. Nietzsche does not deny that this fiction may be indispensable, but this

---

6 Aquinas, '*On Free Choice*' in *Selected Writings of Thomas Aquinas*, trans. Robert P. Goodwin. New York: MacMillan, 1965, p.121.

7 Ibid, p.120.

8 Ibid, p.15.

9 For instance, even if a particular philosopher shared precisely the same view of the 'self' as Nietzsche, it could also be expected that Nietzsche would repudiate his or her *normative* ideals.

10 Nietzsche is not alone in his attack on the freedom of the will. There is a line of similar criticism from Hume to Gilbert Ryle; one found also in Sartre and others. However, if one considers the consequences of their rejection of free will, then none of these philosophers come close to emulating Nietzsche's 'revaluation of values'. Moreover, Nietzsche's rejection of morality was *not* especially preoccupied with the 'error of free will' since he claims that errors of this sort were not what 'horrified' him, but rather the normative content of Christian morality (EH XIV:7). I elaborate on this point later in the chapter.

simply indicates that it is a condition of life, rather than asserting its truth. This seduction of language is described as follows:

> For just as the popular mind separates the lightning from its flash and takes the latter for an *action*, for the operation of a subject called lightning, so popular morality also separates strength from expressions of strength, as if there were a neutral substratum behind the strong man, which was *free* to express strength or not to do so. But there is no such substratum; there is no 'being' behind doing, effecting, becoming; 'the doer' is merely a fiction added to the deed—the deed is everything. (GM I:13, KSA 5:279)

'*Im Anfang war die Tat*'[11] would be a fitting slogan for Nietzsche's view. In exposing the 'subject' as a fiction (i.e. a term which designates a non-existing *unity* underlying the vast array of impulses and drives), Nietzsche has at the same time rejected its component parts, in particular, the 'will'. On this view, the subject is treated as a fable, and is consequently, stripped of its causal power.

The separation of doer from deed is characteristic of the Christian, moral interpretation of existence which isolates the 'subject' as a responsible and accountable agent. Nietzsche rejects this 'metaphysics of the hangman' (TI 6:7, KSA 6:96) by outlining the host of errors involved in this misdiagnoses of the 'will'. To begin with, we naively accepted three 'inward facts': the belief that we knew what a cause is, the belief that we ourselves are causal in the act of willing, and that the causes of an act can be located in consciousness (as 'motives') (TI 6:3, KSA 6:90). We may feel that we are causal in the act of willing, but this experience is owed to a false psychology (i.e. belief in an imaginary causality). Yet, the desire for 'freedom of the will' in the metaphysical sense can be attributed to the desire to bear ultimate responsibility for one's actions (BGE 21, KSA 5:35). This yearning to be the *causa sui* was inculcated by the theologian who possessed an instinct for judging and punishing, and sought to make people responsible. Nietzsche calls this notion of *causa sui* "a sort of rape and perversion of logic" (BGE 21, KSA 5:35) because our actions, he thinks, cannot be based on 'choices' issuing from the 'will' since these choices themselves are determined by facts, that is, by one's physiological constitution. On his view, then, the make-up of our 'will' is owed to physiological and cultural determinants which remove the possibility that the individual is the architect of his will. In claiming that the 'will' cannot be regarded as autonomous, Nietzsche has denied the accompanying notion of 'responsibility'. His point is that we cannot be held accountable for our choices and actions since these are the result

---

11 In the beginning was the deed. Goethe. *Faust*, I. Intro.

of facts belonging to one's nature.[12] Hence, Nietzsche is *not* the philosopher of 'self-creation' as is often asserted, but rather the philosopher of fatalism.[13]

As I have indicated, the 'will', for Nietzsche, is an example of a 'phantom' of the 'inner world', a 'fiction', invented for the purpose of imputing guilt. His task is to cleanse psychology by extricating the concepts of guilt and punishment from the world. And, putting an end to the superstition of free will is left to the '*new* psychologist' (BGE 12, KSA 5:27) in order to make room for new values which will not be rooted in this antiquated and spurious conception of the human subject. However, despite Nietzsche's critique of the 'subject' or 'soul', he refuses to dispense with the term itself. His specific objection is to the 'atomistic need', especially the '*soul atomism*' preached by Christianity. This expression refers to "the belief which regards the soul as something indestructible, eternal, indivisible, as a monad, as an *atomon*" (12). Here, the subject is construed as a unity underlying our various impulses and drives. But, Nietzsche's position is that it is unnecessary to assume that these diverse impulses are the effect of one substratum.

In place of the confused notion of the 'soul atom', Nietzsche turns to the body which he thinks is a "richer, clearer, more tangible phenomenon" (WP 489, KSA 12:205-06). In claiming that the individual is first and foremost a physiological being, Nietzsche treats the body as his starting point: "I am body entirely, and nothing beside; and soul is only a word for something in the body" (Z I:4, KSA 4:39).[14] This shift to the body and its affective existence results in a

---

12 Compatibilists would disagree with Nietzsche's *causa sui* argument, and insist that free will and responsibility are consistent with the causality of the will. They maintain that determinism is true because every event has a cause, but they make room for the idea of freedom by arguing that the distinction between a free (i.e. voluntary) and compelled (i.e. involuntary) act is *not* based on the distinction between the uncaused and the caused. All actions rather are caused but some are caused *internally* (free actions) whereas others have *external* causes (involuntary actions). Nietzsche would respond by claiming that these internal causes, too, are really the product of facts about our nature.

13 Examples of those commentators who read Nietzsche as a philosopher of 'self-creation' include: Karl Jaspers, *Nietzsche: An Introduction to the Understanding of his Philosophical Activity*, trans. Charles F. Wallraff and Frederick J. Schmitz. Baltimore: Johns Hopkins University Press, 1997; Alexander Nehamas, *Nietzsche: Life as Literature.* Cambridge, Mass: Harvard University Press, 1985; Richard Rorty, *Contingency, Irony, and Solidarity.* Cambridge: Cambridge University Press, 1989; Peter Berkowitz, *Nietzsche: The Ethics of an Immoralist.* Cambridge, Mass: Harvard University Press, 1995.

14 It is interesting to compare this statement to Feuerbach's conception of the self in *Grundsatzen der Philosophie der Zukunft* (1849) cited in Friedrich Lange's *History of Materialism*, II, p.523, a work which greatly influenced Nietzsche: "*Ich bin ein wirkliches, ein sinnliches Wesen: der Leib gehört zu meinem Wesen; ja, der Leib in seiner Totalität ist mein Ich, mein Wesen selber*" ("I am a real, a sensible being; the body is part of my being; nay, the body in its totality, is my ego, is itself my essence").

reconceptualization of human subjectivity, where the 'subject' is regarded, *not* as a unity underlying its numerous drives, but as multiplicity. Nietzsche explains:

> But the way is open for new versions and refinements of the soul-hypothesis; and such conceptions as 'mortal soul,' and 'soul as subjective multiplicity,' and 'soul as social structure of the drives (*Triebe*) and affects (*Affekte*),' want henceforth to have citizens' rights in science. (BGE 12, KSA 5:27)

On this view, the human subject is constituted by a multiplicity of competing drives. Rather than serving as a causal agent, the 'subject' is now the site of warring impulses and drives. "Every drive is a kind of lust to rule; each one has its perspective that it would like to compel all the other drives to accept as a norm" (WP 481, KSA 12:315).[15] In other words, the subject consists of what Nietzsche will alternatively refer to as 'drives' (*Triebe*), 'affects' (*Affekte*), 'impulses' (*Reize, Impulse*), 'instincts' (*Instinkte*), 'passions' (*Leidenschaften*), 'feelings' (*Gefühlen*), 'desires' (*Begierden*), 'forces' (*Kräfte*), and the like. Note, however, that this version of the 'soul-hypothesis' explains the form or function of the 'soul', or affective body. In outlining what the 'soul' does, Nietzsche is offering a functionalist account rather than describing the content or ingredients of the 'soul'. The picture of human agency that we are left with, then, is that of a human, biological organism controlled by the constant play and interaction of its drives and impulses. Far from being an active agent, or self-propelled wheel, Nietzsche's 'subject' is, as Conway nicely puts it, "a passive conduit of the undifferentiated vital forces that flow through it [the visible body]."[16]

How does conceiving the 'subject' as a 'subjective multiplicity' or as a 'social structure of drives' help explain what actually takes place during this so-called 'willing'? To avoid the popular prejudice[17] of treating the will as if it were the best-known fact, Nietzsche proceeds cautiously with the following 'unphilosophical' observations: 1. "in all willing there is, first, a plurality of sensations"; 2. "just as sensations are to be recognized as ingredients of the will, so, secondly, should thinking also: in every act of will there is a ruling thought"; 3. "the will is not only a complex of sensation and thinking, but it is above all an

---

15 It is worthwhile to note, however, that there are a multitude of 'ruling' or 'chief' drives so that it is not always the same drive executing the command in the individual. This view allows Nietzsche to explain different experiences as belonging to the 'same' self, but it does not provide an adequate account of personal identity. For instance, how can a multiplicity of drives produce a unitary self that conceives of those drives as its own? There is no effort on Nietzsche's part to account for this possibility.

16 Dan Conway, *Nietzsche's Dangerous Game*, 1997, p.54.

17 Nietzsche makes a specific reference to Schopenhauer (see BGE 19, KSA 5:31–2).

affect, and specifically the affect of a command. That which is termed 'freedom of the will' is essentially the affect of superiority in relation to him who must obey" (BGE 19, KSA 5:32). Here, Nietzsche models 'willing' after the relations of dominance that one might find in 'a well-constructed and happy commonwealth'. However, unlike the political model where a ruler's commands are obeyed by the ruled, the individual's willing means that he simultaneously commands and obeys 'himself'. He notes that this aspect is what is 'strangest' about the will. Indeed, in willing we seem to experience ourselves as the executor of the command who comes to expect a particular action (i.e. the effect of his command). The expectation of the action gives rise to a feeling of the 'necessity of effect'. Nietzsche writes: "he who wills believes with a fair amount of certainty that will and action are somehow one; he ascribes the success, the carrying out of the willing, to the will itself, and thereby enjoys an increase of the sensation of power which accompanies all success" (BGE 19, KSA 5:33). Freedom of the will, then, is explained in terms of the individual who credits himself (i.e. his will) as the executor of the order, and then delights in feeling that '*L'effet c'est moi*'. Just as the rulers identify themselves with the successes of the commonwealth, the individual experiences the same delight as commander. Nietzsche reiterates: "In all willing it is absolutely a question of commanding and obeying, on the basis…of a social structure composed of many 'souls'" (BGE 19, KSA 5:33).

Although Nietzsche claims that the theory of free will is one of the most easily refuted, he does not endorse its opposite, the 'unfree will'. In fact, he insists that the notion of an 'unfree will' represents 'a misuse of cause and effect' (BGE 21, KSA 5:35). The concept of cause and effect is a mere projection on our part, and hence is meaningless when it comes to explaining phenomenon.[18] As conventional fictions, their use should be restricted to designation and communication. In addition, Nietzsche observed that the problem of the 'unfreedom of the will' led to two opposing standpoints from which he quickly dissociated himself. On the one hand, he noted that some individuals will not abandon the view that they have a personal right to their merits at any price, while conversely, another segment of the population feel that they cannot be blamed or held responsible for anything. He associates the latter with "a sort of socialist pity" which occurs, for instance, in their sympathy for criminals (BGE 21, KSA 5:36). Ultimately, thus spoke Nietzsche, the

18 This remark seems to suggest that Nietzsche rejects the notions of 'cause and effect' altogether, but when viewed in its proper context, he is merely undermining the claim that 'cause and effect' can relate to the noumenal world (the world 'in itself'). He makes no claim whatsoever that causation does not occur in the phenomenal world (the world of appearance). See BGE 21.

'unfree will' belongs to mythology, since there are only '*strong* and *weak* wills' (21).[19] The strength or weakness of the will depends, not on an individual's free choice, but rather on the body's measure of vitality which includes its capacity to order and organize its varied assortment of competing drives.

This description of subjectivity permeates Nietzsche's writings (both published and unpublished). In a note from 1884, he explains:

> In contrast to the animals, man has cultivated an abundance of *contrary* drives and impulses within himself:...Moralities (*Moralen*) are the expression of locally limited orders of rank in his multifarious world of drives, so man should not perish through their contradictions. Thus a drive as master, its opposite weakened, refined, as the impulse that provides the stimulus for the activity of the chief drive. The highest man would have the greatest multiplicity of drives, in the greatest strength that can be endured. Indeed, where the plant 'man' shows himself strongest one finds instincts that conflict powerfully (e.g. Shakespeare), but are controlled. (WP 966, KSA 11:289)

Amongst the competing drives, a ruling thought or 'chief drive' will emerge according to the relation of command and obedience, and will determine the order of rank of impulses. It is precisely for this reason that Nietzsche wants to include 'willing' within the sphere of morals, since morals is understood as the "relations of supremacy under which the phenomenon of 'life' comes to be" (BGE 19, KSA 5:34). As mentioned previously, this 'willing' has nothing to do with attributing the command to the deliberate willing of a causal agent. The belief that 'this could have happened differently', or 'I do not have to do this' is based on error (WS 12, KSA 2:547). As Leiter explains, "A person is an arena in which the struggle of drives is played out; how they play out determines what he believes, what he values, what he becomes. But *qua* conscious self or 'agent', the person takes no active part in the process."[20] The notion of 'self-mastery' often credited to Nietzsche simply refers to the 'control' of a master drive, rather than to the volitional capacity of a moral agent.

Nietzsche sometimes speaks of "*my conception of freedom*" where freedom is measured "according to the resistance which must be overcome, according to the exertion required in order to remain on top" (TI 9:38, KSA 6:140). Similarly, he describes 'happiness' as "the feeling that power is *growing*, that resistance is overcome" and the 'good' as "everything that heightens the feeling of power in man, the will to power, power itself" (A 2, KSA 6:170). This idea of 'freedom' as overcoming resistances must not be confused with the *volitional*

---

19 Nietzsche's reference here to 'wills' should not be confused with the traditional conception of the 'will' which he has gone to great lengths to refute.

20 Brian Leiter, 'Fatalism and Self-Creation in Nietzsche' in *Willing and Nothingness: Schopenhauer as Nietzsche's Educator*. Oxford: Oxford University Press, 1998, p.255.

model which recognizes that a person can work at cultivating a degree of self-control previously lacking. At times, Nietzsche's rhetoric of self-creation seems to allow for such a possibility, as for instance in section 290 of *The Gay Science* where Nietzsche counsels the reader to 'give style' to one's character, claiming that this requires that "one survey all the strengths and weaknesses of their nature and then fit them into an artistic plan" adding that the strongest natures will delight "in such constraint and perfection under a law of their own". Yet, what commentators often leave out is the crucial point of the passage which undermines the voluntaristic account. In the end, Nietzsche explains, when one has succeeded in giving style to one's character, "it becomes evident how the constraint of a single taste governed and formed everything large and small." This 'single taste' refers to the psycho-physiological determinants that account for what a human being is. For Nietzsche, this means that the individual is entirely constrained, and is therefore, neither the author of one's acts nor of one's character since these are determined by facts about the person. Ultimately, Nietzsche's critique of human agency resulted in a reconceptualization of human subjectivity with the expressed concern for the type of 'willing' (or configuration of drives) conducive to human flourishing.

Nietzsche's theory of human subjectivity is certainly a major departure from the conception of the subject he targets, even if it resembles a similar line of criticism from Hume to Gilbert Ryle, and others. For instance, as will become evident later in this chapter, Nietzsche's psycho-physiologically based account of human subjectivity provides the ground for his diagnoses and evaluation of 'human types' according to which the instincts and drives of an individual serve as a measure of one's vitality, whether one represents the instincts of decadence or health. In addition, one of the consequences of my reading of Nietzsche as an anti-voluntarist is that it undermines those interpretations which view him as promoting the heroic feats attainable through an act of will. More importantly, however, in undermining the conception of a free, moral agent, the basic question of ethics 'what should I do' is rendered obsolete. As we shall see later, Nietzsche's fatalism is responsible in large part for the absence of any prescriptive moral theory.

Morality as Unconditional and Universal

Despite Nietzsche's critique of the metaphysical view of agency that he takes to be implicit in Christian morality, his primary concern lies in the normative content of morality. Hence, his rejection of this account of human agency plays a subordinate role in his overall attack on morality. For instance, Nietzsche is critical of those philosophers who think that they have criticized morality itself when they have simply exposed the 'superstition of free will' (GS 345, KSA

3:579). The fact that morality has grown out of an error does not address the problem of its *value.* And, referring to Christian morality, he writes:

> It is *not* error as error that horrifies me at this sight [Christian morality]—not the lack, for thousands of years, of 'good will,' discipline, decency, courage in matters of the spirit, revealed by its victory: it is the lack of nature, it is the utterly gruesome fact that *antinature* itself received the highest honors as morality and was fixed over humanity as law and categorical imperative. (EH XIV:7, KSA 6:372)

This passage expresses two objections to morality, that morality is anti-nature (which I shall address later), and that it is 'fixed' or unconditional. A morality is 'unconditional' insofar as it claims to be binding on everyone regardless of their interests, desires, and other distinguishing features. For now, I will concentrate on the latter since it represents one of Nietzsche's most prominent objections.

Nietzsche's rejection of unconditional morality has been the subject of much discussion. However, the emphasis in his critique has been misplaced in the secondary literature. It is common to point out that Nietzsche objects to unconditional morality since it necessarily conflicts with the moral pluralism revealed through his genealogical findings.[21] Recall, for instance, the *Genealogy* where moral absolutism is championed by Christian morality via the slave revolt in morals, in contrast with noble morality. Although Christianity is one example of unconditional morality, it is evident that it is the specific form which preoccupies Nietzsche's critique. "For, confronted with morality (especially Christian, or unconditional, morality) life must continually and inevitably be in the wrong" (BT SC:5, KSA 1:19). And, elsewhere, he explains that Christianity represents the "final lunge in the struggle of the theory of unconditional morality" (AOM 33, KSA 2:396). Still, to claim that Nietzsche's critique of unconditional morality amounts to its insistence that "I am morality itself, and nothing besides is morality" (BGE 202, KSA 5:124) is not only vague, but unpersuasive. When he writes, "there is no such thing as a morality with an exclusive monopoly of the moral, and that every morality that affirms itself alone destroys too much valuable strength and is bought too dear" (D 164, KSA 3:147), he is doing more than proclaiming the right to existence for other moralities. Nietzsche's objection to unconditional morality is that in resisting the possibility of '*higher* moralities' (BGE 202, KSA 5:124), we are deprived of their greatest splendour—a higher 'type' of human being. Therefore, it is *not* Christian morality's imperialistic ambitions, itself, which concerns Nietzsche but rather the undesirable consequence of this morality.

---

21 Karl Jaspers, *Nietzsche: An Introduction to the Understanding of His Philosophical Activity*, Baltimore: Johns Hopkins Univ. Press, 1997, p.140. Dan Conway, *Nietzsche and the Political*, New York: Routledge, 1997, ch. 2.

Nietzsche refers to the taste for the unconditional as the "worst of tastes", but there is a specific sense in which he opposes moral absolutism. He explains that, "what is fair for one *cannot* by any means for that reason alone also be fair for others; that the demand of one morality for all is *detrimental for the higher men*; in short, that there is an order of rank between man and man, hence also between morality and morality" (BGE 228, KSA 5:165 my emphasis). And, similarly, he claims that "when a decadent type of man ascended to the rank of the highest type, this could only happen at the expense of its countertype (*Gegensatz-Art*), the type of man that is strong and sure of life" (EH XIV:5, KSA 6:369). In this way, morality for Nietzsche, becomes the "danger of dangers" (GM P:6, KSA 5:253) for a *particular* type of individual. Briefly, Nietzsche's point is that there are different 'types' of human beings whose flourishing depends on certain needs or conditions of existence which are by no means uniform. Morality proves to be a 'danger' for those 'higher types' whose flourishing is inhibited by the dictates of the reigning morality.[22] Elsewhere, he states, "the question is always who *he* is, and who the *other* person is" and then adds:

> Every unegoistic morality that takes itself for unconditional and addresses itself to all does not only sin against taste: it is a provocation to sins of omission, one *more* seduction under the mask of philanthropy—and precisely a seduction and *injury for the higher, rarer, privileged.* Moralities must be forced to bow first of all before the *order of rank*; their presumption must be brought home to their conscience—until they finally reach agreement that it is *immoral* to say: 'what is right for one is fair for the other'. (BGE 221, KSA 5:156 my emphasis)

In each case, Nietzsche's overriding concern relates to the harm inflicted on the exemplary individual as a result of morality's monopolizing tendency. His objection to unconditional morality, then, does not involve the claim that morality is a danger to *everyone*, or that other moralities are unjustly denied a voice. In fact, he is cognizant of the salutary effects of morality insofar as it promotes the interests and needs of a lowly human type—the herd. However, Nietzsche laments that this morality exists "*at the expense of the future*...so that precisely morality would be to blame if the *highest power and splendor* actually possible to the type man was never in fact attained" (GM P:6, KSA 5:253). The claim that morality has a diminutive effect on higher types is Nietzsche's fundamental objection to Christianity. In a *Nachlaß* note from the late 1880's, he explains: "What I fight against in Christianity? Always only one thing: its human ideal, its demands on humans, its no and its yes in relation to man...All the

---

22 I discuss the 'higher type', including Nietzsche's view of how they are harmed by morality, in the final section of this chapter.

absurd rest of Christian fables, constructed false concepts and theology does not concern us...What we fight against in Christianity? *That it wants to break the strong.*"[23]

These remarks reflect Nietzsche's anti-egalitarianism, and his preoccupation with 'types' of human beings, especially exemplary individuals. Since morality involves the physiological demands for the preservation of a certain type of life (BGE 3, KSA 5:17), and these demands vary according to the 'type' of individual, Nietzsche feels justified in arguing that human inequality is a relevant consideration for not imposing one morality on everyone. Of course, with this view, he has challenged the moral tradition's most agreed upon tenet, that human beings are *equal* from a moral point of view.[24] Yet, this critique requires a more detailed treatment than is implied by Nietzsche's anti-egalitarian discourse. In any case, he must show that it is possible for a 'type' of human being to be harmed by egalitarian practices, and to do this he relies on a physiological analysis of moral values.

Nietzsche's opposition to the unconditional demands of morality is closely associated with his rejection of equality. In spreading the poisonous doctrine of 'equal rights for all', "Christianity has waged war unto death against all sense of respect and feeling of distance between man and man" (A 43, KSA 6:217–18). The crucial point here is that Nietzsche denounces equal rights since it fails to recognize an inherent order of rank among men. He continues to describe the idea of 'equality' in the same terms: "The doctrine of equality! There is no more poisonous poison anywhere: for it seems to be preached by justice itself, whereas it really is the termination of justice" (TI 9:48, KSA 6:150). Instead, Nietzsche offers his own brand of justice, "Equal to the equal, unequal to the unequal...never make equal what is unequal" (48). The theory of 'equal rights', in making everyone similar, "is an essential feature of decline" (TI 9:37, KSA 6:138). On the other hand, a "sign of nobility" for Nietzsche includes, "never thinking of degrading our duties into duties for everybody" (BGE 272, KSA 5:227). His critique of equality is motivated by a desire to re-establish an order of rank among human beings, and hence correct the injustices against the higher type. To do this, Nietzsche introduces the antithetical concept, the *pathos*

---

23 "*Was ich am Christenthum bekämpfe? Immer nur Eins: sein Ideal vom Menschen, seine Forderungenan den Menschen, sein Nein und sein Ja in Hinsicht auf den Menschen...Der ganze absurde Rest von christlicher fabel, Begriffs-Spinneweberei und Theologie geht uns nicht an...Was wir am Christenthum bekämpfen? Daß es die Starken zerbrechen will.*" The first sentence is quoted from KSA 14:750 (this belongs to a draft of KSA 13, 11[55]) and the remainder from KSA 13, 11[55], Nov. 1887–March 1888, p.27–8.

24 This objection is serious, yet Nietzsche's anti-egalitarianism tends to quickly dismiss the forcefulness of appeals to equality as a claim of what is morally valid. I discuss this issue in greater detail in Chapter Four.

of distance, which acknowledges "the cleavage between man and man, status and status, the plurality of types, the will to be oneself, to stand out" (TI 9:37, KSA 6:138). The pathos of distance inspires human flourishing in both the social and personal sphere:

> Without that *pathos of distance* which grows out of the ingrained difference between strata...that other, more mysterious *pathos* could not have grown up either—the craving for an ever new widening of distances within the soul itself, the development of ever higher, rarer, more remote, further-stretching, more comprehensive states—in brief, simply the enhancement of the type 'man,' the continual 'self-overcoming of man', to use a moral formula in a supra-moral (*über- moralischen*) sense. (BGE 257, KSA 5:205)

The recognition of an order of rank among human beings is crucial for the enhancement of the human 'type'. Otherwise, human existence will be plagued by the "degeneration and diminution of man into the perfect herd animal...the dwarf animal of equal rights and claims" (BGE 203, KSA 5:127-28). Or, in the words of Zarathustra: "thus blinks the mob—'there are no higher men, we are all equal, man is man; before God we are all equal.' Before God! But now this god has died. And before the mob we do not want to be equal" (Z IV:13, KSA 4:356). However, when one considers the ideal of contemporary society in light of the death of God, one finds that there has been no reconsideration (let alone, revaluation) of our moral values. Once access is denied to the metaphysical source, in this case God, the status of human beings must be re-evaluated. In other words, for Nietzsche, equality can no longer shine in the shadows of the death of God.[25] Yet, the ideal of equality continues to shine brightly, for it has become embedded into the fabric of culture. Nietzsche makes the following observation regarding contemporary society: "What they would like to strive for with all their powers is the universal green-pasture happiness of the herd, with security, lack of danger, comfort, and an easier life for everyone; the two songs and doctrines which they repeat most often are 'equality of rights' and 'sympathy for all that suffers'—and suffering itself they take for something that must be *abolished*" (BGE 44, KSA 5:61). In short, Nietzsche's defense of inequality will require recognition that the conditions for the preservation of individuals vary depending on the 'type' of person, and that 'equal rights for all' discriminates against the needs of the 'higher, rarer, privileged'. Of the 'two

---

25 The point is not that the notion of human equality is logically dependent on a metaphysical source. Rather, Nietzsche is accounting for its currency by showing that it owes its existence to a belief or appeal to the metaphysical realm. Even if one argues on secular grounds for equality, Nietzsche would claim that this individual has rejected the Christian God, but still bows down to its morality (TI 9:5).

songs', there is no doubt in Nietzsche's mind that the one sung loudest is 'sympathy for all that suffers', and it is the one to which I will now turn.

The 'Unegoistic Drives'—Pity, Altruism, and Selflessness

One of the most recognized features of Nietzsche's critique of morality is his objection to pity (*Mitleid*). However, like many great thinkers, Nietzsche's views evolved and this is particularly true regarding his critique of pity. In what follows, I would like to examine his earlier remarks on pity from his positivist period.[26] In *Human, All-Too-Human* (1878), the work immediately preceding *Daybreak*, Nietzsche attempted to rescue morality from its metaphysical underpinnings. 'Morality' was one of the three "higher activities" (art and religion were the others) which was traditionally explained in terms of human participation in a metaphysical realm (HH 10, KSA 2:30). Nietzsche insisted that these 'higher' things could be attributed to a basic psychological need that could easily be discerned as 'lower', as 'human, all-too-human'. In *Ecce Homo*, he offers an explanation of the book's title: "'where *you* see ideal things, I see what is human, all-too-human!' I know man better" (EH VI:1, KSA 6:322). As well, Nietzsche adds that in this book you will find:

> a merciless spirit that knows all the hideouts where the ideal is at home...One error after another is coolly placed on ice; the ideal is not refuted—it *freezes* to death.—Here, for example, 'the genius' freezes to death; at the next corner, 'the saint'; under a huge icicle, 'the hero'; in the end; 'faith,' so-called 'conviction'; 'pity' also cools down considerably—and almost everywhere 'the thing in itself' freezes to death. (EH VI:1, KSA 2:323)

The aim of this work was to 'overcome metaphysics', a project that included the overturning of traditional valuations that mislead the human mind. In the above passage, Nietzsche emphasizes that these 'ideals' are merely based on human standards, and hence do not possess the 'higher' status that they are usually accorded. The overturning of traditional valuations means overturning the presumption that these valuations, which *humans make*, are really 'God' given. Nietzsche explicitly states that 'the ideal is not refuted—it *freezes* to death', and he describes his approach as 'psychological observation' or 'reflection on the

---

26 In Nietzsche scholarship, it is customary to refer to his 'positivist' or 'Voltairean' period as commencing with *Human, All-Too-Human* (1878), since this work marks a new, yet short-lived, phase in his thinking which involved a commitment to and enthusiasm for science and naturalistic explanation, in contrast with his early attempts at metaphysical philosophy. Nietzsche applied the term 'positivism', himself, to this text. See Erich Heller's Introduction to *Human, All-Too-Human*, trans. R.J. Hollingdale. Cambridge: Cambridge University Press, 1986, p. xiii.

human, all-too-human' (HH 35, KSA 2:57). In other words, he used psychological observation as a weapon to slay metaphysics. Or as Nietzsche puts it, an axe is applied to "the root of the 'metaphysical need' of man" (HH 37, KSA 2:61). The 'higher' is now explicated in terms of the merely human, and there is no longer any concern about whether a metaphysical realm possesses any veridical worth. Once the historical and psychological justification that resides in such ideals has been grasped, a liberation from metaphysics is complete.

It must be emphasized that Nietzsche is not denying the existence of a metaphysical world. Rather than discussing the issue of the truth or falsity of such a world, his project is intended to explain why a belief in a metaphysical world exists. In fact, he concedes that "there could be a metaphysical world" (HH 9, KSA 2:29), but since he thinks that we have no epistemological access to it, we must dispense with reference to metaphysical assumptions. The most we could say is that the metaphysical world is a 'being-other', and as a result, this 'knowledge' could not serve human beings in any important capacity. In eliminating the metaphysical perspective, Nietzsche is limiting himself to offering strictly naturalistic explanations (i.e. psychological observation) for metaphysical assumptions. Since my immediate concern lies with his treatment of one particular idealization, pity, I will now turn to the naturalistic explanation that he offers.

In *Human, All-Too-Human*, Nietzsche attempts to trace 'pity' back to an egoistic source. For instance, he explains that when we are in the presence of a suffering person, "we rid ourselves of our own suffering by performing an act of pity" (HH 103, KSA 2:100). By reducing pity (unegoistic acts) to a form of psychological egoism, Nietzsche denies the possibility of altruistic actions altogether. He writes: "Any being who would be capable of purely selfless actions only is more fabulous than the phoenix", and to this, he adds:

> Never has a man done anything that was only for others and without any personal motivation. Indeed, how *could* he do anything that had no reference to himself, that is, with no inner compulsion (which would have to be based on a personal need)? How could the ego act without ego? (HH 133, KSA 2:126–27)

The fundamental idea in this section is that the very notion of a 'selfless act' is incomprehensible. Since Nietzsche treated the moral and the egoistic as mutually exclusive, we can infer that he accepted Schopenhauer's account of morality as altruism. On this view, Nietzsche's endorsement of psychological egoism did not involve a commitment to *ethical* egoism, since the latter is ruled out by his separation of the moral and egoistic. Instead, in the same passage, he aligns himself with the psychological egoism of Lichtenberg and

LaRochefoucauld—the former claiming that "it is impossible for us to *feel* for others. We feel only for ourselves…we love neither father nor mother nor wife nor child, but rather the agreeable feelings that they give us", and the latter stating that "*Si on croit aimer sa maîtresse pour l'amour d'elle, on est bien trompé.*" Psychological egoism was Nietzsche's naturalistic explanation of human behaviour.

The challenge that Nietzsche offers to unegoistic behaviour is that it is merely a sham—a disguised egoism. This view has prompted Brian Leiter and Maudemarie Clark to remark that even though Nietzsche accepts Schopenhauer's equation of morality with unegoistic acts, he takes for granted their higher value, and "rather than challenging Schopenhauer on the value of unegoistic actions, *Human, All-Too-Human* seems to argue that nothing possessing the higher value that an unegoistic action would have actually makes its appearance in the human world."[27] However, this interpretation is, I believe, mistaken since Nietzsche's critique of pity can be well-documented prior to and during the period in which he was working on *Human, All-Too-Human.*[28] And, in the text itself, there is evidence to suggest, contra Leiter and Clark, that he did *not* view unegoistic acts as having 'higher value', and that he did question their value, albeit infrequently and not in great detail. For instance, section 50 of *Human, All-Too-Human* is specifically directed against Schopenhauer's deification of pity as the highest moral feeling. In this passage, LaRochefoucauld is cited approvingly insofar as he "hits the mark when he warns all reasonable men against pity…For pity, in his (and Plato's) judgment, weakens the soul." And in section 103, Nietzsche writes: "Aside from a few philosophers, men have always placed pity rather low in the hierarchy of moral feelings—*and rightly so.*" These comments reinforce Nietzsche's anti-pity sentiments beyond their reduction to egoism. Thus, it was not a matter of accepting pity's 'higher value', while bemoaning its illusory status. Still, it would be fair to say that the preoccupation of *Human, All-Too-Human* was to explain that egoistic motives underlie all selfless acts, rather than providing a commentary on the value of pity. The closest that he comes to any critical assessment of pity is in his refinement of LaRochefoucauld's view on the subject:

---

27 See B. Leiter and M. Clark's (eds.) Introduction to Nietzsche's, *Daybreak*. Cambridge: Cambridge University Press, 1997, p.xxiv.

28 See, for instance, Nietzsche's notes from the summer of 1875 (KSA 8:181), and from the end of 1876–Summer of 1877 (KSA 8:429,434,437–38). Interestingly, these references from 1876–1877 seem to coincide with his time spent in Sorrento with Rée, Meysenbug, and Brenner, thereby confirming that his low valuation of pity pre-dates the publication of *Human, All-Too-Human.*

> Perhaps one can warn even more strongly against having pity for the unfortunate if one does not think of their need for pity as stupidity and intellectual deficiency, a kind of mental disorder resulting from their misfortune (this is how LaRochefoucauld seems to regard it), but rather as something quite different and more dubious. Observe how children weep and cry, *so that* they will be pitied, how they wait for the moment when their condition will be noticed. Or live among the ill and depressed, and question whether their eloquent laments and whimpering, the spectacle of their misfortune, is not basically aimed at *hurting* those present. The pity that the spectators then express consoles the weak and suffering, inasmuch as they see that, despite all their weakness, they still *have* at least one *power*: *the power to hurt.* When expressions of pity make the unfortunate man aware of this feeling of superiority, he gets a kind of pleasure from it...Thus the thirst for pity is a thirst for self-enjoyment, and at the expense of one's fellow men. It reveals man in the complete inconsideration (*Rücksichtslosigkeit*) of his most intimate dear self, but not precisely in his 'stupidity,' as LaRochefoucauld thinks.[29] (HH 50, KSA 2:70–1)

The point here is that there is no value in pitying or consoling the weak, since their efforts to obtain pity are designed to hurt those present, while at the same time, deriving pleasure from this sense of power. This psychological observation of the unfortunate man's need for pity is not some disinterested statement of fact. By 'strongly' warning against having pity, Nietzsche proves that he is not neutral on the issue—he explicitly devalues pity, agreeing with LaRochefoucauld and Plato that it 'weakens the soul' (HH 50, KSA 2:70). Consequently, Nietzsche did not agree with Schopenhauer's reduction of morality to pity or compassion *because* it possessed 'high value', but *because* it captured the current moral sentiment which he argued was a 'great danger'.[30]

Schopenhauerian 'pity' continued to haunt Nietzsche for the remainder of his academic life. In what follows, I would like to shift attention to his more pronounced repudiation of pity from the period of *Daybreak* (1881) up to his final writings (1888). In a letter dating from 1883, he writes:

> Schopenhauerian '*pity*' (*Mitleid*) has always caused the greatest mischief in my life—so I've every reason to favor moral philosophies which ascribe a few *other* motives to

29 LaRochefoucauld wrote: "*Je suis peu sensible à la pitié et voudrais ne l'y être point du tout...Cependant, il n'est rien que je ne fisse pour le soulagement d'une personne affligée...Mais je tiens aussi qu'il faut se contenter d'en témoigner et se garder soigneusement d'en avoir. C'est une passion qui n'est bonne à rien au dedans d'une âme bien faite, qui ne sert qu'a affaiblir le coeur, et qu'on doit laisser au peuple, qui, n'exécutant jamais rien par raison, a besoin des passions pour le porter à faire les choses.*"

30 Consider, for instance, the context in which these remarks on pity were made. They [sections 50 and 103] come from a chapter in *Human, All-Too-Human* devoted to the history of the moral sensations.

> moral conduct, and don't try to reduce all human excellence to 'fellow-feelings'. For this isn't just effeminacy…but a serious practical *danger*.[31]

The seriousness in which Nietzsche condemns 'pity' as a moral sentiment should not be underestimated. In the above passage, 'pity' is not only identified as the source of much grief, but is specifically rejected as a vehicle to human excellence. Presumably, this means that Nietzsche wants to focus his attention on other avenues to human flourishing, ones which do *not* represent a 'danger'. Interestingly, the same sentiments are expressed four years later in his Preface to the *Genealogy of Morals* where Nietzsche admits that his preoccupation with the value of morality meant having to comes to terms with "my great teacher Schopenhauer" who deified "the value of the 'unegoistic,' the instincts of pity, self-abnegation, self-sacrifice…" (GM P:5, KSA 5:251–52). In order to expose 'pity' as "the *great* danger to mankind", Nietzsche questioned its value in furthering man's advancement and prosperity. His conclusion was that the morality of pity was a "symptom of regression…through which the present was possibly living *at the expense of the future*". In this way, "morality would be to blame if the *highest power and splendor* actually possible to the type man was never in fact attained" (GM P:6, KSA 5:253). This is precisely the sense in which Nietzsche views morality as the great danger. We can expect, then, that his arguments against pity would address its negative value in relation to the conception of human flourishing he aims to promote.

It is important to clarify Nietzsche's use of the term *Mitleid* (literally, 'suffering with'), translated throughout as 'pity'. When Nietzsche refers to the morality of pity, he is quite explicit as to its intended meaning. For instance, he often uses such terms as "self-sacrifice" (HH 49, KSA 2:69), "selflessness" (EH VII:2, KSA 6:332), "disinterested" (D 132, KSA 3:123), "altruistic" (TI 9:35, KSA 6:134), "neighbour-love" (TI 9:37, KSA 6:138), "*vivre pour autrui*" (D 132, KSA 3:123), "sympathetic" (D 132, KSA 3:123), and the Latin "*misericordia*" as alternative ways of expressing the current moral fashion. In fact, all of these terms fall under the rubric of "unegoistic drives". There is certainly a distinct family-resemblance among these expressions (they are all 'other-directed'). More importantly, however, he thinks that this morality of pity is an offshoot of Christianity, and points out that a philanthropic state of mind persisted even among those who rejected Christianity. In addition to Schopenhauer, Nietzsche cites John Stuart Mill and the French freethinkers from Voltaire up to Auguste Comte, all of whom advanced the teaching of the sympathetic affections (D

31 "Letter to Malwida von Meysenbug" (July 1883) given in translation in *Nietzsche: A Self-Portrait from His Letters*, ed. and trans. Peter Fuss and Henry Shapiro, Cambridge, MA: Harvard University Press, 1971, p.75.

132, KSA 3:123). While some readers may feel that Nietzsche is offering a limited view of the existing morality when he describes it as a morality of pity, others have come to his defense. Kai Nielsen writes, "This morality of 'turning the other cheek', this morality of mercy, humility and meekness is indeed, culturally speaking, our official morality."[32] Note, however, that even if Nietzsche's *identification* of the prevalent morality is correct, it does not follow that so too is his critique of it.

So far I have expressed Nietzsche's antipathy towards the morality of pity. But what are his arguments to support the claim that pity is the 'danger of dangers'? When Nietzsche refers to 'pity' as the 'virtue of decadents' (EH I:4, KSA 6:270), he is not resorting to mere name-calling. Instead, this remark is consistent with his discrimination of human 'types'. The virtues of an inferior type will conflict with those of an exemplary human being. Or, as Nietzsche puts it: "What serves the higher type of men as nourishment…must almost be poison for a very different and inferior type" (BGE 30, KSA 5:48). Far from being 'nourished' by 'pity', "the noble type", according to Nietzsche, "is not made for pity" (BGE 260, KSA 5:210). However, this is not to say that the noble individual is immune from contamination. In this sense, co-existing with such practitioners of pity would increase "the danger that he might suffocate from pity" (BGE 269, KSA 5:222-23). Still, it is curious as to why Nietzsche would think that 'pity' is capable of such corruption, why it "is more harmful than any vice" (A 2, KSA 6:170). He explains:

> But whenever people *notice* that we suffer, they interpret our suffering superficially. It is the very essence of the emotion of pity that it strips away from the suffering of others whatever is distinctively personal…one simply knows nothing of the whole inner sequence and intricacies that are distress for *me* or for *you*. The whole economy of my soul and the balance effected by 'distress', the way new springs and needs break open, the way in which old wounds are healing, the way whole periods of the past are shed—all such things that may be involved in distress are of no concern to our dear pitying friends; they wish to *help* and have no thought of the personal necessity of distress, although terrors, deprivations, impoverishments, midnights, adventures, risks, and blunders are as necessary for me and for you as are their opposites. It never occurs to them that…the path to one's own heaven always leads through the voluptuousness of one's own hell. (GS 338, KSA 3:566)

Insofar as 'pitying' someone is intended to alleviate suffering, the 'pitier' misinterprets the 'personal necessity of distress'. These 'dear pitying friends' rush to help without realizing that the road to one's successes is paved with suffering and adversity. Christianity, as the 'religion of pity', implores people to come to the aid of the suffering since suffering and displeasure are regarded as

---

32 Kai Nielsen, "Nietzsche As A Moral Philosopher", *Man and World* 6, 1973, pp.182-205.

evil, 'worthy of annihilation' and 'a defect of existence' (GS 338, KSA 3:566). Further, this negative evaluation of suffering entails, *eo ipso*, a promotion of happiness. But, for Nietzsche, this interpretation displays an ignorance regarding human happiness, "for happiness and unhappiness are sisters and even twins that either grow up together or…*remain small* together" (338). The mistake, then, is to treat happiness and unhappiness, pleasure and pain as antipodes. Instead, Nietzsche hypothesizes that pleasure and displeasure are so intimately connected "that whoever *wanted* to have as much as possible of one *must* also have as much as possible of the other—that whoever wanted to 'jubilate up to the heavens' would also have to be prepared for 'depression unto death'" (GS 12, KSA 3:383). In failing to recognize the positive value of suffering, "pitying hands can interfere in a downright destructive manner in a great destiny, in the growing solitude of one wounded" (EH I:4, KSA 6:270).

Pity, however, does not pose a danger for everyone. It is a weakness from the standpoint of every noble morality (A 7, KSA 6:173). Recall, for instance, the First Essay of the *Genealogy* where slave morality affirmed the opposite qualities possessed by the nobles. In doing so, this morality was successful at easing existence for those who suffer. We could even say that 'pity' is 'good' for the herd insofar as it is necessary to their preservation and advancement. When Nietzsche refers to 'pity' as a "parasite harmful to moral health" (WP 368, KSA 12:268), he is alluding to the health risk for the strong, higher type. As with any 'parasite', it is crucial that one avoid infection at all cost. The higher type "finds all kinds of disguises necessary to protect itself against contact with obtrusive and pitying hands and altogether against everything that is not its equal in suffering" (BGE 270, KSA 5:225). Therefore, it is incumbent upon the noble type that he avoid contact with any threatening element. He is no stranger to suffering, but rather welcomes it with open arms, secure in the knowledge of its profound effects—"profound suffering makes noble; it separates" (BGE 270, KSA 5:225). In addressing the devotees of pity, Nietzsche adds: "You want…to *abolish* suffering. And we? It really seems that *we* would rather have it higher and worse than ever" (BGE 225, KSA 5:161). This comment is based on his view that suffering is a prerequisite for human greatness, not that it is intrinsically valuable. "Brave and creative men *never* consider pleasure and pain as ultimate values—they are epiphenomena: one must *desire* both if one is to achieve anything" (WP 579, KSA 12:328).

The noble type needs 'hardness' and 'cheerfulness' as a protective against such pitying hands. A morality of pity or altruism is harmful insofar as it leads to a deterioration of 'self-interest'. "The best is lacking when self-interest begins to be lacking" (TI 9:35, KSA 6:133). Nietzsche associates an attraction to 'disinterested' motives with decadence. To ignore or overlook one's own advantage betrays a physiological state of affairs—the disgregation (*Disgregation*) of the instincts (35). The exemplary human being resists decadence realizing that "man is finished when he becomes altruistic" (35). The noble individual wants to avoid the bad consequences of both being pitied, and feeling pity. The danger of being the 'pitier' is that we risk losing our 'own way'. Nietzsche explains, "All such arousing of pity and calling for help is secretly seductive, for our 'own way' is too hard and demanding and too remote from the love and gratitude of others, and we do not really mind escaping from it—and from our very own conscience—to flee into the conscience of the others and into the lovely temple of the 'religion of pity'" (GS 338, KSA 3:567). Christian morality facilitates this distraction from our 'own way'.[33] On account of the unhealthiness of Christian pity, Nietzsche announces some protective measures. In this same passage, he introduces the notion of 'my morality' (*meine Moral*) as a way of counteracting the effects of pity. He writes:

> And while I shall keep silent about some points, I do not want to remain silent about my morality which says to me: Live in seclusion so that you *can* live for yourself. Live in *ignorance* about what seems most important to your age. (GS 338, KSA 3:568)

Nietzsche's solution to the infectious virus of 'pity' is to quarantine those unaffected. In this way, one is removed from the infected area and is able to live for oneself rather than for others. At the same time, he counsels an indifference toward the fundamental concerns of one's age. And, finally, in one of his most poignant remarks directed at the preachers of pity, Nietzsche proclaims, "I want to teach them what is understood by so few today, least of all by these preachers of pity: *to share not suffering but joy*" (338). Here, joy is associated with a level of vitality which allows the individual to treat suffering as an energetic *stimulus* for life. The contrast between these conflicting emotions illustrates nicely Nietzsche's critique of pity. For instance, when he writes that "pity stands opposed to the tonic emotions which heighten our vitality", he is drawing a distinction between emotions conducive to human flourishing and those that

---

33 It is important to note that the attention that Nietzsche gives to self-interest and living for oneself is not to be construed as an incessant or unreserved selfishness. In fact, he draws a distinction between two types of selfishness, a healthy kind expressed by the 'gift-giving virtue' where "You force all things to and into yourself that they may flow back out of your well as the gifts of your love…" And, secondly, Nietzsche refers to a 'degenerate' kind of selfishness: 'sick selfishness' which views the world solely in relation to itself, "a degenerate sense that says, 'Everything for me'." Rather than hunger after things like a predator, the gift-giving virtue has acquired a thirst of its own. "This is your thirst: to become sacrifices and gifts yourselves; and that is why you thirst to pile up the riches of your soul" (Z I:22). This is not to say that there are not objectionable features belonging to this noble bestower.

impede it. As we have just seen, the feeling of joy represents a 'tonic emotion', and as such, is an expression of vitality. Pity, on the other hand, is harmful since "we are deprived of strength when we feel pity" (A 7, KSA 6:172-73). Further, since pity is a matter of 'suffering with', it increases the amount of suffering in the world, or as Nietzsche puts it, "pity makes suffering contagious" (7). The point here is that by continually being called upon to pity the suffering, we are being pained by the pain of others, and as a result, suffering becomes multiplied.

There is yet another damaging consequence of pity. Nietzsche describes its perilous nature as follows:

> Quite in general, pity crosses the law of development, which is the law of *selection*. It preserves what is ripe for destruction; it defends those who have been disinherited and condemned by life; and by the abundance of failures of all kinds which it keeps alive, it gives life itself a gloomy and questionable aspect. (A 7, KSA 6:173)

In protecting the weak, pity becomes an instrument for the advancement of decadence. It crosses those opposing instincts which aim at the enhancement of life. For this reason, Nietzsche describes pity as "the *practice* of nihilism" (7). Pity is not simply *a* virtue, but owing to Schopenhauer and other preachers of morals, "it has been made *the* virtue, the basis and source of all virtues" (7). As such, morality becomes preoccupied with the things for which people are to be pitied, to the exclusion of other considerations. Nietzsche is not convinced that the ensuing 'cult of suffering' is the pinnacle of human achievement. Suffering, he contends, should not be taken as an objection to existence, but rather as an inseparable component of life.

Martha Nussbaum has argued that Nietzsche's assertion that pity augments the suffering in the world is "the weakest of his [anti-pity] claims."[34] Her refutation is based on counterexamples which show that the suffering of pity gives rise to acts of benevolence, which in turn, produce societies which improve the circumstances of the worst off. However, it seems to me that Nietzsche would agree that pity does in fact benefit the particular group to which Nussbaum refers. But, I think Nietzsche's response would be that this sort of society does not address the needs of the higher type—needs which would not include pity. And, for Nietzsche, the value of morality is not restricted to "the preservation of the greatest number" but to "producing a stronger type" (GM I:17n, KSA 5:289). In fact, the egalitarian society that she has in mind fails to acknowledge a difference in human 'types'. If Nussbaum

---

34 Martha C. Nussbaum, "Pity and Mercy: Nietzsche's Stoicism" in R. Schacht (ed.), *Nietzsche, Genealogy, Morality: Essays on Nietzsche's* Genealogy of Morals. Berkeley: University of California Press, 1994, p.157.

had shown that the emotion of pity was a vital component of the *aristocratic* societies which Nietzsche repeatedly eulogizes, her critique would be fatal. For now, her encomium for egalitarian societies merely begs the question. It is important to point out, however, that there may be other reasons, as I believe there are, for rejecting Nietzsche's critique of pity.

So far the main point of Nietzsche's critique of pity seems to be that in overvaluing selflessness, morality does not encourage sufficient attention to the care of one's 'self'. But, this sort of conclusion overlooks many deficiencies in Nietzsche's account of suffering. To begin with, the notion that we actually benefit from suffering is not only counter-intuitive, but is rather ambiguous since it is not obvious what kind of suffering Nietzsche is referring to, or whether the 'merits' of suffering warrant its infliction on others. In a recent account of Nietzsche's views on suffering, Brian Leiter claims that Nietzsche is not arguing that suffering is *intrinsically* valuable, but that its value is *extrinsic*.[35] Leiter goes on to quote the following passage to explain that Nietzsche's position is that suffering is a prerequisite of 'all enhancements of man', not that all forms of suffering are meritorious. "The discipline of suffering…do you not know that only *this* discipline has created all enhancements of man so far" (BGE 225, KSA 5:161)? The problem, however, is that this citation merely shows that Nietzsche's view is that suffering is a necessary component of human greatness without elaborating on the *nature* of this suffering—what kind of suffering, and for whom? Leiter's answer is limited since he focuses on Nietzsche's own experiences with suffering in order to show that his views on suffering function on a personal level. For instance, Leiter quotes a few passages[36] where Nietzsche expresses his gratitude towards his ill-health for contributing to the production of numerous philosophical works, as well as its role in generating his Dionysian attitude toward life.

The problem with Leiter's account of Nietzsche's view of suffering is that it is far too narrow, and also leaves unanswered the type of suffering that he has in mind. Nietzsche was fortunate that his own degree of suffering, however intense, did not prevent him from writing a philosophical work, but had his illness been more severe, there may have been little for which to feel grateful. What becomes of suffering, one may ask, if it proves much more debilitating? And, what good are Nietzsche's twin affirmative ideals: eternal return and *amor fati*? Unfortunately, Nietzsche failed to distinguish clearly between various forms of suffering. At times, he seems content to claim that morality's low evaluation of suffering tends to mask its extrinsic value, but he never provides a

---

35 Brian Leiter, "Morality in the Pejorative Sense: On the Logic of Nietzsche's Critique of Morality", *British Journal of the History of Philosophy*, Vol.3/No.1, 1995, p.138.

36 EH I:1; EH VI:4; cf. GS P:3.

detailed account of the nature of suffering. Nietzsche's supporters may wish to protest that he is not promoting the gross, unmerited suffering of others at the hands of another, or praising *l'homme méchant* of Gobineau[37] as the pinnacle of human achievement, but rather the creative exploits of a Goethe. However, this sanitized version of Nietzsche is mistaken as is evidenced by his praise of cruelty, the sacrifice of others, slavery, and the absence of any notion of universal rights or respect for all. Nowhere in Nietzsche's writings does he offer a safety-net which would protect against such undesirable outcomes.

False Presuppositions: Morality as 'Error'

In the early 1880's, Nietzsche had become increasingly interested in questioning the *value* of altruistic acts, as his focus shifted away from psychological egoism. The transition from *Human, All-Too-Human* (1878) to *Daybreak* (1881), however, did not signal an abandonment of egoism. Nietzsche still acknowledged that egoistic acts were "the most frequent actions", but he now wanted to restore "their *value*" (D 148, KSA 3:140). But, to do this, he had to confront an unreceptive moral audience which knew morality only in terms of "the sympathetic, disinterested, generally useful social actions", the values imparted by a long Christian heritage (D 132, KSA 3:123).

Daybreak represented Nietzsche's coming of age as a moral philosopher. He was no longer writing and studying in the shadows of his 'moral' educator, Paul Rée[38], whose method of psychological observation, and enthusiasm for LaRochefoucauld, had insinuated their way into *Human, All-Too-Human*. Between 1880–1881, Nietzsche began his own independent study of moral philosophy including works on Christian ethics.[39] *Daybreak*, then, can be viewed

---

37 This refers to the individual who takes pleasure in the suffering of others.

38 At the invitation of a mutual friend, Malwida von Meysenbug, Nietzsche, Rée, and Brenner formed a study group at her home in Sorrento in late October, 1876. Already an established moralist, Rée stimulated Nietzsche's interest in French and English thought, and in my view, moral matters as a whole. Prior to their meeting, Nietzsche did not appear to have a *strong* interest in ethics. It was in this household where Nietzsche worked on *Human, All-Too-Human*. For an excellent discussion of Nietzsche's relation to Rée, see Brendan Donnellan's "Friedrich Nietzsche and Paul Rée: Cooperation and Conflict", *Journal of the History of Ideas*, October, 1982, pp.595–612.

39 Some of his readings in ethics during this period included: Comte, Plato, Spencer (*Die Thatsachen der Ethik*), John Stuart Mill, J.J. Baumann (*Handbuch der Moral*), H.L. Martenson (*Grundriß des Systems der Moralphilosophie*), and many books on Christian morality. (KSA 15, Chronik zu Nietzsches Leben, p.113; Karl Schlechta, *Nietzsche-Chronik: Daten zu Leben und Werke zusammengestellt*, p.70–1; Letter to his mother, March 27, 1880; Thomas Brobjer, *Nietzsche's Ethics of Character*, 1995, pp.137, 145, Table 2 from Ch.6)

as the product of his own philosophical labours. As a result, he was able to acquire a greater sense of independence. One way to gain an appreciation of Nietzsche's development as a moral thinker, is to consider his *new* effort to clarify his rejection of morality. In section 103 of *Daybreak*, Nietzsche contrasts his denial of morality with that of "LaRochefoucauld and those other French masters of soul searching (whose company a German, the author of *Psychological Observations*,[40] has recently joined)". He explains that rather than following these 'French masters' (as he had previously done) in asserting that apparent moral motivations are mere deceptions, his own view involves a *denial* that:

> moral judgments are based on truths. Here it is admitted that they really are motives of action, but that in this way it is *errors* which, as the basis of all moral judgment, impel men to their actions. This is *my* point of view...Thus I deny morality as I deny alchemy, that is, I deny their premises: but I do *not* deny that there have been alchemists who believed in these premises and acted in accordance with them.—I also deny immorality: *not* that countless people *feel* themselves to be immoral but there is any *true* reason so to feel. It goes without saying that I do not deny unless I am a fool—that many actions called immoral ought to be avoided and resisted, or that many called moral ought to be done and encouraged—but I think the one should be encouraged and the other avoided *for other reasons than hitherto.* We have to *learn to think differently*—in order at last, perhaps very late on, to attain even more: *to feel differently.* (D 103, KSA 3:91-2)

This new approach focuses on the motivating errors of morality, rather than the 'French' tendency to explain such errors in terms of misunderstandings of motivation (i.e. obscuring the true motivation of a moral action). Nietzsche can now make room for moral motives whereas in *Human, All-Too-Human*, his *non*-moral psychological egoism (inspired by Rée and LaRochefoucauld) ruled out the possibility of such motives. An understanding of his 'campaign against morality', then, will require an examination of the 'errors' which impel human beings to their moral actions.

What does Nietzsche mean by claiming that moral premises are based on errors? To begin with, his use of the plural 'errors' indicates that there is not one fundamental error underlying all moral premises, although the sorts of errors to which he refers could be subsumed under the category of 'intellectual mistakes'. Even still, these mistakes or delusions, can be attributed to various aspects of morality, even to different moralities. For instance, in *Daybreak*, Nietzsche's discussion of the morality of mores (i.e. the earliest or original morality) will account for the errors as to its *origin* in addition to the errors which sustain it. In other words, it will outline the intellectual mistakes responsible for primitive man being under the 'spell' of custom. On the other hand, there are intellectual mistakes associated with the current morality, the

---

40 Paul Rée.

errors responsible for our acceptance of the morality of selflessness. It seems to me that it would be important to keep these two moralities separate, since their respective errors pertain to distinct motives, 'obedience to custom' in the case of the morality of mores, and 'pity or selflessness' for the current morality.[41] I will begin by considering the errors underlying the acceptance of the morality of mores.

In the preceding chapter, I emphasized Nietzsche's historical reflections on morality, whereby the morality of custom (*Sittlichkeit der Sitte*) was introduced as the means for evaluating human conduct in the pre-moral period. Now, I want to revisit Nietzsche's concept of the morality of mores before moving on to discuss the underlying errors which account for its emergence. In section 9 of *Daybreak*, we find the clearest articulation of the morality of custom. He explains:

> In comparison with the mode of life of whole millennia of mankind we present-day men live in a very immoral age: the power of custom is astonishingly enfeebled and the moral sense so rarefied and lofty it may be described as having more or less evaporated. That is why the fundamental insights into the origin of morality are so difficult for us latecomers, and even when we have acquired them we find it impossible to enunciate them...because they seem to slander morality! This is, for example, already the case with the *chief proposition*: morality is nothing other (therefore *no more*!) than obedience to customs, of whatever kind they may be; customs, however, are the *traditional* way of behaving and evaluating. In things in which no tradition commands there is no morality; and the less life is determined by tradition, the smaller the circle of morality. The free human being is immoral because in all things he is *determined* to depend upon himself and not upon a tradition...if an action is performed *not* because tradition commands it but for other motives (because of its usefulness to the individual, for example)...it is called immoral and is felt to be so by him who performed it: for it was not performed in obedience to tradition. What is tradition? A higher authority which one obeys, not because it commands what is *useful* to us, but because it *commands*. (D 9, KSA 3:21-2)

The crucial point here is not simply that the origin of morality is traced to custom, or that it conflicts with our modern moral sensibilities, but rather that the *only* legitimate moral motive occurs when an act is performed out of 'obedience to tradition'. The remainder of the passage goes on to account for the authority of the tradition. Nietzsche adds:

> What distinguishes this feeling in the presence of tradition from the feeling of fear in general? It is fear in the presence of a higher intellect which here commands, of an

41 This separation of the two moralities is in keeping with Nietzsche's effort to draw a distinction between the morality of mores, and the contemporary moral sense where the power of custom has become enfeebled (see D, 9)

> incomprehensible, indefinite power, of something more than personal—there is *superstition* in this fear...Originally, therefore, everything was custom, and whoever wanted to elevate himself above it had to become a lawgiver and medicine man and a kind of demi-god: that is to say, he had to *make customs*...The most moral man is he who *sacrifices* the most to custom...Self-overcoming is demanded, *not* on account of the useful consequences it may have for the individual, but so that the hegemony of custom, tradition, shall be made evident in despite of the private desires and advantages of the individual: the individual is to sacrifice himself: that is the commandment of morality of custom...Everywhere that a community, and consequently a morality of custom exists, the idea also predominates that punishment for breaches of custom will fall before all on the community: that supernatural punishment whose forms of expression and limitations are so hard to comprehend and are explored with so much superstitious fear...it [the community] can also take a kind of revenge on the individual for having as a supposed after-effect of his action, caused the clouds and storms of divine anger to have gathered over the community—but it feels the individual's guilt above all as *its own* guilt and bears the punishment as *its own* punishment... (D 9, KSA 3:23-4)

The fear or reverence towards tradition is explained in terms of the commanding power of a 'higher intellect' whose authority is owed to 'superstitious fear'. Obedience to tradition, as the sole moral motive, meant observing prescriptions without regarding oneself as an *individual.* Although the commandment of the morality of mores is that one sacrifice oneself to custom, this self-sacrifice can be attributed to the superstitious fears common to primitive human beings. For instance, the morality of mores includes the notion that breaches of custom are met with 'supernatural punishment'. The fact that it is an individual transgression is irrelevant since individual misdeeds affect the entire community—to punish the one means punishing the other. On the occasion of such breaches, primitive human beings believe that they will face God's wrath. Of course, this threat of an almighty terror can be minimized by respecting custom.

The validity or invalidity of a moral prescription is generally determined by its success in living up to its promise. But, how can these prescriptions hold sway when it would appear that these superstitious beliefs which sustain them can be undermined by empirical observation? Nietzsche asks us to consider the following prescription: "you shall not throw an animal bone into the fire or give it to the dogs—its validity is demonstrated with: 'if you do so you will have no luck in hunting'" (D 24, KSA 3:35). In alluding to the difficulty in *refuting* the validity of prescriptions, he adds that it is almost always the case that in some respect one has 'no luck in hunting'. And, if obedience to moral prescriptions produced unexpected results, say for instance, misery resulted instead of the promised good fortune, then this mishap would be explained away: "something was overlooked in the way it was *performed*" or even, "it is impossible to perform the precept properly" (D 21, KSA 3:33). According to Nietzsche, these early human beings either lacked a sense of causality or showed contempt towards it. He writes, "Whenever an evil chance event—a sudden storm or a crop failure or a plague—strikes a community, the suspicion is aroused that custom has been offended in some way…this species of suspicion and reflection is thus a direct avoidance of any investigation of the real natural causes of the phenomenon: it takes the demonic for granted" (D 33, KSA 3:42). Nietzsche attributes this 'perversity of the human intellect' to the 'pressure of superstitious fear' which focused man's attention on supernatural explanations rather than the 'real natural *consequences* of an action' (33). In time, however, "as the sense for causality increases, the extent of the domain of morality decreases", since we can now dispense with those "*imaginary causalities* hitherto believed in as the foundations of morality" (D 10, KSA 3:24). In sum, Nietzsche is critical of the morality of mores insofar as he denies its false premises. Specifically, he claims that the beliefs regarding traditional valuations that impel individuals to their moral actions are based on error. This error involves accepting the notion of imaginary causalities (e.g. the belief that misfortunes are the result of gods who are angered by the violation of custom, see D 33), and hence, misinterpreting natural events.

Nietzsche's account of 'imaginary causalities' may do well to explain the false premises of the 'morality of mores', but what are the false presuppositions belonging to our present-day 'rarefied and lofty' moral sense? Indeed, it is this latter question which is his more pressing concern. After all, Nietzsche's 'campaign against morality' was *not* directed against the morality of mores, but the current morality of selflessness. In his 'review' of *Daybreak*, he writes: "With *Daybreak* I first took up the fight against the morality that would 'unself' (*die Entselbstungs-Moral*) man" (EH VII:2, KSA 6:332). In what sense, does the morality of selflessness rest on error? Section 148 of *Daybreak* offers an important clue:

> If only those actions are moral which are performed for the sake of another and only for his sake, as one definition has it, then there are no moral actions!...What is it then which is so *named* and which in any event exists and wants explaining? It is the effects of certain intellectual mistakes.—And supposing one freed oneself from these errors, what would become of 'moral actions'? By virtue of these errors we have hitherto accorded certain actions a higher value than they possess: we have segregated them from the 'egoistic' and 'unfree' actions. (D 148, KSA 3:139)

It may appear that Nietzsche is reverting to the position he held in *Human, All-Too-Human* that selfless acts are fictitious, as 'fabulous as the phoenix'. But, this is not the case since he is now prepared to admit that selflessness 'exists' and can function as a motivational belief. Note, however, that he still maintains that selflessness is a covert form of egoism. As Richard Schacht notes, "If 'moral actions' are construed as actions *serving* primarily to benefit others (either individually or generally), and only secondarily if at all to benefit the agent, then of course *there are* such actions."[42] To this, I would add that to the extent that we believe in the value of selfless acts, and act on this belief, they could not possibly be imaginary. It is precisely for this reason that Nietzsche claims, "Thus I deny morality as I deny alchemy, that is, I deny their premises: but I do *not* deny that there have been alchemists who believed in these premises and acted in accordance with them" (D 103, KSA 3:91). The 'intellectual mistake', then, occurs when one goes beyond acknowledging their motivational significance and grants them an other-worldly, metaphysical, or religious status. The segregation of selfless acts from egoistic ones resulted in the valorization of the former. By denying their spurious metaphysical grounding, he hopes to realign selfless acts with egoistic ones, thereby restoring *value* to the latter.

Nietzsche does not offer a complete listing of every possible error, but rather his general point is that moral actions are motivated by the intellectual mistakes that he identifies as moral premises. Thus, he denies morality insofar as the moral actions of human beings are dependent on certain motivating errors—acting according to moral judgements rooted in superstitious beliefs. The idea that morality is based on error is a rather broad critique discussed throughout Nietzsche's corpus. The false presuppositions of morality are not confined to the psychological error of interpreting human actions and motives as selfless or unegoistic. The claim that morality is the work of error also includes the error of 'free will'.[43] "If only those actions are moral which are performed out of freedom of will, as another definition says, then there are likewise no moral actions!" (D 148, KSA 3:139). An example of the sorts of metaphysical errors that Nietzsche has in mind can be gleaned from the following passage:

> In Christianity neither morality nor religion has even a single point of contact with reality. Nothing but imaginary *causes* ('God', 'soul', 'ego', 'spirit', 'free will'—for that matter, 'unfree will'), nothing but imaginary *effects* ('sin', 'redemption', 'grace', 'punishment', 'forgiveness of sins'). Intercourse between imaginary *beings* ('God', 'spirits', 'souls'); an imaginary *natural* science (anthropocentric; no trace of any concept of natural causes); an imaginary *psychology* (nothing but self-misunderstandings, interpretations of agreeable or disagreeable general feelings…). (A 15, KSA 6:181)

---

42 Richard Schacht. *Nietzsche*. London and New York: Routledge, 1995 (first published 1983), p.449.

43 This specific objection was dealt with previously in my discussion of Nietzsche's critique of human agency.

Nietzsche's objections to these metaphysical presuppositions are best viewed in light of his naturalism. From the standpoint of Christian morality, life, nature and history are non-moral. As a result, in order to salvage morality it is necessary to posit an 'other world', a 'beyond' in opposition to the non-moral naturalistic world. The erroneous belief in the existence of a metaphysical world exhibits an ignorance of reality, and the concept of natural causes.

This component of Nietzsche's critique is preoccupied with the motivating forces (intellectual mistakes) of morality. His position in respect to moral actions including their motives and intentions is that "Moral actions are in reality 'something other than that'—more we cannot say: and all actions are essentially unknown" (D 116, KSA 3:109). Nietzsche is not interested in countering these erroneous presuppositions with the *true* motives of moral actions. Instead, his view entails that "*there are altogether no moral facts*...Morality is merely an interpretation of certain phenomena—more precisely, a misinterepretation" (TI 7:1, KSA 6:98). Although the idea that morality is based on error permeates his writings, there is good reason not to accord it too much weight in his overall critique of morality. He states: "Even if a morality has grown out of an error, the realization of this fact would not as much as touch the problem of its *value*" (GS 345, KSA 3:579 my emphasis). It is precisely the *value* of morality which is Nietzsche's fundamental concern (GM P:5, KSA 5:251). Since moral judgements can never be taken literally, he goes on to evaluate moralities in the only possible way—semeiotically, as sign-language of the affects.

Morality as Life-Negating, Anti-Natural

In order to legitimize the demand for a revaluation of values, Nietzsche must show that what passes for our 'highest values' are really quite low in a *Rangordnung*. Since a convincing response will no longer include the claim that morality is based on errors, some other evaluative standpoint is needed. In Nietzsche's post-Zarathustran writings, the crucial question concerning the value of existence now becomes: "what, seen in the perspective of *life* (*der Optik des* Lebens), is the significance of morality" (BT SC:4, KSA 1:17)? Specifically, the evaluation of morality will depend on whether it is a sign of ascending or declining life, as is evidenced in Nietzsche's most basic typology of morals, where he pronounces the following verdict on master and slave morality: "Master morality is...the sign language of what has turned out well, of *ascending* life, of the will to power as the principle of life" whereas slave morality "impoverishes, pales and makes uglier the value of things, it *negates* the world" (CW 'E', KSA 6:50–1). Morality, then, is attacked to the extent that it affirms values which are life-negating. The question as to its 'truth-claims' is a non-issue since the standpoint of 'life' does not entail any epistemic privilege: "Judgments, value judgments concerning life, for or against, can in the last resort never be true: they possess value only as symptoms…" (TI 2:2, KSA 6:68). In fact, Nietzsche will affirm the *falseness* of a judgement provided that it proves indispensable for the enhancement of life (BGE 4, KSA 5:18).[44]

While one might very well agree with Nietzsche that life demands that we posit values of some sort (TI 5:5, KSA 6:86), and that a human being is, first and foremost, 'an evaluating animal' (KSA 12:182), the force of his critique rests on the much larger claim that morality is 'hostile to life'. Some commentators, however, have denied this opposition between morality and life. For example, Thomas Mann explains Nietzsche's error in terms of the "utterly false relationship into which he puts life and morality when he treats them as antagonists."[45] And, as Mark Platts states succinctly, "*Morality versus Life* is not the best defined of battle lines."[46] It is apposite, then, that we come to an understanding of what Nietzsche means by morality being life-negating. Yet, the answer to this question is complicated by the fact that he is not particularly forthcoming in his explanation of how 'life' can function as a criterion of value.

It may be useful, then, to review Nietzsche's concept of 'life' and how it relates to the 'will to power'. The 'will to power' is often encountered as the fundamental character of existence as when Zarathustra states: "Wherever I found a living thing, I found will to power" (Z II:12, KSA 4:147). In place of self-preservation as the cardinal instinct of organic beings, Nietzsche continually reasserts that "A living thing seeks above all to *discharge* its strength—life itself is *will to power*" (BGE 13, KSA 5:27). The notion that 'life is will to power' is expressed elsewhere in his writings, but should be dealt with cautiously. The expression itself connotes an equivalence between 'life' and 'will to power' which is not entirely accurate: "For life is merely a special case of the will to power" (WP 692, KSA 13:301). Whereas the 'will to power' is an active agent in both the organic and inorganic realms, 'life' is restricted to the former but exists in multiple forms. In addressing the ambiguity of Nietzsche's references to 'life', Michel Haar quotes the following 'definitions':

---

44 Nietzsche's willingness to endorse judgements that are false (if they are life-promoting) appears to be inconsistent with his critique of the morality of mores (from *Daybreak*) which alluded to its erroneous presuppositions. Note, however, that Nietzsche's critique of the morality of mores occurred in his positivistic period, and that by the time he wrote *Beyond Good and Evil*, he had developed a new view—symptomatology.

45 Thomas Mann. *Reflections of a Non-Political Man* quoted in Ernst Behler's "Nietzsche in the twentieth century" in *The Cambridge Companion to Nietzsche*. (eds. B. Magnus and K. Higgins), Cambridge: Cambridge University Press, 1996, p.304.

46 Mark Platts, *Moral Realities*, New York: Routledge, 1991 p.220.

> Life itself is essential assimilation, injury, violation of the foreign and the weaker, suppression, hardness, the forcing of one's own forms upon something else, ingestion and—at least in its mildest form—exploitation. (BGE 259, KSA 5:207)
> Doesn't living mean evaluating, preferring, being unjust, being limited, wanting to be different? (BGE 9, KSA 5:22)
> Life operates *essentially*, i.e., in its basic functions, through injury, assault, exploitation, destruction and simply cannot be thought of at all without this character...From the highest biological standpoint, legal conditions can never be other than *exceptional conditions.* (GM II:11, KSA 5:310–11)[47]

Haar proceeds to outline the variations in meaning. On the one hand, Nietzsche appeals to 'life' as simultaneously "an organic process...and as the social existence of man entailing the concept of *right*", and "on the other hand, they have a meaning that is ontological, descriptive...and also a normative and prescriptive meaning."[48] As Haar notes, it would be a mistake to construe Nietzsche's understanding of 'life' as strictly ontological and lacking any ethical consequences. Despite the rather diverse application of the term 'life', Nietzsche takes *human* life as his point of departure when his discussion shifts to moral concerns.[49]

In a note from 1885–1886, Nietzsche applies the concept of 'life' to the task of evaluating our moral values. He writes:

> What are our evaluations and moral tables really worth? What is the outcome of their rule? For whom? In relation to what?—Answer: for life. But *what is life*? Here we need a new, more definite formulation of the concept 'life'. My formula for it is: Life is will to power. (WP 254, KSA 12:161)

A human being, too, is fundamentally, will to power. But, in this case, the will to power does not refer to the essence of reality, but to a human being (i.e. a real entity) in its reality.[50] From the standpoint of the large realm of the organic, *human* life is simply *one* form of life. Yet, because moral values belong exclusively to the human domain, it is this specific form of life to which Nietzsche devotes his attention. The question of the value of morality is always

---

47 Michel Haar, *Nietzsche and Metaphysics*, (tr. Michael Gendre), Albany: State University of New York Press, 1996, p.118.

48 Ibid, p.118.

49 Brian Leiter (1995) reduces Nietzsche's standard of life as a criterion of morality to the value of life for human beings, without considering its other diverse applications. I think that Leiter is correct to highlight the question of the value of life for human beings, but in doing so, it gives a false impression that this is the only possible interpretation of the term 'life'.

50 At times, Nietzsche will oscillate between an understanding of 'will to power' as characteristic of the world in its organic and inorganic nature.

a question of the 'value for life', specifically, the value of life *'for whom'*. In expressing the formula 'life is will to power' within the context of an evaluation of morality, Nietzsche is asserting that the will to power is instrumental in determining morality's value for life (i.e. the value for human lives) insofar as the enhancement of an individual's life will reflect the essential nature of reality. This relation is expressed in the following remarks where Nietzsche opposes the 'will to life' as self-preservation: "A living thing seeks above all to discharge its strength" (BGE 13, KSA 5:27), and the "really fundamental instinct of life…aims at the *expansion of power*" (GS 349, KSA 3:585). For Nietzsche, the 'will to life' always comes down to "superiority…growth and expansion…power" (349).

This account of the 'living thing' as a perpetual squanderer of power does not preclude the notion of a ruthless, barbarian type who engages in heinous acts which increase his feeling of strength, but Nietzsche's principle of 'will to power' includes a more general application. For instance, in his discussion of the ascetic ideal[51] in the *Genealogy*, he explains that no one is immune from the 'will to power': "Every animal…too—instinctively strives for an optimum of favorable conditions under which it can expend all its strength and achieve its maximal feeling of power" (GM III:7, KSA 5:350). If all human beings are products of the 'will to power', then this will hold true equally for the tame, weak, decadent type of human being. What is relevant for our immediate discussion is the manner in which Nietzsche argues against certain manifestations of the 'will to power'. If we consider, for instance, the valuation that the ascetic priest places on our life, we encounter a denunciation of certain basic needs of the human organism. Since these needs are fundamental to life, condemning them indicates that life is viewed as "a wrong road on which one must finally walk back to the point where it begins, or as a mistake that is put right by deeds" (GM III:11, KSA 5:362). The power-will of the ascetic priest does not want to become master over something in life, but over life itself; over its basic conditions. Hence, the self-contradiction, and physiological absurdity of 'life *against* life'. Nietzsche's revised formulation is stated as follows: "*the ascetic ideal springs from the protective instinct of a degenerating life* which tries by all means to sustain itself and to fight for its existence" (GM III:13, KSA 5:366). The ascetic ideal is explained physiologically as the work of a degenerate, sickly type of human being. Ultimately, the ascetic priest, the "apparent enemy of life, this *denier*—precisely he is among the greatest *conserving* and yes-creating (*Ja-schaffende*) forces of life" (13). There are consequences when the highest values of a culture are represented by the physiologically inhibited. The more a culture

---

51 The term 'ascetic ideal' refers to any ideal that requires one to frustrate the basic needs of a human being (e.g. poverty, humility, and chastity, GM III:8, KSA 5:352).

becomes accustomed to sickliness among men, "the higher should be the honor accorded the rare cases of great power of soul and body, man's *lucky hits*; the more we should protect the well-constituted from the worst kind of air, the air of the sickroom" (13). Unfortunately, the 'lucky hits' do not receive such honours, nor are they protected from the degenerate type. The result is that "the sick represent the greatest danger for the healthy; it is not the strongest but the weakest who spell disaster for the strong" (13). Nietzsche's repudiation of the ascetic ideal culminates in a concern over its damaging effects for the healthy type of human being.

This critique of morality as hostile to life is informed by the more general opposition between the supernatural and the natural (i.e. the 'true world' of the metaphysicians versus the 'this-worldly'). On many occasions, Nietzsche will claim that Christian morality negates life insofar as its metaphysical principles serve to undermine our affective existence (BGE 258, KSA 5:206). For instance, he writes: "The concept of 'God invented as a counterconcept of life…the whole hostility unto death against life…The concept of the 'beyond', the 'true world' invented in order to devaluate the only world there is…invented in order to despise the body, to make it sick…" (EH XIV:8, KSA 6:373-74). This hostility against life occurs, for example, in Christianity's means for overcoming the vehemence of a passion. Instead of considering how the passions may be 'beautified' or 'deified', Christianity opts for their extirpation: *il faut tuer les passions*. In regard to sexuality, Nietzsche asks us to recall the Sermon on the Mount from the New Testament where it is remarked: "If thy eye offend thee, pluck it out". The idea of destroying the passions as a preventative measure against their stupidity is as misguided as a dentist who 'plucks out' teeth so that they will no longer hurt (TI 5:1, KSA 6:83). These examples aim to show that "an attack on the roots of passion means an attack on the roots of life: the practice of the church is *hostile to life*" (1). Far from suggesting that we give free reign to the passions, Nietzsche's point is that in condemning them, one is necessarily condemning life.

The superiority of the (pre-Socratic) Greeks was evident in their success at integrating the passions within culture without being extirpated or repressed. The Hellenic 'instinct of life', expressed in the Dionysian mysteries, of "*eternal* life, the eternal recurrence of life; the future promised and consecrated in the past; the triumphant Yes to life beyond death and change; *true* life as collective continuation of life through procreation, through the mysteries of sexuality" (TI 10:4, KSA 6:159) is put forth as a contrast to the anti-affective, and hence, life-negating teachings of the Church. In this way, Nietzsche continually stresses the conflict between Christian morality and the instincts of life. There is certainly some truth to this critique of Christianity, although it does not justify, in itself, an appeal to 'life' as a standard of evaluation. As Krell astutely observes, the physiological decadence behind Christian *ressentiment* appears validated in the plea of the chorus in Georg Friedrich Händel's cantata, "*Ach Herr, mich armen Sünder*", with a text which reads: "Heal me, dear Lord, for I am sick and weak; my heart is sore and afflicted and suffers great adversity. My bones are a-tremble, full of anxiety and alarm, my soul is all a-tremble, O Lord, why so long?"[52] The source of Nietzsche's inspiration comes from Saint Paul who remarked: "God hath chosen the weak things of the world to ruin what is strong."[53] In fact, the First Essay of the *Genealogy* is a commentary on this citation, and includes additional references to Christian vengeance attributed to Tertullian and Thomas.[54]

The normative thrust of the concept of 'life' is featured in the chapter entitled 'Morality as Anti-Nature' from *Twilight of the Idols*:

> Every naturalism in morality—that is, every *healthy* morality (*gesunde* Moral)—is dominated by an instinct of life; some commandment of life is fulfilled by a determinate canon of 'shalt' and 'shalt not'; some inhibition and hostile element on the path of life is thus removed. *Anti-natural* morality (*widernatürliche* Moral)—that is, almost every morality (*Moral*) which has so far been taught, revered, and preached—turns, conversely, *against* the instincts of life; it is *condemnation* of these instincts...When it says, 'God looks at the heart,' it says No to both the lowest and the highest desires of life, and posits God as the *enemy* of *life*. The saint in whom God delights is the ideal eunuch. Life has come to an end where the 'kingdom of God' begins. (TI 5:4, KSA 6:85)

In this passage, Nietzsche appeals to 'life' as a criterion for the evaluation of two distinct types of morality—natural or healthy, and the more pervasive, anti-natural. In this way, the determination of a particular morality will depend on its relation to life, whether it represents the instincts of life or their deterioration. A morality is healthy or natural insofar as it is 'dominated by an instinct of life' which, for Nietzsche, means that 'some commandment of life is fulfilled by a determinate canon of 'shalt' and 'shalt not'; some inhibition and hostile element on the path of life is thus removed.' But, in what sense does life issue commands? A certain command of life is fulfilled when 'some inhibition and hostile element on the path of life is thus removed'. Conversely, anti-natural morality, rather than promoting life, always strives to condemn the affective existence of human life. By calling for the extirpation of life's instincts, anti-natural morality is, at the same time, condemning life itself.

---

52 David Farrell Krell's *Infectious Nietzsche*, Bloomington and Indianapolis: Indiana University Press, 1996, p.4.

53 Paul, I Corinthians, 1:20 cited in A 45, KSA 6:223.

54 See GM I:15, KSA 5:283–85.

The specific conception of 'life' from the above passage may not be immediately obvious. However, it is evident from the following section that Nietzsche's account of 'life' is primarily affiliated with *human* lives. He explains,

> When we speak of values, we speak with the inspiration, with the way of looking at things, which is part of life: *life itself forces us to posit values*; life itself values through us when we posit values. From this it follows that even that anti-natural morality which conceives of God as the counter-concept and condemnation of life is only a value judgment of life—but of what life? of what kind of life? I have already given the answer: of declining, weakened, weary, condemned life. (TI 5:5, KSA 6:86 my emphasis)

In keeping with his semeiological approach, judgements concerning life are merely symptoms of a certain kind of life. Thus, there is no vantage point external to life which permits any definitive solutions to the problem of life's value. Regardless, life demands that we posit values of some sort. After all, a person is first and foremost, 'an evaluating animal' (KSA 12:182). The question that needs to be asked is always what 'kind of life' (i.e. what type of person) underlies one's moral values. As is most often the case, Nietzsche will diagnose the crusader of Christian morality as a weak, degenerative type, lacking "the really fundamental instinct of life which aims at *the expansion of power*" (GS 349, KSA 3:585).

What does Nietzsche hope to accomplish by unmasking a decadent type of individual behind Christian morality? He cannot argue that this morality is a threat to human existence. On the contrary, the ascetic ideal has served the weak quite well as "an artifice for the *preservation* of life" (GM III:3, KSA 5:366), albeit a degenerating life. Nietzsche's chief complaint, rather, is that "Christianity…has waged a *war to the death* against this *higher* type of man, it has excommunicated all the fundamental instincts of this type, it has distilled evil, the *Evil One*…it has made an ideal out of the preservative instincts of strong life" (A 5, KSA 6:171). And, in explaining how this came to be, he adds, "it has depraved the reason even of the intellectually strongest natures by teaching men to feel the supreme values of intellectuality as sinful, as misleading, as temptations" (5). Nietzsche's critique of morality as anti-life, then, is fueled by his interest in the flourishing of 'this higher type of man'. Christianity is rejected on account of its harmful consequences for the exemplary human being. In a note from 1888, he writes,

> Whoever reflects upon the way in which the type man can be raised to his greatest splendor and power will grasp first of all that he must place himself outside morality (*Moral*); for morality (*Moral*) has been essentially directed to the opposite end: to obstruct or destroy that splendid evolution wherever it has been going on…the weaker, more delicate…existences need to take sides *against* that gloriousness of life (*Glorie von*

> *Leben*) and strength; and to that end they have to acquire a new valuation of themselves by virtue of which they can condemn life in this highest plenitude, and where possible destroy it. A tendency hostile to life is therefore characteristic of morality (*Moral*), in so far as it wants to overpower the types of life. (WP 897, KSA 12:225–26)

In this passage, Nietzsche sets up an antithesis between morality and the higher type. When he attacks morality as being 'hostile to life', the specific reference is to its damaging consequences for that 'splendid evolution'. The weak retaliate against this higher type by devising a new valuation designed for the purpose of condemning the existence of the strong.

This new mode of valuation, as we have seen, amounts to the *denaturing* of natural values. To counter this denaturalization of morality, he describes his fundamental innovation as follows: "In place of 'moral values', purely naturalistic values" (WP 462, KSA 12:342), and Goethe and Napoleon are often cited as the embodiments of naturalism. Although Nietzsche, following Rousseau, speaks of a 'return to nature', he is eager to distance himself from the latter's naturalistic tendencies. In *Twilight of the Idols,* Rousseau is counted among Nietzsche's "impossible ones", as he writes: "*Rousseau*: or the return to nature *in impuris naturalibus*"[55] (TI 9:1, KSA 6:111). Properly speaking, Nietzsche's 'return to nature' "is really not a going back but an *ascent*—up to the high, free, even terrible nature and naturalness where great tasks are something one plays with, one *may* play with. To put it metaphorically: Napoleon was a piece of 'return to nature', as I understand the phrase" (48). This account of an 'ascent' to nature is disappointingly vague. Rather than providing substance to his thought, Nietzsche seems content to merely invert Rousseau's position. The ambiguity surrounding this notion of 'nature' has a potentially crippling effect on his efforts to distinguish moralities, and their overall orientation to 'life'. Even if Nietzsche can emerge unscathed from this Scylla, the method which he employs to evaluate moralities (i.e. symptomatology), will shipwreck him on a Charybdis of rhetoric.

Both the rejection of anti-natural morality and the affirmation of natural morality not only depend on the plausibility of the concepts 'life' and 'nature', but require an interpreter—someone skilled in the art of semeiology, an expert at reading the signs of moral judgements. What I find problematic and even ironic is that while insisting that human beings lack an 'organ of truth', Nietzsche, *qua* 'philosopher of life', pronounces his own expertise on moral matters by appealing to his 'organs'! How is it that he is sensitive to the ascending and declining instincts of life? At this critical moment when we expect Nietzsche to provide justification for his insights into decadent and

55 In natural dirtiness.

healthy morality, he defends the view that 'morality negates life' by claiming to have developed "a keen eye for the symptoms of decline" (CW P, KSA 6:11), while elsewhere claiming to have "a subtler sense of smell for the signs of ascent and decline than any other human being before me" (EH I:1, KSA 6:264). It may have been no joke when one commentator remarked that Nietzsche was the first to philosophize with his 'nostrils'. Consider these thoughts from *Ecce Homo*:

> What is it, fundamentally, that allows us to recognize *who has turned out well?* That a well-turned out person pleases our senses, that he is carved from wood that is hard, delicate and at the same time smells good. (EH I:2, KSA 6:267)

Can it be that the advocate of the 'organic' has his 'organs' confused? Or, has fate dictated that all his organs are attuned to the instincts of life? David Farrell Krell has expressed a similar objection relating to Nietzsche's appeal to 'life'. He states, "However, we will want to know by what sort of intuition Nietzsche is convinced that life, nature, and history rest upon deception. Has he been reading too much Schopenhauer, too much Darwin, too much Ranke? Can we escape the dilemma through the following bit of cleverness: in order to *know* that life rests upon deception, Nietzsche would have to be undeceived in his intuition of life."[56] The difficulty, then, has to do with Nietzsche's claim to occupy a non-epistemically, privileged position in assessing the value of morality. While one might share many of his 'sensibilities', as I certainly do, the appeal to life as a standard of evaluation must include his personal stamp of approval, and there seems to be no justification for accepting his final judgements. Put differently, it would appear that anyone could exercise his or her veto. At other times, when Nietzsche is not trying to convince readers of his insightful organs, he enlists his own skills as a philologist to justify his critical perspective. A philologist, he explains, can see *behind* the 'sacred books' (A 47, KSA 6:226).[57] Yet, given the fundamental importance of the question of the value of existence, a response relying on one's credentials either as a philologist or as a gifted sensitive type remains unconvincing.

Despite the inadequacies involved in trying to rest on his laurels, there might be some sort of saving grace for Nietzsche's critique. To begin with, it is worth noting here that morality, for Nietzsche, is more a cultural phenomenon

---

56 Krell, *Infectious Nietzsche*, p.5.

57 Nietzsche's remarkable contributions as a philologist have been well-documented, but at the same time, his *Birth of Tragedy* was considered a disgrace to the study of philology, and was greeted with much ridicule (recall, for instance, the Wilamowitz-Nietzsche debate). So, an appeal to his skills as a philologist cannot serve as a convincing response.

than a theoretical discipline, and as such, will affect the attitudes of people. The crucial question, then, is what are the consequences of morality for individuals, and is it possible that Christian morality actually harms certain 'types' of people? This question is legitimate even if Nietzsche's appeal to 'life' as a standard for evaluating moralities is seriously flawed. As a result, we can reject his criterion of morality without denying that there may be 'types' of human beings who are in fact harmed by morality, even if we disagree with Nietzsche on who these higher types are. Dan Conway has attempted, in a different way, to rescue Nietzsche's position from its epistemic shortcomings by suggesting that if we accept his view that all philosophers resort to mythmaking, and eventually come to accept the tales they tell, then: "Following his [Nietzsche's] own lead, we might reject the myth on epistemic grounds, while endorsing it nonetheless on pragmatic grounds—for example, as the philosophical armor that affords us our best chance of surviving the twilight of the idols."[58] Before we can gauge the efficacy of these various options, Nietzsche's general assertion that morality is a threat to the well-being of 'higher types' must be accompanied by an account of who these 'higher types' are, and how they are distinguishable from the decadent, lower type. And, it will be necessary to explain the exact sense in which these exemplary types are harmed.

Who are the 'Higher Types'?

Having shown that Nietzsche's critique of morality underlies a preoccupation with great human beings, the next question that arises is: 'who are these *higher types*' and how are they distinguished from their antithesis—the lower men?' Nietzsche's references to exemplary individuals occur in two forms, either as specific historical examples (e.g. Goethe, Napoleon, Thucydides, Caesar, Bizet, Borgia, etc.) or as more general classifications such as free spirits, aristocrats of the spirit, higher men, philosophers of the future, the genius, highest exemplars, stronger type, great men, lucky strikes, *Übermensch*, a well-turned-out person, etc. Regardless of certain distinctions that commentators are apt to point out among these various expressions of greatness, the basic point is that the highest value resides in human flourishing. Great human beings, however, are not understood in terms of ideals, but as concrete living examples. For Nietzsche, it is always possible to determine the order of rank of each person since "Every individual may be scrutinized to see whether he represents the ascending or the descending line of life" (TI 9:33, KSA 6:131). In other words, the value of an individual is a measure of his physiological success or failure. An individual who

---

58 Daniel W. Conway, "Returning to Nature: Nietzsche's *Götterdämmerung*" in *Nietzsche: A Critical Reader* (ed. Peter R. Sedgwick), Oxford: Blackwell, 1996 (First Published 1995), p.48.

attains such heights will be in select company since higher types are a rare breed. Since a detailed treatment of Nietzsche's affirmative ethics including his understanding of human flourishing will be the focus of Chapter Five, I will now provide a general account of 'higher types'.

While Nietzsche often teases the reader with a sample of certain admirable traits[59], there are no defining characteristics of this 'higher type', or specific formula for becoming an *Übermensch*—a point which has not escaped the attention of his critics. Unlike Aristotle, who listed the virtues belonging to the great-souled man, Nietzsche determines the order of rank among men according to their 'quanta of power'. The highest type would possess the greatest multiplicity of drives where the strongest instincts conflict powerfully, but are controlled (WP 966, KSA 11:289). Human flourishing, then, involves the capacity to discharge one's natural energies. In this way, Nietzsche is offering a formal account of the exemplary individual. He writes:

> The genius, in work and deed, is necessarily a squanderer (*Verschwender*): that he squanders himself, that is his greatness. The instinct of self-preservation is suspended, as it were; the overpowering pressure of outflowing (*ausströmenden*) forces forbids him any such care or caution...He flows out, he overflows, he uses himself up, he does not spare himself... (TI 9:44, KSA 6:146)

The economics of the genius indicates that his involuntary vitalistic expenditures include a capacity for excess. Like a cup that has overflowed, human greatness is described as a natural outpouring of one's native vitality. Note, however, that these higher types may command admiration, but cannot be praised or censured for assuming the role assigned by their physiological fate. Although there is nothing in this passage which explicitly rules out cruelty towards others as an expression of one's overflowing vitality, Nietzsche's admiration for various historical figures is evidence that power over others is not the quality in which he reserves his highest esteem.[60] Instead, his admiration extends to those who are creative, overrich in 'will', and have mastered the conflicting drives. "He shall be greatest who can be loneliest, most-concealed, beyond good and evil, master of his virtues, overrich in will" (BGE 212, KSA 5:147).

In place of a fixed table of virtues, Nietzsche considers concrete living exemplars of greatness (many of whom are listed above). These paradigms of human flourishing possess a Dionysian attitude towards life. He writes:

---

59 E.g. Hardness, solitude, strength, power, self-mastery, gift-giving virtue, cheerfulness, etc.

60 Yet, the fact that he does not rule out cruelty will prove to be a problematic feature of his ethics.

> Saying Yes to life even in its strangest and hardest problems; the will to life rejoicing over its own inexhaustibility even in the very sacrifice of its highest types—that is what I called Dionysian, that is what I understood as the bridge to the psychology of the tragic poet. Not in order to get rid of terror and pity, not in order to purge oneself of a dangerous effect...but in order to be oneself the eternal joy of becoming, beyond all terror and pity... (TI 10:5, KSA 6:160)

The solution to the question of the value of existence, then, includes a tragic view of life, 'tragic' because there is no effort to redeem or alleviate suffering in life. Together, with its sister concept, *amor fati*, Nietzsche's tragic wisdom offers an account of the exemplary type's orientation to life: a joyous, complete affirmation of existence. He explains:

> My formula for greatness in a human being is *amor fati*: that one wants nothing to be different, not forward, not backward, not in all eternity. Not merely bear what is necessary, still less conceal it—all idealism is mendaciousness in the face of what is necessary—but *love* it. (EH II:10, KSA 6:297)

The enormity of such a task can hardly be disguised. It would not only entail a Stoic 'hardness' towards the unavoidable hardships in life, but also a *love* of them on account of their necessity. Although one might wish to challenge this conception of human flourishing, it is certainly not difficult to appreciate Nietzsche's motivation for offering a formula for greatness which expresses a profound gratitude towards life in all its colours. It is his hope to erase two millennia of anti-nature which has, he insists, deprived human beings of a greater glory. In other words, Nietzsche wants to articulate the conditions under which the affirmation of life is possible after the death of God. Schopenhauer had failed to provide such a justification for life because he remained entangled in the moral-Christian ideal. Ironically, Christian morality *survived* the death of God, and continues to hold sway despite Nietzsche's ambitions to awaken the unrealized, liberating consequences of this great event. While one may admire Nietzsche's motivations for offering an affirmative ideal to counter Christian morality, one may equally challenge *the* ideal that he seeks to put in its place. Affirming life amidst all its sufferings is an unrealistic ideal, which we would do well to reject even if we are sympathetic to Nietzsche's critique of Christian morality. However, this does not rule out the possibility of constructing alternative ideals to respond to the threat of nihilism.

Among the list of exemplary human beings, Goethe is often singled out as the most beautiful expression of a life-affirmer. The references to Goethe provide the clearest statements of the conception of human flourishing that Nietzsche promotes insofar as he displays the features of the Dionysian philosophy at the heart of Nietzsche's affirmative ethics. Goethe, according to

Nietzsche, possesses a Dionysian faith, for he "stands amid the cosmos with a joyous and trusting fatalism, in the *faith* that only the particular is loathsome, and that all is redeemed and affirmed in the whole—*he does not negate any more.* Such a faith, however, is the highest of all possible faiths: I have baptized it with the name of *Dionysus*" (TI 9:49, KSA 6:151-52). For Nietzsche, Goethe's existence was untimely yet he sought to overcome the eighteenth century by a return to nature, by *ascending* to the naturalness of the Renaissance. Goethe's 'ascent' to nature was made possible by his affective economy which consisted of drives of great intensity that allowed the dominant drive at any given time, to go to its limit: to excess. In this way, Goethe realized his creative potential. Moreover, his *virtù* can be attributed to the fact that "he disciplined himself to wholeness, he *created* himself" (49).

It is worth noting here that this anti-voluntaristic model of human flourishing is a significant departure from traditional concerns regarding the moral worth of our *actions*. It is not actions which determine nobility: "*The noble soul has reverence for itself*" (BGE 287, KSA 5:233). In possessing an instinct for rank, the noble type, itself, will be a determiner of values. Rather than "brooding about the moral value of our actions", Nietzsche explains, "We…want to become those we are—human beings who are new, unique, incomparable, who give themselves laws", and who, like Goethe, "create themselves" (GS 335, KSA 3:563). In denying an external authority dictating who one is to become, and with an eye full of good will towards sensuality, Goethe and Dionysus are united in their opposition to Christianity. For Nietzsche, Goethe's experience of Christianity was similar to that of the Noble Romans who regarded it as a *foeda superstitio* (CW 'E', KSA 6:52).[61] In the confrontation between 'Dionysus versus the Crucified', Goethe stood on the side of the amoral Greek god in his artistic and anti-Christian valuation of life. In short, Goethe embodied various life-affirming qualities such as a saying-Yes to life in its totality, self-control, strength, and reverence toward himself.[62] Yet, at the same time, such qualities resist any moral codification since what will be demanded of the higher type depends on an ever-changing, shifting context. The inappropriateness of moral prescriptions, then, can be attributed to their unconditional or fixed nature which stands opposed to Dionysian flux.

---

61 In his translation and commentary of *The Case Of Wagner*, Kaufmann quotes from Goethe's *Venetian Epigrams*:

Much there is I can stand, and most things not easy to suffer
I bear with quiet resolve, just as a god commands it.
Only a few I find as repugnant as snakes and poison—
These four: tobacco smoke, bedbugs, garlic, and †. (quoted in CW 'E', n.7)

62 See TI 9:49, KSA 6:151.

The construction of a Dionysian perspective was intended to supplant the nihilistic world-view mired in *ressentiment.* In particular, the exemplary human being was to replace the 'world-weary' inhabitants of modernity—*all-too-* human beings who instead of expressing gratitude towards life and remaining faithful to the earth, take leave of the 'this-worldly' to embrace the metaphysical comforts located in the 'beyond', the 'other-world'. At this point, it is necessary to turn our attention to the 'lower type'. In so doing, we find once again that Nietzsche uses various terms to denote this brand of individual: fettered spirits, weak, decadent, mediocre, herd-animal, lower men, world-weary, incomplete fragmentary men, and the last man. Fortunately, it is less difficult to determine the identity of this lower type of individual owing to Nietzsche's candid remarks. Recall, for instance, the explanation of his self-professed immoralism where he identified the type of man whom he negates. "I negate a type of man that has so far been considered supreme: the good, the benevolent, the beneficent" (EH XIV:4, KSA 6:367). The morality accompanying this decadent type is none other than Christian morality (4). After describing goodness and benevolence as symptoms of weakness, Nietzsche specifically identifies the last men (*die letzten Menschen*), as "good human beings", "herd animals", "or as Herbert Spencer would have it, altruistic", and then equates altruism with morality (4). In the same passage, Nietzsche criticizes 'the good' for regarding all kinds of distress as an objection, for prevailing at the expense of the *future,* and for their inability to create.

The 'last man' (*letzste Mensch*) is introduced in the Prologue to *Zarathustra* as the antipode of the *Übermensch.*[63] Both the last man and the *Übermensch* are the possibilities presented to humanity after the death of the Christian God. In his speech on the last man, Zarathustra warns the people against idealizing this degenerative type of individual. However, his words fall on deaf ears as his rather obtuse audience herald the coming of the last man. Failing to heed the warning of a disappointed Zarathustra, the herd go on to live a comfortable, utilitarian existence within an egalitarian society prizing uniformity, love of the neighbour, happiness, and equal rights for all. In expressing the virtues of the herd, the last man considers himself the epitome of perfection. Zarathustra's ignored message was that these characteristics do not signify human excellence, but instead represent human degradation. The proliferation of the last man will set humanity on a course for an irreversible spiritual nihilism, hence permanently eliminating the seed of man's highest hope, the *Übermensch.* Zarathustra spoke thus:

---

63 In the first edition of *Zarathustra*, the Prologue was entitled "On the Overman and the Last Man" (W. Kaufmann, *The Portable Nietzsche.* New York: Viking Press, 1964, p.116).

> The time has come for man to set himself a goal…His soil is still rich enough. But one day this soil will be poor and domesticated, and no tall tree will be able to grow in it. Alas, the time is coming when man will no longer shoot the arrow of his longing beyond man, and the string of his bow will have forgotten how to whir! (Z P:5, KSA 4:19).

This passage leads to the issue of whether human flourishing is even possible in late modernity, or whether the *Übermensch* necessarily belongs to an uncharted future. Although further discussion on this point would take me far afield from my present concern, suffice it to say that Nietzsche thought that great human beings can appear in any period yet they have thus far only surfaced as accidents (i.e. 'lucky strikes') and never as something willed or bred. The danger of the last man, then, involves the permanent jeopardizing of the *Übermensch* as the *goal* of humankind.

The term 'last man' drops out after the Prologue before reappearing in Part Three where it is then replaced by the related expression, 'the good and the just'. "Oh my brothers, who represents the greatest danger for all of man's future? Is it not the good and the just?" (Z III:12:§26, KSA 4:265). Zarathustra's quarrel with the 'good and the just' has to do with their conception of goodness and justice, and their disdain for *creators*, those who break tablets and old values. "The good", Zarathustra proclaims, "are *unable* to create…they crucify him who writes new values on new tablets" (§26). In doing so, their great danger lies in sacrificing man's future. This last remark is consistent with Nietzsche's view that "the *goal of humanity* cannot lie in its end but only *in its highest exemplars*" (UADH 9, KSA 1:317). But, instead of society concerning itself with creating the conditions for the production of exemplary individuals, it has remained committed to striving for the happiness of the greatest number. For this reason, Nietzsche usually associates democracy with man's diminution. The weak can maintain and develop themselves most easily in a democratic society (WP 887, KSA 12:493). This is the case because they possess qualities which are "the most useful"—"qualities…which serve to ease existence for those who suffer: here pity, the complaisant and obliging hand, the warm heart, patience, industry, humility, and friendliness are honored" (BGE 260, KSA 5:211). Nietzsche, on the other hand, values greatly the discipline of suffering since "only *this* discipline has created all enhancements of man so far" (BGE 225, KSA 5:161). This view is in keeping with his fundamental ethical assertion that only human flourishing is intrinsically valuable.

'Types' of persons are distinguished by their attitude towards life. In the section "On Redemption" from *Zarathustra*, the point is made that an affirmation of life occurs when one is able to accept the totality of his life. Nietzsche writes:

> To redeem those who lived in the past and to recreate all 'it was' into 'thus I willed it'—that alone I should call redemption...Willing liberates; but what is it that puts this liberator in fetters? 'It was'—that is the name of the will's gnashing of teeth (*Willes Zähneknirschen*) and most serious melancholy. Powerless against what has been done, it is an angry spectator of all that is past. The will cannot will backwards; and that it cannot break time and time's covetousness, that is the will's loneliest melancholy. (Z II:20, KSA 4:179–80)

This passage offers an important contrast between the life-affirmer and the life-negater. The fettered spirit's loneliest melancholy is attributed to his inability to affirm the past, the 'it was'. This lower type is filled with anger and resentment, wanting desperately to change the unchangeable—the past. Rather than displaying gratitude towards life, he stands before existence in a state of denial. In refusing to accept the world in its totality, his anger and melancholy represent his vindictive need to slander life. Conversely, Nietzsche's formula for greatness, *amor fati*, however idealistic it may be, precludes any *ressentiment*.

In distinguishing between 'types' of individuals, Nietzsche is claiming that they have different needs, interests, attitudes, and values. Herd morality, as an expression of the needs of one particular group (the values of the weak), means that the interests of exemplary human beings (their instincts of growth) are neglected. The values espoused by Christian morality permeate society as a whole, affecting the attitudes of *all* its citizens. Morality, then, is harmful insofar as it exposes exemplary human beings to values that conflict with their means of flourishing, and thus, threaten their potential for greatness. For instance, if a society promotes such values as altruism, equal rights for all, happiness, extirpation of the passions, pity, and social utility, then these values will influence the attitudes of everyone. It is precisely in its demanding one morality for all that Christian morality proves devastating for the higher type. As Leiter explains, "he [Nietzsche] thinks a culture in which such norms prevail as morality will be a culture which eliminates the conditions for the realization of human excellence."[64] The value of Leiter's reading lies in its treatment of Nietzsche's understanding of morality as a *cultural* (rather than a *theoretical*) phenomenon. Otherwise, Nietzsche would be open to an objection which would run as follows: even if suffering is necessary for human flourishing, moral prescriptions need not (and historically, do not) interfere with one's artistic achievements. If an artist discovers, for instance, that his powers of creativity are heightened every time he inflicts pain on himself, then morality will not intervene to thwart his creativity. It would appear, then, that morality and artistic achievement can peacefully co-exist suggesting that there is no need to undermine Christian morality to attain greatness. This objection to

---

64 Brian Leiter, 1995, p.136.

Nietzsche, however, has been circumvented by placing his critique within the context of *culture*. Exemplary individuals are harmed not in virtue of morality's *theoretical* principles, but because morality insinuates itself into the fabric of a culture, shaping the thoughts and attitudes of those whose flourishing resides elsewhere. Morality is a danger, then, insofar as it prevents the higher type from realizing his potential for human flourishing. Moreover, since the reigning moral ideal is based upon what is useful to the herd, the affliction of all higher types occurs because everything that distinguishes them enters their thoughts accompanied by a feeling of diminution and discredit. In this way, exemplary individuals have been corrupted by Christian morality.

There is a more serious objection relating to the dreadful things sanctioned by Nietzsche's noble morality of the 'few', which pose a danger not only to the weak majority, but also to the 'higher types' that it is supposed to allow to flourish. By offering no safeguards to prevent against cruelty, the noble few are as much at risk as are the masses. The focus of this chapter, however, has been to demonstrate that the various strands of Nietzsche's critique are united by this fundamental opposition to morality: that morality is inimical to human flourishing.

*

"Have I been understood?—*Dionysus versus the Crucified...*" (EH XIV:9, KSA 6:374). These closing remarks of *Ecce Homo*, not only bring to a conclusion Nietzsche's philosophical autobiography but sum up his deepest reflections on morality. In many ways, my second chapter can be read as an exegesis of this statement. The 'Crucified' is a metaphor for the normative content of Christian morality (whose dominant components were catalogued—i.e. altruism, unconditional and absolutist, and anti-natural), as well as the individual personified by this morality—the 'lower type'. Conversely, 'Dionysus' is emblematic of Nietzsche's major preoccupation with 'higher types', in particular their beatific attitude towards life. The crucial distinction between these antithetical types is that the weak seek redemption from life whereas Dionysus offers a promise of life.

I would like to point out in closing that a critical concern could not possibly be Nietzsche's foremost task. As I have shown throughout, his objections to morality emanate from a positive interest in human flourishing. Even his critique of the free and responsible moral subject was related to his affirmative thinking. In place of the moral agent, Nietzsche treated the 'body' as his starting point from which he developed a person-oriented ethics culminating in a jubilant affirmation of existence in all its forms. This affirmation of life is symptomatic of physiological well-being and is based on Nietzsche's discrimination of 'types' of human beings. However, this view of human flourishing is undermined by Christian morality's normative agenda which conflicts with the ingredients necessary for the production of exemplary human beings. His declaration of war on morality springs entirely from his hope of re-instilling a sense 'for those who have ears to hear' of what men can aspire to—the affirmation of life in its totality.

My reading of an essentially affirmative Nietzsche conflicts with his traditional reception as merely a critic of morality. For instance, one is reminded of the American artist David Levine's caricature of Nietzsche in *The New York Review of Books*, as a mad dog, foaming at the moustache and growling at the world. Yet, as recently as 1990, one commentator challenged the phalanx to write on Nietzsche's positive morality noting that, "Because Nietzsche is generally received as primarily a critic of morality, my concern with his positive moral teaching may seem perverse."[65] In the last decade, however, there has been change in Nietzsche scholarship such that it is no longer 'perverse' to encounter readings of his affirmative ethics.[66] Still, my view is more radical in the sense that it is not intended to *add* an affirmative dimension to a prevailing critique, but rather to overcome the critical/affirmative dichotomy, and view Nietzsche's ethics as strictly affirmative. The French philosopher, Clément Rosset comes closest to expressing a similar view. He writes, "To make of Nietzsche a thinker essentially concerned with criticizing Christian, Judaic, or Platonic morals is to miss what is 'radical' in him, that is, both what interests him in the first place and, second, what is precisely the root and reason for being of the entire Nietzschean critical effort."[67] Unlike my view, Rosset simply reverses the onus, claiming that Nietzsche is primarily an affirmative thinker, and only secondarily, a critic.

In any case, it would be useful (not just for David Levine) to reconsider Nietzsche's own description of his *Feldzug* from *Ecce Homo*:

> With this book my campaign against morality begins. Not that it smells in the least of powder: you will smell far different and much lovelier scents in it, assuming your nostrils have some sensitivity. Neither big nor small guns: if the effect of the book is negative, its means are anything but that...the whole book contains no negative word, no attack, no spite... (EH VII:1, KSA 6:329)

---

65 Dan Conway, "A Moral Ideal For Everyone And No One", *International Studies in Philosophy*, XX/2, 1990, p.18.

66 For instance, it is not uncommon to find Nietzsche's ethics described as a 'virtue ethics' (Thomas Brobjer, 1995), 'moral perfectionism' (Dan Conway, 1997), or 'Dionysian morality' (Peter Murray, 1999).

67 Clément Rosset, *Joyful Cruelty: Toward a Philosophy of the Real.* (tr. David F. Bell). New York and Oxford: Oxford University Press, 1993, p.55.

With these words, Nietzsche is clarifying the nature of his 'attack' on morality, explicitly trying to avoid any negative connotation surrounding his 'campaign'. In this sense, he is an opponent of morality *de rigueur.* The 'lovelier scents' of the book have to do with its overall affirmative tone which may appear to be an astonishing admission for those accustomed to the traditional portrait of Nietzsche as a critic of morality. But, what Nietzsche means by 'criticism' is entirely consistent with the description of his campaign. He writes:

> When we criticize something, this is no arbitrary and impersonal event; it is, at least very often, evidence of vital energies in us that are growing and shedding a skin. We negate and must negate because something in us wants to live and affirm—something that we perhaps do not know or see as yet.—This is said in favor of criticism. (GS 307, KSA 3:545)

The act of negating is understood as a condition for affirming where the priority is given to the latter. What lives within Nietzsche himself are the vital energies propelling him towards a vision of the production of higher types.
What seems *prima facie* to be a hateful attack on morality turns out to be a genuine love of exemplary human beings. "The task is to bring to light what we *must ever love and honor* and what no subsequent enlightenment can take away: great individual human beings" (PTG, p.24, KSA 1:802).

In addition to arguing that Nietzsche repudiates Christian morality on account of its detrimental consequences for exemplary individuals, I wanted to capture the spirit of his inquiry which I take to be *affirmative.* Still, it seems to me that Nietzsche's methodology, his evaluation of morality, suffers from certain shortcomings. Most notably, in the absence of objective criterion for determining the ascending and declining instincts of life (and hence, the higher versus the lower man), he often flatters himself by presupposing 'a perfectly uncanny sensitivity' to such instincts. How is it that Nietzsche is granted a penetrating eye into the psychology of the 'good', while all other philosophers have remained blind? He attributes his uniqueness to being the *first* to uncover Christian morality, but even this is a contentious point since he fails to acknowledge two anti-christian precursors, Voltaire and Feuerbach. As we shall see in the next chapter, Nietzsche found few philosophical allies within the moral tradition, insisting rather that moral philosophers are stuck within the prejudices of their environment from which only Nietzsche, apparently, was able to escape.

3

The 'Preachers of Morals'

Moral predigen ist leicht, Moral begründen schwer.
—Schopenhauer, *Preisschrift Über Die Grundlage Der Moral*

May I be forgiven the discovery that all moral philosophy so far has been boring and was a soporific, and that 'virtue' has been impaired more for me by its *boring* advocates than by anything else...
—BGE 228, KSA 5:163

Die Moral-Philosophie ist die scabreuse Partie in der Geschichte des Geistes.
—KSA 13:292

To see and to demonstrate the problem of morality—that seems to me the new principal task. I deny that it has been done in previous moral philosophy.
—WP 263, KSA 11:522

In addition to his critique of morality, Nietzsche's 'campaigning' spirit extends to his evaluations of moral philosophers, to whom he often refers as 'the preachers of morals' (*Moralprediger*). In this chapter, my aim is to consider Nietzsche's evaluations of certain key figures within the history of moral philosophy in order to question whether it is possible to situate his thinking within the moral tradition. Or, whether he would sooner echo the sentiment expressed by Lope de Vega, "*yo me sucedo a mi mismo.*"[1] Since it is certainly not possible to examine his relation to every moralist discussed in his writings, some justification needs to be made for my selection of the following: Schopenhauer, Rée, Mill, Kant, and Aristotle. The Preface and the note attached to the end of the First Essay of the *Genealogy* reveal that Nietzsche's interest in morality was primarily twofold: questioning the *origin* of morality, and more importantly, determining the *value* of morality. Schopenhauer is Nietzsche's most formidable

---

1 Lope de Veda (1562–1635), Spanish dramatist. "I am my own successor."

influence, and figures prominently in the latter concern over the problem of the value of morality. Rée was responsible in large part for developing Nietzsche's interest in *rebus moralibus.* There is considerable discussion of Kant as a moralist throughout Nietzsche's corpus, and there is no justification for leaving out modern philosophy's most influential moral philosopher. Rée and Mill represent the meagre, prototypical 'English' effort to present a history of the origin of morality, and they have a dominating presence in Nietzsche's texts. Only my inclusion of Aristotle may come as a surprise to readers since Nietzsche did not make many explicit references to Aristotle's ethics. Why then did I deem it necessary to include Aristotle? The answer has to do with the frequent comparisons between Nietzsche's and Aristotle's ethics, as well as the recent attempts to situate Nietzsche's ethics within the tradition of virtue ethics.[2] In short, the moral philosophers that I selected are not only featured prominently in his writings (with the exception of Aristotle), but also represent the three major moral traditions[3] within which a comparison can be made.

An understanding of Nietzsche's relation to the moral tradition is crucial for assessing his contribution to moral philosophy. The lack of comparative studies can be attributed to a history of Nietzsche scholarship which has only recently recognized his affirmative morality. One noteworthy exception is Thomas Brobjer's excellent study of Nietzsche's ethics and its place in the history of moral thinking. However, despite claiming that Schopenhauer is Nietzsche's most important influence,[4] Brobjer offers no discussion of his ethics. Instead, Schopenhauer is used as a source for Nietzsche's objections to Kant owing to his lengthy critique of Kant's ethics in *On the Basis of Morality.* With the inclusion of Schopenhauer and Rée, and my reluctance (after comparing Nietzsche's ethics to Aristotle's) to seat Nietzsche on the throne of the aretaic tradition, I part company with Brobjer's work.

General Remarks on the 'Preachers of Morals'

In the late 1870's, Nietzsche introduced the expression 'preachers of morals' (*Moralprediger*) to avoid confusing their efforts with that of 'moralists' (*die Moralisten*). In drawing a distinction between 'preachers of morals' and 'moralists', he commended the latter for their commitment to the dissection of morality while chastizing the former's desire to serve as a model and ideal to be

---

2 Lester Hunt, *Nietzsche and the Origin of Virtue*, New York: Routledge, 1985, Thomas Brobjer, *Nietzsche's Ethics of Character*, 1995, Michael Slote, "Nietzsche and Virtue Ethics", *Int. Studies in Philosophy*, 1998, Robert C. Solomon, "A More Severe Morality: Nietzsche's Affirmative Ethics", 1986.

3 Deontological ethics, Consequentialism (Utilitarianism), and Virtue ethics (Aretaics).

4 Thomas Brobjer, *Nietzsche's Ethics of Character*, 1995, p.69.

imitated (WS 19, KSA 2:553). In a note from 1885, Nietzsche retains this distinction claiming that the distinguishing feature of a moralist is that he regards morality as questionable, in short, as a problem. The moralist then is the opposite (*Gegenstück*) of a preacher of morals since the latter never treats morality as a problem.[5] In general, the terms 'moralist' and the French '*moraliste*' are referred to in a non-pejorative fashion[6] while the derogatory expression 'preachers of morals' belongs to a group consisting of 'moral philosophers', 'priests', 'moral fanatics', 'preachers of virtue', and 'teachers of the purpose of existence', all of whom offer a deficient analysis of morality. Nietzsche attributes their meagre contributions to various shortcomings including their lack of an historical sense, knowledge of physiology, and a future goal (WP 408, KSA 11:176–77), their eagerness to offer prescriptions to everyone (D 194, KSA 3:167), their attempts to convince people that that they are in a bad state and require a radical cure (GS 326, KSA 3:553), and their efforts to 'improve mankind' in their own image (TI 7:2, KSA 6:99).

The most serious objections to the 'preachers of morals' tend to follow from their 'lack of an historical sense'. This accusation is often directed against the English historians of morality, whom according to Nietzsche, bungled the only attempts thus far "to arrive at a history of the origin (*Enstehungsgeschichte*) of morality" (GM I:1, KSA 5:257). Failing to recognize that 'the good' themselves were the initial determiners of value, the English erroneously traced the origin of the concept 'good' to unegoistic actions and labeled them 'good' from the perspective of those to whom these acts were done, those to whom these acts were *useful* (1). What these historians of morality 'uncovered' was simply a confirmation that 'unegoism' accounts for the origin of morality as well as the prevailing morality. Therefore, morality throughout the ages has remained constant, or so these incompetent genealogists had thought. The absence of an 'actual' historical sense explains this supposed continuity between the current and original morality. For Nietzsche, this false evaluation has had a lasting effect on moral philosophy. Rather than living up to their name as true 'historians', these philosophers are "still quite unsuspectingly obedient to one morality and, without knowing it, serve that as shield-bearers and followers—for example, by sharing that popular superstition of Christian Europe…that

5 KSA 11:509. "*Ein Moralist ist das Gegenstück eines Moral-Predigers nämlich ein Denker, welcher die Moral als fragwürdig, fragezeichenwürdig, kurz als Problem nimmt. Ich bedaure hinzufügen zu müssen, daß der Moralist, eben deshalb, selber zu den fragwürdigen Wesen gehört.*"

6 The only exception that I was able to find comes from the Preface to *The Case of Wagner* (*Der Fall Wagner*, 1888) where Nietzsche uses the term 'moralist' (*die Moralisten*) in a pejorative sense after having distanced himself from the perspective of the 'moralist'. He writes: "If I were a moralist, who knows what I might call it…—But the philosopher has no love for moralists" (CW P, KSA 6:11).

what is characteristic of moral actions is selflessness, self-sacrifice, or sympathy and pity" (GS 345, KSA 3:578). According to Nietzsche, moral philosophers remain under the spell of the morality of their environment, merely offering a rational foundation for the current morality (BGE 186, KSA 5:105). In doing so, these rather pretentious moralists go so far as to attach the arrogant term 'science of morals' to their botched analysis. In this way, we can see how morality as a cultural phenomenon influences not only the attitudes and beliefs of the general public, but also the thinking of its philosophers. The only morality that they know is the current morality of selflessness. "Indeed, those who now preach the morality of pity even take the view that precisely this and only this is moral..." (GS 338, KSA 3:567).

It may be that there is more diversity in the views of moral philosophers than Nietzsche is prepared to admit, but he remains convinced that philosophers have never treated morality as a *problem.* In section 345 of *The Gay Science* entitled "*Morality as a problem*", Nietzsche offers an important summary of the problems in moral philosophy. He distinguishes three ways that morality can be studied. One can offer:

1. A *critique* of moral valuations.
2. A *history of the origins* of moral valuations.
3. A history of ethical systems. (GS 345, KSA 3:578)

For Nietzsche, only a *critique* of morality is the true task of the philosopher, and this requires that one approaches morality in a 'personal way', as a 'problem'. It is worth noting, however, that a *critique* of morality involves much more than a criticism of "the foolish opinions of a people about their morality...opinions about its origin, religious sanction, the superstition of free will, and things of that sort" (345). In other words, it is not enough to offer a criticism of the opinions of 'thou shalt' commands, but instead a critique of the *value* of a command 'thou shalt' is needed. Nietzsche writes, "just as surely as the value of a medication for a sick person is completely independent of whether he thinks about medicine scientifically or the way old women do" (345).

The second approach relates to the attempts at a history of the origins of moral valuations. As we have seen, Nietzsche is critical of all previous efforts, but he still endorses this approach provided that it is carried out with an 'actual' historical sense. However, he finds that this approach, in itself, would represent an incomplete study of moral matters since it "is something quite different from a critique" (345). His loftier ambition was to provide an historical approach to morality while also questioning the *value* of morality. This task is stated most clearly in the note appearing at the end of the First Essay of the *Genealogy* where

Nietzsche pleads for the promotion of *valuative* historical studies in morality. Of particular importance, here, is his claim that questions pertaining to the *value* of existing morality demand the services, not just of the genealogist, but also "physiologists and doctors" (GM I:17n, KSA 5:289). The point, however, is that the feeble attempts at exploring the origins of morality precluded a concern over its value, and consequently, morality has never been regarded as a problem. The same deficiency is apparent in the third and final approach which provides a history of ethical systems. This approach would involve an examination of various moral views or ethical systems expressed throughout the history of philosophy, and hence, it too would fail to address Nietzsche's evaluative concerns. Moral philosophy, then, appears to be nothing more than a repository of one great prejudice which it aims to promote: that morality is nothing other than acting for the sake of the other (i.e. selflessly) which it attempts to codify and systematize. Nietzsche's critique of moral philosophy is not reducible to the rather general pronouncements discussed above. Hence, it is necessary to consider his evaluations of specific moral philosophers if we are to attempt to situate his own ethics within the moral tradition.

Schopenhauer as *Moral* Educator?

The extent to which Schopenhauer's ethics influenced Nietzsche's views on morality can hardly be underestimated. As early as 1873, Nietzsche regarded Schopenhauer as "the only serious moralist of our century" (PTG, p.46, KSA 1:818), attributing his success as a moralist to the fact that he arrived at the most profound problems of ethics, raising the question of the *value* of existence (KSA 7:425). To many readers, such lavish praise simply serves as yet another example of the sycophantic ravings scattered throughout Nietzsche's early writings. As is well-known, Nietzsche would later renounce his discipleship and become Schopenhauer's 'antipode'. In a letter to Wagner dated December 19, 1876, just three years after praising Schopenhauer's exploits as a moralist, Nietzsche confessed that he now disagreed with Schopenhauer's teaching on virtually all general propositions. This confession was made public in *Human, All-Too-Human* (1878) and in his subsequent writings, as Nietzsche went on to repudiate key aspects of Schopenhauer's moral philosophy. A comparison of their respective views on morality certainly yields tremendous oppositions. Perhaps, the most glaring contrast lies in their treatment of pity (*Mitleid*) which is aggrandized by Schopenhauer as the sole source of moral worth, while vehemently denounced by Nietzsche.

Despite the significant differences in their moral philosophies, it would be rather shortsighted to view Nietzsche's relation to Schopenhauer's ethics as that of a mere 'antipode', or youthful devotee.[7] Consider, for instance, Nietzsche's Preface to *On the Genealogy of Morals* (1887) where he refers back to his writing of *Human, All-Too-Human*, claiming that during this period "what was at stake was the *value* of morality—and over this I had to come to terms with my great teacher Schopenhauer, to whom that book of mine...addressed itself as if to a contemporary" (GM P:5, KSA 5:251-52). With this remark, Nietzsche is acknowledging the role that Schopenhauer played in his development as a moral philosopher. Since, for Nietzsche, there is nothing more important than the problems of morality (GM P:7, KSA 5:254), by stating that he had to 'come to terms' with his former 'educator', the implication is that Nietzsche's views on morality were influenced greatly by Schopenhauer's morality of compassion. Schopenhauer issued a challenge important enough to demand Nietzsche's serious attention, suggesting that Nietzsche's affirmative reflections on morality will involve an overcoming of Schopenhauer's ethics. Still, Nietzsche is aware of a certain debt owed to his mentor although he remains openly hostile to Schopenhauer's philosophy. Specifically, the indelible lesson that Schopenhauer had imparted to Nietzsche was the problem of the 'value of existence'. It was this problem which would serve as the focal point of Nietzsche's moral philosophy. Of course, they offered very different solutions, but in the words of Zarathustra: "one repays a teacher badly if one always remains nothing but a pupil" (Z I:22, KSA 4:101). Before dismissing Nietzsche's early remarks on Schopenhauer as the views of an overzealous disciple, we need to question what Nietzsche had inherited from his former 'educator'—only then can we appreciate Nietzsche's relation to Schopenhauer's moral philosophy. I will begin then with an overview of Schopenhauer's ethics.

As he prepared to write his *magnum opus*, *Die Welt als Wille und Vorstellung* (*The World as Will and Representation*, 1818), Schopenhauer announced his philosophical ambition to unify ethics and metaphysics.[8] However, Schopenhauer's attempt to develop a metaphysical ethics is featured most prominently in his essays *Über die Freiheit des Willens* (*On the Freedom of the Will*, 1838) and *Über die Grundlage der Moral* (*On the Basis of Morality*, 1839) published together in 1841 under the title, *Die beiden Grundprobleme der Ethik* (*The Two Fundamental Problems in Ethics*). The latter provides the deepest insights into

---

7 In fact, in an early unpublished essay "On Schopenhauer" ('*Zu Schopenhauer*', 1868), Nietzsche was highly, yet respectfully, critical of Schopenhauer. This essay has been translated by Christopher Janaway in *Willing and Nothingness: Schopenhauer as Nietzsche's Educator*, Oxford: Oxford University Press, 1998, Appendix I, pp.258–65.

8 Arthur Schopenhauer, *Manuscript Remains: Early Manuscripts (1804–1818)*, trans. E.F.J. Payne, Oxford: Berg, 1988, §92, p.59.

Schopenhauer's moral philosophy, and is crucial for understanding Nietzsche's philosophical engagement with Schopenhauer's ethics of compassion.

On the Basis of Morality was Schopenhauer's submission to a prize essay contest offered in 1837 by the Royal Danish Society of Scientific Studies. The Society posed the following question: "Is the source and foundation of morality (*Moral*) to be looked for in an idea of morality (*Moralität*) which lies immediately in consciousness (or conscience), and in the analysis of the other principal notions of morality springing from this, or is it to be sought in another ground of knowledge?" Schopenhauer's essay focuses on 'morality in the narrower sense', which includes an explanation of moral psychology and a topology of character, leading to the claim that pity or compassion (*Mitleid*) is the sole motive for actions possessing moral worth. The remainder of the essay offers a metaphysical foundation for morality to justify Schopenhauer's fundamental principle of ethics which he writes in Latin: *Neminem laede, imo omnes, quantum potes, juva* (Injure no one; on the contrary, help everyone as much as you can, OBM 69). The 'basis' of morality will be established once the metaphysical grounding for this moral principle has been explained.

Before presenting his own theory of the 'basis of morality', Schopenhauer devotes considerable attention to a detailed critique of Kant's ethics, "the last important event to occur in ethics" (OBM 47). Indeed, Schopenhauer's book-length essay can be read as a response to Kant's moral philosophy. Although familiar with most of Kant's ethical writings, Schopenhauer focuses on Kant's *Grundlegung zur Metaphysik der Sitten* (*Groundwork of the Metaphysics of Morals*, 1785) whose content he thinks mirrors the question posed by the Royal Danish Society. Schopenhauer immediately takes issue with Kant's conception of ethics, his 'first false step'. "In a practical philosophy we are not concerned with stating reasons for what happens, but with giving laws as regards what *ought to happen, even though it may never happen.*"[9] Schopenhauer charges Kant with a *petitio principii* since Kant assumes from the outset what he has yet to prove, specifically, that there are moral laws which command obedience, despite the fact that these laws may dictate behaviour that may have never happened. For Schopenhauer, Kant's theoretical (i.e. non-empirical, *a priori*) conception of morality (*Moral*) is without "real substance" since it is far removed from morality (*Moralität*) as practice (what actually 'happens')—hence, the terminological distinction between '*Moral*' and '*Moralität*'. Schopenhauer ridicules this non-empirical, *a priori* element of Kant's ethics claiming that it is "entirely abstract, wholly insubstantial, and likewise floating about entirely in air" (OBM 62). It is not clear, however, that Kant's ethics is as 'abstract' and 'insubstantial' as Schopenhauer seems to think. For instance, Schopenhauer

9 OBM 52, quoting from Kant's *Grundlegung*, with Schopenhauer's emphasis.

ignores Kant's repeated claim that purely rational beings of a theoretical nature would be under no moral obligations. The Kantian moral subject (i.e. 'persons') must have other attributes[10] than theoretical reason before they are full-fledged members of the moral universe.

A second objection relates to Kant's application of such ethical concepts as 'law', 'command', 'duty' and 'obligation'. For Schopenhauer, any law-morality requires a law-giver, and since Kant denies that this law-giver is human, it must therefore be God. He argues that, "Separated from the theological hypotheses from which they came, these concepts [command and obedience, law and duty] really lose all meaning…" (OBM 54–5). However, in insisting that Kant's ethics is really a theological notion in disguise, Schopenhauer has misrepresented Kant's position. While it is certainly the case that Kant's Protestant Christian moral environment influenced his thinking, the arguments found in his *Groundwork* and the *Critique of Practical Reason* are *non-theological*. Schopenhauer errs, then, in claiming that Kant was perpetuating the following spurious philosophical trend: "In the centuries of Christianity, philosophical ethics has generally taken its form unconsciously from the theological" (OBM 54).

Since Schopenhauer argued that egoism is at the root of theological ethics, he concluded that Kant's ethics is egoistic. Although they both agree that acts motivated by egoism cannot possess moral value, Schopenhauer accuses Kant's ethics of being couched in egoism since the only real incentive for acting in accord with the categorical imperative[11] is its desired effect.[12] In other words, imperatives can only be of the *hypothetical* variety since egoism underlies Kant's moral principle. As support for this claim, Schopenhauer considers some examples from Kant's *Grundlegung* such as the man who is 'flourishing', but surrounded by others who are not well-off and could use his assistance. Kant denies that this man could consistently will indifference towards others as a universal law of nature. Schopenhauer cites Kant's argument: "A will that decided on this would contradict itself, since cases can occur in which a man needs the love and sympathy of others, and in which, through such a natural law that is evolved from his own will, he would deprive himself of all hope of

---

10 In Kant's *Tugendlehre* (*Doctrine of Virtue*), the four moral attributes to which he explicitly refers are: moral feeling, conscience, love of one's neighbour, and respect for oneself (self-esteem).

11 "Act only according to that maxim which you *can* at the same time *wish* will become a universal law for all rational beings."

12 In claiming that every action is motivated by egoism, malice, or compassion (or possibly asceticism), Schopenhauer had no place in his theory of motivation for 'noncompassionate disinterestedness'. Hence, what Kant calls 'respect for the moral law', including the familiar notions of 'impartiality' or 'fairness', are ruled out under the Schopenhauerian scheme of things.

the help he desires for himself' (quoted in OBM 90). If this man should choose to help others, then, according to Schopenhauer, it is only because he desires the help of others. In this case, the agent is not obeying a universal law of indifference, but is thinking of how he would stand to suffer living in an indifferent world, and so his actions are motivated by his own self-interest. For Schopenhauer, this is an example of a disguised hypothetical imperative. In order for the categorical imperative, 'You ought not to be indifferent to the fate of others' to exert any influence it must be expressed as 'If you want others to help you, you ought not be indifferent to the fate of others'. In this example, a desire to receive help is the selfish motive underlying the categorical imperative.

The final objection relevant to my present concern has to do with Schopenhauer's critique of Kant's emphasis on reason. *Pace* Kant, Schopenhauer maintains that reason plays an *instrumental* role in human affairs. In place of reason, the focal point of Schopenhauer's ethics is the 'will', "which alone is metaphysical and indestructible" (OBM 64), and is representative of one's moral personality. Reason, on the other hand, functions as the means for attaining one's desired ends. Schopenhauer challenges Kant's appeal to a rational foundation of morality on the grounds that an individual can be both "reasonable and vicious" and "unreasonable and noble-minded" (OBM 83). These shortcomings of Kant's moral philosophy inspired Schopenhauer to offer an alternative basis of morality.

In order to derive the true basis or foundation of morals, we must ascertain how human beings *really* act, rather than how they *ought* to act. In this way, Schopenhauer approaches the study of morality as an empirical inquiry. He explains:

> The purpose of ethics is to indicate, explain, and trace to its ultimate ground the extremely varied behavior of men from a moral point of view. Therefore there is no other way for discovering the foundation of ethics than the empirical, namely, to investigate whether there are generally any actions to which we must attribute *genuine moral worth*...Consequently, we have to indicate the peculiar motive that moves man to actions of this kind, a kind specifically different from any other. This motive together with the susceptibility to it will be the ultimate ground of morality, and a knowledge of it will be the foundation of morals. This is the humble path to which I direct ethics; it contains no construction a priori, no absolute legislation for all rational beings *in abstracto*. (OBM 130)

This 'humble path' takes the reader into a rich labyrinth of moral psychology, a topology of character, and concludes with a metaphysics of morals to justify the basic phenomena of his ethics. An implicit assumption of this methodology is that an empirical study would yield the same results regardless of the human beings under consideration, and hence, historical studies would be unnecessary.

Schopenhauer's analysis begins with a description of three classes of actions, those that are 'morally reprehensible' (*moralisch verwerflich*), of 'moral worth' (*moralischer Wert*), and, the largest class, considered 'morally indifferent' (*moralisch indifferente*). Schopenhauer claims that all human actions are intentional, motivated by 'weal (*Wohl*) and woe (*Wehe*) in general' which signifies 'in agreement with or contrary to a will' (OBM 141). Consequently, the end to which all actions aim will be the individual's well-being or misfortune. To each action, one finds these corresponding incentives: egoism (*Egoismus*), which desires the agent's own well-being,[13] is the motive behind 'morally indifferent' acts; malice (*Bosheit*), which desires another's misfortune is the incentive belonging to 'morally reprehensible' acts, while acts possessing 'moral value' spring from the motive of compassion (*Mitleid*). All three incentives are found in each individual in varying degrees, but one still retains his or her individuality, or uniqueness.

Schopenhauer outlines an axiology of character whereby the types of motives to which a person is swayed is a reflection of his will, or character (the two are identical). A person's character is unalterable and innate such that he will always retain the moral disposition with which he was born. Actions, then, are caused by a combination of one's unalterable character and a specific motive. As a result, all actions are determined and the belief in the freedom of the will is based on error, mere deception. In his *Preisschrift über die Freiheit des Willens* (*Prize Essay on the Freedom of the Will*, 1839), Schopenhauer writes on the error of free will:

> ...let us think of a man in the street who says to himself: 'It is six o'clock; the day's work is over. I can now go for a walk, or go to the club; I can also climb the tower to see the sun set; I can also go to the theater, I can also visit this or that friend...All that is entirely up to me; I have complete freedom; however, I do none of them, but just as voluntarily go home to my wife.' This is just as if water were to say: 'I can form high waves (as in a storm at sea); I can rush down a hill (as in the bed of a torrent); I can dash down foaming and splashing (as in the waterfall)...however, I do none of these things now, but voluntarily remain calm and clear in the mirroring pond.' Just as water can do all those things only when the determining causes enter for one or the other, so is the condition just the same for that man with respect to what he imagines he can do. (FW 37)

---

13 There is actually a fourth 'unnamed' incentive which is the desire for one's own misfortune, but this incentive is not discussed in *On the Basis of Morality* because it has ascetic (not moral) value, and Schopenhauer suggested that it would not be received well by the Royal Danish Society since it conflicted with the reigning moral sentiment in Protestant Europe.

The notion of *voluntas* is a deception since actions are decided according to their causal conditions. Our ineradicable character conjoined by a motive occurring in one's consciousness renders meaningless the concept of free will. As an expression of his determinism, Schopenhauer adopts the scholastic motto '*operari sequitur esse*' ('what we do follows from what we are'). For Schopenhauer, the will is that which is most valuable from an ethical standpoint since it is responsible for one's actions, and the moral quality of these actions. The will of a morally bad character will be affected by malice and extreme egoism, but the morally good character will feature a will expressing compassion.

Given Schopenhauer's claim that egoism is "the chief and fundamental incentive in man…the craving for existence and well-being" (OBM 131), his challenge will be to explain how acts of moral worth (compassionate acts) are possible. Egoism, he insists, completely lacks moral value, "by its nature, *egoism* is boundless…it towers above the world" (OBM 131-32). To serve as the criterion of an action of moral worth, my action must be completely devoid of egoism or malice. But, if moral acts are those which are done solely for the sake of another, how is it possible that the well-being and misfortune of another are capable of moving my will? How is it possible to meet the objection of the moral sceptic who argues that there is no natural morality apart from human convention, which is an artificial construct designed out of necessity to curb the selfish and wicked appetites (OBM 121)? Schopenhauer's response is that while civil law can successfully enforce justice, it cannot legislate philanthropy and beneficence, yet these we know to exist. Although acknowledging with such moralists as Holbach, Helvétius, d'Alembert, and others that morality is reducible to egoistic motives, Schopenhauer parts company by insisting that there are also cases of disinterested philanthropy and of voluntary justice. To buttress his argument, Schopenhauer appeals to several experiences, one of which is a case where there was no opportunity for punishment yet a poor man returned the property of a rich man. But, do these examples really strengthen his argument? How is it, we might ask, that empirical observation can provide a direct line to another's motivation? Perhaps, the poor man was motivated strictly by the anticipation of a reward for his good deed, or from the encomium which was sure to follow. Schopenhauer was cognizant of this difficulty, and concedes that "this question cannot be decided altogether empirically…hence there is always left the possibility that an egoistic motive had influenced the doer of a just or good action" (OBM 138). Still, Schopenhauer reiterates his faith in moral acts with the example of Arnold von Winkelried, the soldier who in the battle of Sempach (1386), served as a human pincushion, clasping in his arms as many hostile spears as he could grasp to sacrifice himself for his comrades in an act of pure, self-sacrifice (OBM 139).

Schopenhauer appeals to the metaphysical realm to ground the compassionate attitude. His task is to arrive at the metaphysical theory that is advanced by the compassionate character, and then refer back to that theory to explicate the compassionate act. Ultimately, *Mitleid* reflects a view of oneself and the nature of reality which is diametrically opposed to the one found in egoism. Schopenhauer's literal rendering of *Mitleid* as 'suffering-with' indicates that compassion is valuable in its tendency to decrease the amount of suffering in the world, in addition to offering a truer metaphysical viewpoint. Feeling compassion for another human being "presupposes that to a certain extent I have identified myself with the other man, and in consequence the barrier between the ego and non-ego is for the moment abolished" (OBM 166). There is no other way to explain this 'mysterious occurrence', but to admit that the other's suffering and well-being becomes my own concern.

For an accurate metaphysical picture, Schopenhauer appeals to Kant's *Transcendental Aesthetic* (the doctrine of the ideality of space and time) which had shown that the conditions for the possibility of plurality and diversity, space and time (what Schopenhauer calls the *principium individuationis*), belong merely to phenomenal appearances, not to things in themselves. Having established that plurality is only apparent, Schopenhauer asserts that however numerous, all individuals are *one* insofar as they possess the same essence. This point of view not only betrays Schopenhauer's Buddhistic influence (e.g. his reading of the Upanishads), but echoes a popular philosophical teaching found for instance in the Eleatics, Neoplatonists, and Scotus Erigena. The behaviour of the compassionate person exemplifies a belief in the unity of being, a knowledge of one's own self in the other person, whose formula expressed in Sanskrit reads: *tat tvam asi* (this art thou). Conversely, the bad character adopts a false metaphysical view where the other is treated as a distinct individual ('non-ego'), rather than as an 'I once more' (OBM 211).

Unfortunately for Schopenhauer, despite being the lone entry, the Royal Danish Society did not award him the prize, judging unsatisfactory his metaphysical foundation of morality. Their decision confirmed the author's own motto stated at the beginning of his essay: "*Moral predigen ist leicht, Moral begründen ist schwer*" (Moral preaching is easy, to found it difficult, OBM, title page). If moral philosophers were evaluated strictly by their success at providing a metaphysical ground for morality, then they would all receive a failing grade. We can discuss Schopenhauer's contribution to moral philosophy independently of its commitment to *archē*. For instance, David Cartwright claims that *On the Basis of Morality* "presents a descriptive virtue ethics, concentrating on moral character and moral psychology."[14] On account of Schopenhauer's theories of determinism and the unalterable character, his moral philosophy rules out any prescriptive ethics. The idea that 'you *ought* to do this, or refrain from doing that' is nonsensical for Schopenhauer, since moral rules cannot influence one's character. It is pointless, then, to preach morals in an effort to make a bad human being into a good or virtuous person. As Charles Andler writes:

> *L'intention de Schopenhauer n'a jamais été de formuler une morale: elle était de donner une interprétation philosophique des faits…Il est vain de nous proposer des impératifs qu'il ne nous est pas loisible de suivre, s'ils ne coïncident pas avec l'élan naturel de notre tempérament et il est vain de nous demander un repentir au sujet d'actes que nous n'étions pas libres de ne pas accomplir.*[15]

The proper task of moral philosophy cannot be 'moral improvement' (WW I, 301,368; WW II, 223,597) since *velle non disitur* (willing cannot be taught). For Schopenhauer, the subject matter for ethics is not how human beings *ought* to act, but how they actually do act. In adopting an empirical standpoint, Schopenhauer's emphasis shifts to the individual's character ('will'), which explains his association with virtue ethics.[16] Although morality is a major concern throughout Schopenhauer's philosophy, he does not think that the *morally* good character is the pinnacle of human achievement.

In highlighting the ideal of a good character, *On the Basis of Morality* seems to be suggesting that the greatest human accomplishment would be to possess a compassionate character. However, elsewhere, Schopenhauer is adamant that moral goodness cannot compensate for the suffering inherent in life. The individual does not merely identify with the suffering of another person, but "regards the endless sufferings of all that lives as his own, and thus take upon himself the pain of the whole world" (WW I, 379). The ubiquitous nature of suffering makes it impossible for a human being to affirm this life, especially its "constant recurrence" (WW I, 284). The will now turns away from life as "man attains to the state of voluntary renunciation, resignation, true composure and complete will-lessness" (379). The individual now develops an aversion to the

---

14 David E. Cartwright, "Schopenhauer's Narrower Sense of Morality" in C. Janaway (ed.), *The Cambridge Companion to Schopenhauer*, Cambridge: Cambridge University Press, 1999, p.253.

15 Charles Andler, *Nietzsche, Sa vie et sa pensée* (I), Paris: Éditions Gallimard, 1999, p.98.

16 Richard Taylor, a proponent of a return to virtue ethics, has acknowledged the significant influence of Schopenhauer on his own moral thinking. This influence can be detected in such works as *Good and Evil*, New York: Macmillan, 1970 and *Reason Faith and Ethics*, Englewood Cliffs, N.J.: Prentice Hall, 1985; reprinted as *Virtue Ethics: An Introduction*, Interlaken, N.Y.: Linden Books, 1991.

will-to-live, and renounces his inner nature. This event marks the transition from virtue to *asceticism.*

In the foregoing account of Schopenhauer's ethics, I have presented an overview of its essential features as a preparatory task leading to a discussion of Nietzsche's relation to Schopenhauer's moral philosophy. While their approach to morality is motivated by a shared concern over practical morality in place of the abstract, theoretical moralizing of philosophers (e.g. Kant), Schopenhauer opts for a 'science of morals', a descriptive, empirical methodology penetrating into the recesses of human nature, and supported by a metaphysics of the will. Nietzsche, on the other hand, thought that the best way to understand the morality that people actually lived by, was to question under what conditions human beings devised their value judgments, and for this he utilized a genealogical and physiological methodology. Nietzsche rejected Schopenhauer's non-historical approach to morality, while noting a certain epistemological shortcoming associated with his moral psychology. In particular, Nietzsche would deny Schopenhauer's insistence on the accessibility of moral motives since all actions, moral or otherwise, "are essentially unknown" (D 116, KSA 3:109). As a result, Schopenhauer's attempt to describe the motives belonging to a specific class of action indicates, for Nietzsche, that he suffered from the primeval delusion of thinking that one knows in precisely all cases how human action is brought about (116). Rather than profess ignorance as to the inner workings of the 'subject', philosophers have presupposed that there exists knowledge as to the essential nature of an action. In this way, they have gone on not just to indicate the motives belonging to acts, but to preach which motives we 'should' be acting from. In Nietzsche's later writings, he will emphasize that philosophical explanations cannot enlighten us on any 'truths' since every philosophy is merely "the personal confession of its author and a kind of involuntary and unconscious memoir" (BGE 6, KSA 5:19).

Despite his objections to Schopenhauer's approach to morality, Nietzsche shares Schopenhauer's contempt for moral philosophy, and agrees with him that Kant's ethics is rooted in theology. However, Nietzsche turns this criticism against Schopenhauer, accusing him of being under the dominion of Christian values despite his rejection of Christian dogma. While Nietzsche admired Schopenhauer's "honest atheism" (GS 357, KSA 3:600), he regarded him as "the heir of the Christian interpretation" (TI 9:21, KSA 6:125) in his perpetuation of its 'cult of philanthropy'. Of course, Schopenhauer would deny that compassionate acts belong exclusively to Christian morality, but he acknowledges that *On the Basis of Morality* was written in the spirit of the ethics prevailing in Protestant Europe (WW II, 607). In addition, Schopenhauer argued that the fundamental proposition of morality: *Neminem laede, imo omnes, quantum potes, juva* (Injure no one; on the contrary, help everyone as much as you can, OBM 69) "is really the proposition whose establishment is the constant endeavor of all teachers of morals; this is the common result of all their deductions" (69). This admission may have fueled Nietzsche's objection that the 'basis' of Schopenhauer's ethics was attributable to his faith in the prevailing morality. In claiming that "each one of us is truly a competent and perfectly moral judge, with an exact knowledge of good and evil,"[17] Schopenhauer attempted to present his *Mitleids-Moral* as 'scientific'. For Nietzsche, this effort to reduce the history of all moral phenomena to *Mitleid* shows a complete absence of an historical sense. And, only philosophers denuded of all historical instinct, he claims, would arrive at such an absurd conclusion. In contrast to a 'science of morals', Nietzsche recommends a 'typology of morals', that is, an historical approach aimed at exploring the differences in moral values throughout past ages. In other words, a typology or genealogy of morals would show that moral values are in flux, and are therefore, *un*scientific. Neither Nietzsche's moral genealogy nor his anti-pity arguments need to be rehashed here.[18] However, it is worth pointing out that Nietzsche's critique of Schopenhauer's ethics of compassion was more than a mere disagreement of opinion between two thinkers on the question of the fundamental principle of morality. Nietzsche praises Schopenhauer for taking seriously the problem of the value of existence (D 52, KSA 3:56), and for identifying the true task of the philosopher—the determination of value (WP 422, KSA 11:531). However, he rejects the specific moral value (i.e. *Mitleid*) that Schopenhauer had advanced. Thus, Nietzsche had to 'come to terms' with his 'great teacher' over the question of the *value* of morality.

In regard to their views on traditional moral philosophy, both Nietzsche and Schopenhauer were convinced that moral prescriptions are useless for making individuals conform to a preconceived notion of the 'good', and so they were united in their rejection of imperativistic ethics.[19] For this reason, Schopenhauer denied that moral rules could 'improve' humankind.[20] And,

---

17 D 116, KSA 3:109 quoting from Schopenhauer's *Nachlaß*.

18 These arguments are discussed in Chapter Two in the section "The 'Unegoistic Drives'—Pity, Altruism, Selflessness."

19 In fact, even the early Nietzsche (1874) was critical of the "ethical aristocracy" who "reproach Schopenh<auerian> ethics (*Ethik*) for not having an imperativistic form, indeed, for openly rejecting such a form" (KSA 7:809). And, in Nietzsche's early essay *Philosophy in the Tragic Age of the Greeks* (1873), he insists that "man is necessity" against critics who attack Heraclitus for offering no imperativistic ethics. "Who could possibly demand from such an ethic (*Ethik*) with its necessary imperatives 'thou shalt,' or worse yet, accuse Heraclitus of lacking such" (PTG, p.62–3, KSA 1:831)!

20 See WW I, 301, 368; WW II, 223, 597.

heeding the wisdom of his great teacher, Nietzsche explains, "The last thing I should promise would be to 'improve' mankind" (EH P:2, KSA 6:258). Nietzsche was quite fond of this term and borrowed it on many occasions to describe the untenable goal of moral philosophy. For example, in the chapter entitled "The 'Improvers' of Mankind" from *Twilight of the Idols*, Nietzsche claims that the effort to 'improve' human beings has been a perennial task, whether improvement meant to 'tame' (e.g. Christian morality) or to 'breed' (e.g. the Law of Manu, Plato) human beings. Since both thinkers agree that expressions such as 'man *ought* to be such and such' and 'Change yourself!' are nonsensical, it is necessary to consider their reasoning behind such claims. Nietzsche's answer is that "the single individual is a piece of *fatum* from the front and from the rear, one law more, one necessity more for all that is yet to come and to be" (TI 5:6, KSA 6:87). Schopenhauer's response to the moral philosopher's attempt to 'improve' human beings has been to reassert the inalterability of character. Quite simply, this entails the view that our character is innate and fixed, and so immune from moral persuasion.

While both deny the freedom of the will, Nietzsche's position on the inalterability of character is somewhat ambiguous. For instance, in the section entitled "The unalterable character" from *Human, All-Too-Human*, a work steeped in Schopenhauerian allusions, Nietzsche writes:

> That the character is unalterable is not in the strict sense true; this favourite proposition means rather no more than that, during the brief lifetime of a man, the effective motives are unable to scratch deeply enough to erase the imprinted script of millennia. If one imagines a man of eighty-thousand years, however, one would have in him a character totally alterable...The brevity of human life misleads us to many erroneous assertions regarding the qualities of man. (HH 41, KSA 2:65)

It is not clear from this passage that Nietzsche is deviating from Schopenhauer's position even though he denies that it is true 'in the strict sense'. Given the short duration of a human life, Nietzsche would accept, or so it seems, the inalterability of character. In fact, even when he describes Schopenhauer's doctrine of the inalterability of character as an 'error', Nietzsche is careful to add "in the sense in which *he* [Schopenhauer] understands it" (AOM 5, KSA 2:382). At times, however, Nietzsche will refer to character as 'alterable', yet 'necessary' (HH 274, KSA 2:226).

The extent to which Nietzsche's preferred '*necessary* character' differs from Schopenhauer's '*unalterable* character' becomes less significant when we consider their mutual acceptance of 'determinism'. Perhaps both expressions converge on this very point, that a necessary *or* unalterable character implies the impossibility that 'I could have done otherwise'. Not only do both philosophers agree on this point, but Nietzsche appeals to the same analogy, taking a page out of Schopenhauer's essay *On the Freedom of the Will*,[21] to make his case. Following Schopenhauer, Nietzsche uses the example of a 'waterfall' with its various movements (curvings, twistings, breakings of the waves) to claim that these movements are as necessary as human actions (HH 106, KSA 2:103). While both concur that the necessity of human actions renders absurd their praise or censure, Schopenhauer insists, in Humean fashion, that we are responsible for our *character* (will). For Schopenhauer, our causal necessity is part of our empirical reality, but there is also a metaphysical component to our being, our intelligible character, for which we are responsible. All our actions proceed from this intelligible character. Still, it is not clear how this transposition of character into the metaphysical realm offers a convincing account of responsibility given Schopenhauer's view that one's character is innate and fixed.

Nietzsche referred to Schopenhauer's view of the strict necessity of human actions as his "mighty insight", but reeled when Schopenhauer claimed that the inner nature of the whole of things must necessarily coincide with the ethical significance of human behaviour (AOM 33, KSA 2:395). As Nietzsche maintained, the doctrine of necessity strips the world of any ethical significance.[22] Underlying such a critique is Nietzsche's disdain for Schopenhauer's metaphysics as a whole, a metaphysics which purports to offer a description of the world capable of accommodating an ethics. For instance, in the Second Book of *The World as Will and Representation*, Schopenhauer proclaims that the essence of the world is 'will' where 'will' is understood as a general principle of (blind) striving belonging to everything in the world including humans, stones, plants, and animals. Our desires, the gravitational force, the vegetative processes in plants, and the appetites of animals are all manifestations of the same will. Schopenhauer's conception of the will as "the innermost essence, the kernel, of everything particular thing and also of the world" (WW I, 110) is often directed specifically at the human manifestation of this will which we discover as "the kernel of our true being" (WW II, 293). The 'real self' is the 'will to life' (*Wille zum Leben*) since it pertains to the bodily individual's blind striving for existence and reproduction (WW II, 606).

---

21 Arthur Schopenhauer, *Essay on the Freedom of the Will* (FW), trans. Konstantin Kolenda, New York: Bobbs-Merrill, 1960, p.43.

22 Interestingly, in the chapter "On Ethics" from *Parerga and Paralipomena*, Schopenhauer used the term 'antichrist' to describe those individuals who deny that the world has a moral significance. Nietzsche, of course, would later go on to write a book with the same title, and on various occasions would even refer to himself as the 'antichrist'.

Schopenhauer's metaphysics of the will takes on a decisively moralistic tone since he claims that we should not rejoice over the existence of the world, but rather prefer its non-existence. The realization of our blind striving produces suffering, and suffering is viewed as evil, and by extension, so too, is life. Salvation depends on our capacity to deny the will, resign from life, and oppose nature. Schopenhauer's philosophy promotes the elimination of suffering, and treats its augmentation as evil. For Nietzsche, it was not so much Schopenhauer's description of the will[23] which he found problematic as it was his pessimistic evaluation of it. Rather than negating life, Nietzsche *affirms* it in light of the suffering that is essential to life. Although Nietzsche's concept of the will to power was intended as a correction of Schopenhauer's will to life,[24] their differences are primarily attitudinal and evaluative. Nietzsche's foremost concern is expressed in the last section of the *Genealogy*, "Man, the bravest of animals and the one most accustomed to suffering, does *not* repudiate suffering as such; he *desires* it, he even seeks it out, provided he is shown a *meaning* for it, a *purpose* of suffering" (GM III:28, KSA 5:411). Humanity's problem did not lie in suffering, but in its perception of suffering as 'meaningless', and in particular its proposed solution to this problem—*the ascetic ideal.* According to Nietzsche, the ascetic ideal offered the only meaning so far of suffering, and although its solution to the problem of man's suffering was additional suffering, humankind now had an answer as to the meaning of their existence. While Nietzsche admired Schopenhauer for taking seriously the sufferings of humankind, he vehemently rejected Schopenhauer's *ascetic* antidote. Insofar as the ascetic ideal aims to do away with all appearance, change, becoming, death, and wishing, it proceeds from a 'will to nothingness', an aversion to life, but in the end, "it is and remains a will" (GM III:28, KSA 5:412). On Nietzsche's reading, Schopenhauer's ascetic ideal is ultimately self-refuting since the purported task of willing nothingness does not result in the cessation of willing, but rather requires the very act of willing.

Schopenhauer briefly considered the possibility of a life-affirming ideal, but only to reject its plausibility. For example, he denies that one could will "that the course of his life as he had hitherto experienced it should be of endless duration or of *constant recurrence*" (WW I, 283–84, my emphasis) provided that

---

23 Nietzsche would accept Schopenhauer's claim that the force operating in nature is identical with the will in ourselves, but for Nietzsche, this force is not 'will to life', but 'will to power'. In regard to the human manifestation of the will, Nietzsche claims that Schopenhauer failed to comprehend that the will is something complicated, and as a result, he simply accepted the popular prejudice of the 'will', and exaggerated it (BGE 19).

24 See *Zarathustra*, II, 'On Self-Overcoming'. "Only where there is life is there also will: not will to life but—thus I teach you—will to power."

one realized that suffering is essential to life. Nietzsche's doctrine of the eternal return appears to have been motivated by Schopenhauer's position in regard to one's capacity to will eternal return in light of the prevalence of suffering in life.[25] In section 56 of *Beyond Good and Evil*, Nietzsche attempts to liberate pessimism "from the half-Christian, half-German narrowness and simplicity in which it has finally presented itself to our century, namely, in the form of Schopenhauer's philosophy" (BGE 56, KSA 5:74). In response to Schopenhauer who suffered under the delusion of morality, Nietzsche proposes an opposite ideal: "the ideal of the most high-spirited, alive, and world-affirming human being who has not only come to terms and learned to get along with whatever was and is, but who wants to have *what was and is* repeated in all eternity" (56). That Nietzsche's affirmative ideal was intended as a solution to Schopenhauer's pessimism can be gleaned from a further example found in Book V of *The Gay Science* where Nietzsche presents his '*Dionysian* pessimism' as a direct response to Schopenhauer's '*romantic pessimism*' (GS 370, KSA 3:622). The Dionysian, as presented in the later writings, entails "Saying Yes to life even in its strangest and hardest problems; the will to life (*Wille zum Leben*) rejoicing over its own inexhaustibility even in the sacrifice of its highest types" (EH IV:3, KSA 6:312). The formula 'Dionysian' represented Nietzsche's move away from Schopenhauer toward a "justification of life" (WP 1005, KSA 12:354). In articulating this life-affirming ideal, Nietzsche offers an alternative to the problem of suffering by showing that suffering does not necessarily lead to Schopenhauer's pessimistic conclusions. In fact, Nietzsche uses Schopenhauer's expression (*Wille zum Leben*) to assert his affirmative ideal (saying-yes to life amidst suffering). Through a confrontation with Schopenhauer's pessimism, Nietzsche claimed that he not only "deepened" pessimism, but ultimately "devised its antithesis" (WP 463, KSA 11:532).

In his overcoming of Schopenhauerian pessimism, Nietzsche was not replacing a false ethics with his own 'true' account. Since Nietzsche denied, in his later writings, that there are moral facts, he could not evaluate morality according to its truth claims. The difficulty with Schopenhauer's metaphysical ethics is that it offered a 'science of morals', an *external* standpoint from which to assess the value of life. But, such a perspective would require a position *outside* of life, a position to which we have no access. For this reason, Nietzsche emphasizes that the positing of values is part of life, that life values through us

25 Nietzsche explicitly credits the Stoics and Heraclitus as having already articulated this doctrine of the eternal return. However, he was certainly aware of Schopenhauer's comments from *WW* and his application of the doctrine was intended as a direct response to Schopenhauer's pessimism (see BGE 56). In Chapter Five, I criticize Nietzsche's notions of '*amor fati*' and 'eternal return' as formulas of life-affirmation.

when we posit values (TI 5:5, KSA 6:86). By turning to 'symptomatology' where he treats morality as a sign-language of the affects, Nietzsche was able to avoid the metaphysical baggage of an external standpoint while preserving an evaluative dimension. In asserting that moral values are either symptomatic of ascending or declining life, Nietzsche was prepared to pass judgement on Schopenhauer's ethics. In what appear to be *ad hominem* attacks, Nietzsche lists various formulations put forth by Schopenhauer such as 'life is not worth anything', and his understanding of morality as the 'denial of the will to life', and asserts that these pronouncements represent an instinct of decadence (TI 5:5, KSA 6:86; 9:35, KSA 6:134). In adding that "Schopenhauer was hostile to life; therefore pity (*Mitleid*) became a virtue for him" (A 7, KSA 6:174), and that Schopenhauer's morality of pity proved to be "the real movement of decadence in morality...profoundly related to Christian morality" (TI 9:37, KSA 6:138), Nietzsche offered an even more damning evaluation than that of the Royal Danish Society. In undermining Schopenhauer's morality of pity and offering an affirmative ideal, Nietzsche had now reversed their roles, as it was he who was 'educating' Schopenhauer, giving his 'great teacher' a lesson on the *value* of morality.

Nietzsche and 'Higher Réealism': The Influence of Paul Rée

In 1873, Nietzsche had met the moralist Paul Rée in Basel, through a mutual friend, Heinrich Romundt, but it was not until 1875 after having read Rée's *Psychologische Beobachtungen*, (*Psychological Observations*, 1875) that he developed an enthusiasm for Rée's reflections on morality. In fact, just two years after claiming that Schopenhauer was the *only* serious moralist of the century, Nietzsche would praise Rée as "an astute moralist."[26] Nietzsche formed a friendship with Rée in 1876, at approximately the same time that he broke ties with Wagner, and his instincts had turned away from Schopenhauer. In reflecting back on this period of his life, Nietzsche writes: "Only with my instinctive cunning, I avoided the little word 'I' once again and bathed in world-historical glory—not Schopenhauer or Wagner this time but one of my friends, the excellent Dr. Paul Rée" (EH VI:6, KSA 6:327–28). In October 1876, Nietzsche and Rée were re-united as they (along with Albert Brenner) accepted the invitation of their friend Malwida von Meysenbug to form a study group at her villa in Sorrento. The nine months spent in Sorrento were devoted to reading and discussing philosophical texts, in particular, the French moralists and ancient Greek writings. Both Rée and Nietzsche used this time to develop their ideas for their forthcoming works which were later published respectively

---

26 Letter to Rohde, 8 December 1875 in C. Middleton (ed./trans.), *Selected Letters of Friedrich Nietzsche*, 1969, p.138.

as *Origin of the Moral Sentiments* (*Der Ursprung der moralischen Empfindungen*, 1877) and *Human, All-Too-Human* (*Menschliches, Allzumenschliches*, 1878), and each writer acknowledged his indebtedness to the other. Rée's book contained the following hand-written dedication: "To the father of this work, with the deepest thanks, from its mother" while Nietzsche returns the compliment with the expression: "*Vive le Réealisme*!" Nietzsche pays homage to Rée in the text itself, regarding him as a modern-day LaRochefoucauld on account of his sceptical moral observations which make him a master of soul-examination in the tradition of the French moralists (HH 36, KSA 2:59). In the next section of *Human, All-Too-Human*, Nietzsche quotes one of Rée's chief psychological insights from *On the Origin of the Moral Sentiments*: "Moral man stands no closer to the intelligible (metaphysical) world than does physical man". It was Rée, then, who supplied Nietzsche the axe to attack the roots of the 'metaphysical need' of human beings. The two thinkers were united in their commitment to psychological observation (or as Nietzsche would say, 'reflection on the human, all-too-human') as a means of undermining the deceptiveness of idealistic metaphysics.

Apart from Rée and Jacob Burckhardt, the appearance of *Human, All-Too-Human* was not received favourably by Nietzsche's friends, many of whom feared that Nietzsche had 'become' Rée. To quell such fears, Nietzsche offered the following assurance:

> Incidentally: only look for *me* in my book and not for our friend Rée. I am proud to have discovered his splendid aims and qualities, but he *did not have the slightest* influence on the conception of my "Philosophia in nuce": this was *complete* and a good part already put down in writing when I got to know him better in the Fall of 1876. We found each other at the same stage of development.[27]

Despite declaring his independence from Rée, there is no question that Rée exerted an influence on Nietzsche.[28] For instance, prior to his association with Rée, a serious interest in ethics could hardly be discerned from Nietzsche's

---

27 Nietzsche to Rohde, June 1878, *Gesammelte Briefe* (vol. II), Leipzig: Alfred Kröner, 1907, in 5 volumes, p.549.

28 This view contradicts the assertion of Karl Jaspers who, taking too seriously Nietzsche's claim to independence, wrote: "To be sure, Nietzsche scarcely learned anything from Rée (since prior to their acquaintance his own positions were already decisive)…" (Jaspers, *Nietzsche*, p.71). On the other hand, Lou Salomé emphasizes their philosophical similarities: "…*Nietzsche et Rée exprimaient exactement les mêmes idées, car depuis longtemps, en tout cas depuis que Nietzsche avait rompu avec Wagner, ils avaient la même ligne de pensée.*" (Lou Andreas-Salomé, *Ma vie*, trad. Dominique Miermont et Brigitte Vergne, Paris: Presses Universitaires de France, 1977, p.84) It seems that both views are far too extreme.

writings apart from his burgeoning critique of Schopenhauer's *Mitleids-Moral.* He was familiar with the French moralists, yet LaRochefoucauld's name does not appear in print until *Human, All-Too-Human* (his 'Rée-days'), and there is no evidence of any prior commitment to psychological dissection.

In addition to these similarities, there were also significant differences in their views which Nietzsche was only too happy to announce. Rée reappears in Nietzsche's writings nearly a decade after the complimentary remarks from *Human, All-Too-Human*, yet this time the comments on Rée are not nearly as cordial.[29] After crediting Rée's *On the Origin of the Moral Sentiments* as his inspiration to publish his hypotheses concerning the origin of morality, Nietzsche describes Rée's *Büchlein* as:

> an upside-down and perverse species of genealogical hypothesis, the genuinely *English* type, that attracted me—with that power of attraction which everything contrary, everything antipodal possesses. The title of this little book was *The Origin of the Moral Sentiments*; its author Dr. Paul Rée...Perhaps I have never read anything to which I would have said to myself No, proposition by proposition, conclusion by conclusion, to the extent that I did to this book... (GM P:4, KSA 5:250)

Here, Nietzsche speaks of his relation to Rée as if it was ancient history, a period or stage in his development which he acknowledges only to highlight the differences. Rée's book provided Nietzsche with the impetus to publish his views on the origin of morality, but their genealogical results differed markedly. In fact, in the remainder of the passage quoted above, Nietzsche lists the views they disagreed on from their days in Sorrento, specifically citing, among others, their differences in moral genealogy, as Nietzsche contrasted his view of the "morality of mores" with Rée's "altruistic mode of evaluation" (GM P:4, KSA 5:251).

A brief survey of some of the ideas from Rée's *On the Origin of the Moral Sentiments* will serve to accentuate their differences, while minimizing their similarities. In the Preface, Rée explains his approach as a scientific theory which assigns an origin to the observed empirical phenomena. It is the task of moral philosophy, he claims, to examine those human actions felt to be good and bad. In particular an explanation is needed to account for the fact that bad actions produce guilt, and feelings of justice call for punishment. In place of Kant and Schopenhauer who traced the moral conscience to a transcendent source, Rée appeals to the insights of Darwin and Lamarck who have shown

---

29 One could certainly speculate, and perhaps with some truth, that Nietzsche's later criticisms of Rée had been partially motivated by personal events relating to his friendship with Rée and Lou Salomé which ended on poor terms. However, the biographical details of their friendship is not my present concern.

that moral phenomena, like the physical, can be traced to their natural causes. This prompts the claim previously quoted that: "The moral man stands no closer to the intelligible world than the physical man."[30] Although this citation was quoted favourably by Nietzsche, he criticizes his readers for thinking that they understood the whole book [*Human, All-Too-Human*] as "higher Réealism" on the basis of this passage (EH VI:6, KSA 6:328).

The first chapter of Rée's book entitled "The Origins of the Concepts 'Good' and 'Bad'" opens with the claim that in each person, there are two instincts: the egoistic and unegoistic drives. The egoistic instinct means that each individual sees to his own welfare, in particular, to self-preservation, the satisfaction of the sexual instincts, and the satisfaction of his vanity. On the other hand, the unegoistic instinct indicates that the individual considers the welfare of others as the ultimate end of his actions. In general, this unegoistic person displays compassion, fellow-feelings, and neighbour-love. Following Schopenhauer, Rée claims that the unegoistic instinct is generally the weaker of the two, and not as prevalent as the egoistic instinct. By accepting disinterested compassion, Rée denies the view held by Helvétius and others that unegoism is merely a disguised form of the egoistic instinct. From there, he takes up the same question that preoccupied Schopenhauer in *On the Basis of Morality*: How are unegoistic actions possible? Rée is not satisfied with Hutcheson's and Hume's contention that unegoistic actions originate from an innate sentiment, since this response does not explain the origin of this innate sentiment itself. Schopenhauer, on the other hand, recognized correctly the question but Rée rejected the metaphysical explanation that he offers to show that unegoistic actions are possible. For Rée, the correct account of the origin of unegoistic actions is expressed by Darwin who had proven that many species of animals (e.g. bees, ants, and monkeys) possess a social instinct. This social instinct is an extension of the maternal and paternal instinct which has then been maintained and reinforced by natural selection.[31] Thus, human beings inherited this social instinct from their animal ancestors. Through his Darwinian influence, Rée has *naturalized* Schopenhauer.

The two categories of actions are described as follows: egoistic actions are those in which the individual acts for his own good at the expense of other human beings. Unegoistic actions are those in which one acts with the intent to help others, sometimes at the expense of his own detriment. The first class of actions are considered by each one of us as morally bad and blameworthy, the second by contrast, are deemed morally good and praiseworthy, and so the

---

30 From Rée's Preface to *On the Origin of the Moral Sentiments.*

31 The idea here is that those species of animals which are the most tightly bound by the social instincts will supplant the other species.

distinction between 'good' and 'bad' resides exclusively in these oppositions: only the egoistic actions are called 'bad', only the unegoistic actions are called 'good'. Egoism is labeled 'bad' on account of its being harmful to or compromising the well-being of one or several members of the community, while unegoistic behaviour is useful. However, Rée recognizes that it is not only unegoistic behaviour that is useful to others, but also, as is quite often the case, interested behaviour. He asks us to consider the example of a doctor who in treating patients for money, is as useful to them as is the unegoistic individual. In order to determine why unegoistic actions belong exclusively to the moral domain, Rée claims that we must examine how these actions function in a social setting. Since egoistic instincts are understood as harmful, human society has always recognized the need to repress them. On account of their profligacy, the egoistic motives are countered by the systematic inclusion of habits which promote unegoistic behaviour. Following Lamarck and Darwin, Rée believes that these acquired habits can be transferred to successive generations as innate traits. According to Rée, our moral sentiments have evolved over time from a concern over the consequences of our actions to a preoccupation with their motives. The degree of unegoism in feelings and behaviour thus becomes the criterion of moral value. With this account of altruistic behaviour, Rée has accomplished what none of his predecessors could, by explaining that good actions are made possible by the fact that we have inherited from our animal ancestors this instinct which pushes us to attend to the well-being of others.

As we have seen, Nietzsche tells quite a different story of the origin of morality, and so the extent to which his moral philosophy relates to Rée's contribution to the subject requires discussion. In *Human, All-Too-Human*, Nietzsche was influenced by Rée's psychological approach especially its anti-metaphysical standpoint. Interestingly, however, in the same passage that Nietzsche praises Rée's 'penetrating analyses of human action' from the *Origin of the Moral Sentiments*, Nietzsche lists, as one of the merits of psychological observation, its effectiveness at revealing the erroneousness of the so-called unegoistic actions (HH 37, KSA 2:60). So, although Nietzsche was swayed by Rée's psychological approach, he never accepted the results of this approach, namely that there are two instincts, the egoistic and unegoistic. Just as Schopenhauer defended the existence of unegoistic actions, so too did Rée, but from a biological standpoint. There is good reason then to accept Nietzsche's admonishment to his readers that one ought not confuse his 'higher Réealism' with a complete endorsement of Rée's views on morality. In fact, when asked by Siegfried Lipiner if he and Nietzsche shared the same views, Rée was careful to point out that in addition to their widespread agreement, there were also many views which belonged exclusively to Nietzsche.[32]

Given Nietzsche's remarks from the Preface to the *Genealogy*, it would appear that there was less agreement between himself and Rée than the latter was prepared to admit. For instance, in calling attention to his reflections on the twofold prehistory of good and evil in the sphere of the noble and in the slaves (HH 45, KSA 2:67), Nietzsche traces the terms 'good' and 'evil' to the power of the ruling group, anticipating his later genealogy.[33] More importantly, however, these concepts include an evaluative component that is entirely at odds with Rée's dry, disinterested, scientific explanation of moral phenomena. Even as early as 1876, Nietzsche's 'psychological observation' extended beyond its descriptive scope to include a sense for evaluative differences between these original moral concepts of 'good' and 'evil'.

On Rée's account, the origin of morality can be traced to utility where a good action is synonymous with one that is useful while the bad action is harmful. Eventually, he claims, human beings *forgot* that 'good' originally meant 'useful', and unegoistic actions (since they were generally regarded as useful) became accepted as good in themselves, independent of their consequences. The original moral categories ('useful' versus 'harmful') have given way to the more recent 'unegoistic' versus 'egoistic' dichotomy. By contrast, Nietzsche maintains that there is a much older species of morality than the altruistic mode of evaluation put forth by Rée, and is recognized as such in *Human, All-Too-Human*. For instance, in section 96 of that work, Nietzsche writes:

> To be moral, to act in accordance with custom, to be ethical means to practise obedience towards a law or tradition established from of old...'Egoistic' and 'unegoistic' is not the fundamental antithesis which has led men to make a distinction between 'in accordance with custom' and 'in defiance of custom', between good and evil, but adherence to a tradition, a law, and severance from it...(HH 96, KSA 2:92–3)

Again, this is one of the three passages relating to the origin of morality that Nietzsche refers to in the Preface to the *Genealogy* to accentuate his differences with Rée. The emphasis on custom as the original morality is dealt with more extensively in *Daybreak*. For Nietzsche, Rée's views on the origin of morality were not only historically false, but his acceptance of disinterested compassion was rejected as a piece of mythology. Nietzsche does not, however, as we might expect him to, present his own views as a corrective, but rather states that he had no interest in refutation (GM P:4, KSA 5:250–51).

---

32 Rée to Nietzsche, beginning of June 1877. (Lipiner, an Austrian, was an admirer of Nietzsche and Wagner).

33 Cf. *Beyond Good and Evil*, 260 and especially the First Essay of *On the Genealogy of Morals*.

In addition to critiquing Rée's 'upside-down and perverse' genealogy of the concepts 'good' and 'bad', Nietzsche alluded to other philosophical differences. For instance, their views on justice and punishment conflicted as Nietzsche, following Thucydides, claimed that "justice (*Gerechtigkeit*) originates between parties of approximately *equal power*" (HH 92, KSA 2:89). The fundamental component of this conception of justice is '*exchange*' (or requital) in the sense that each party gives to the other what it wants to have, and in return receives from the other what it desires, and as a result, mutual injury is circumvented. Over time, human beings *forgot* the original purpose of just actions, and through habituation children had learned to respect and imitate such actions until finally, just and fair actions were equated with unegoistic ones. In adding that the 'high value' accorded to a just or unegoistic act is now glorified as something to strive for without realizing that the reverence for these moral acts rests, oddly enough, on our *forgetfulness*—"How little moral would the world appear without forgetfulness!", it is worth repeating that Nietzsche's observations on the origin and development of justice are not restricted to a disinterested analysis (92).

In his discussion of the history of punishment from the Second Essay of the *Genealogy*, Nietzsche notes that punishment has served various ends, and consequently cannot be reduced to a single meaning. Eugen Dühring is wrong, then, to single out *ressentiment* as the original motive underlying punishment. Nietzsche cites numerous examples of the various meanings of punishment such as "punishment as a means of rendering harmless, of preventing further harm…as recompense to the injured party for the harm done…as the isolation of a disturbance of equilibrium, so as to guard against any further spread of the disturbance…as a means of inspiring fear of those who determine and execute the punishment…as a kind of repayment for the advantages the criminal has enjoyed hitherto," and the list continues with Nietzsche acknowledging its incompleteness. However, he specifically rejects the notion that punishment awakens a feeling of guilt in the offender, claiming instead that it is likely to make him cold and hard (GM II:14, KSA 5:319).

According to Rée, determinism does not serve to undermine the justification for punishment because on his view the essence of punishment does not lie in accountability, but in deterrence. In other words, we can acknowledge that human behaviour is determined, and hence deny moral responsibility without producing the undesirable consequence of unbridled egoism. For example, the issue of how society is going to legislate or influence behaviour is still an issue independent of the notion of responsibility. As a means of curbing the stronger egoistic drives, Rée argues that the original lawmakers, concerned solely with deterrence, introduced the motive of 'fear of punishment' to ensure the protection of society. Nietzsche, however, explicitly denies that intimidation or fear accounts for the essence or source of punishment (GM P:4, KSA 5:251). Rée goes on to show that this original goal of punishment was eventually forgotten, and replaced with the view that punishment was intended as retribution for past misbehaviour. But, he describes the sense of justice as the product of two *false* assumptions: 1. the routine character of punishment understood as retribution for past misbehaviour, and 2. the belief in free will. Rée's position is that the sense of justice does *not* provide a justification for punishment (as is often maintained) since it only comes *after* punishment as a recent development, a 'parvenu'. Consequently, this account of the sense of justice reveals that punishment cannot be based on retribution, but rather to deter potentially harmful incidents. In effect, then, Rée has separated the institution of punishment from the sense of justice. It was only after the publication of the *Origin of the Moral Sentiments* that Rée expressed his regret for refusing to take Nietzsche's advice that these phenomena should *not* be separated, but rather explained together. In a letter to Nietzsche dated October 10, 1877, Rée writes:

> The wrongest thing about my latest work (*as you said already, but I did not want to admit*—probably because in that case I would have had to revise a lot) is the historical development of punishment (although I still hold that the philosophical view of punishment as merely a means to an end is correct)...[34]

Aside from their correspondence, Nietzsche's differing view on punishment is expressed in section 33 of *The Wanderer and His Shadow* (*Der Wanderer und sein Schatten,* 1880), to which he refers the reader (GM P:4, KSA 5:251). Just as there was no way to reduce punishment to a single meaning, there is also no specific definition of 'revenge' capable of identifying its underlying motives. Yet, Nietzsche regards punishment as a social institution, and he thinks that there is an overlap between punishment and revenge, as opposed to Rée's view that they are distinct.

So far I have explained differences in their respective views on morality in order to account for Nietzsche's later attempts to deny Rée's influence. Even if it can be shown that Nietzsche appropriated certain aspects of Rée's thought within *Human, All-Too-Human*, their moral agendas lie worlds apart. Of significant importance is Nietzsche's task which is not confined to 'hypothesis mongering' on the origin of morality, but rather to questioning the *value* of morality. It is this problem, I believe, that comprises their fundamental difference as moral philosophers. Unlike the cold, disinterested, scientific methodology of Rée, Nietzsche could never resist the opportunity to point out

---

34 Nietzsche, *Kritische Gesamtausgabe: Briefwechsel* [hereafter KGB], ed. G. Colli and M. Montinari, Berlin, 1975–, Band 6/2, pp.718–19, my emphasis.

qualitative differences in moral evaluation. There is no better passage to illustrate this dimension of his thought than section 345 of *The Gay Science* (which makes an implicit reference to Rée). In describing the efforts of moral philosophers to date, Nietzsche is referring to Rée (among others) when he writes: "I have scarcely detected a few meager preliminary efforts to explore the *history of the origins* (*Entstehungsgeschichte*) of these [moral] feelings and valuations (which is something quite different from a critique…)," but when he adds "In one particular case I have done everything to encourage a sympathy and talent for this kind of history—in vain it seems to me today" (GS 345, KSA 3:578), this remark is directed towards Rée as is evidenced by the comments from the Preface of the *Genealogy*. While it is true that Nietzsche claims that these historians of morality are "mostly Englishmen", this does not exclude Rée (a German-Jew) since *The Origin of the Moral Sentiments* is described as offering a moral genealogy of "the genuinely *English* type" (GM P:4, KSA 5:250). The crucial limitation of Rée's approach to morality as psychological observation is that in revealing that morality has grown out of an error, it does not address the problem of its *value*. Moreover, Nietzsche mocked Rée's Darwinian influence on his genealogical hypothesis:

> *This* [an actual history of morality] was unknown to Dr. Rée; but he had read Darwin—so that in his hypotheses, and after a fashion that is at least entertaining, the Darwinian beast and the ultramodern unassuming moral milksop who 'no longer bites' politely link hands, the latter wearing an expression of a certain good-natured and refined indolence… (GM P:7, KSA 5:254)

In this passage, Nietzsche is simply claiming that Darwin's theories contributed to Rée's perverse moral genealogy, 'perverse' because, in addition to being false, Nietzsche denies that the contemporary, altruistic man represents an evolutionary advancement.[35] Rée was not silent on Nietzsche's later evaluative remarks on morality, as he "dismissed Nietzsche's transvaluation of values as a 'mixture of insanity and nonsense'."[36]

Nietzsche's criticism of the social-Darwinian hypothesis that contemporary man, as a selfless, other-regarding type, is the epitome of perfection owing to its victory in the 'struggle for life' is certainly not directed exclusively at Rée. In maligning Rée for too closely resembling the English psychologists, Nietzsche certainly has in mind such British philosophers as Herbert Spencer, and the Utilitarians (e.g. John Stuart Mill). The English Utilitarians, in particular, were the subject of Nietzsche's animosity.

---

35 Nietzsche's critique of Darwin is expressed nicely in TI 9:14, KSA 6:120f.

36 Ted Honderich (ed.), *The Oxford Companion to Philosophy*, 'Paul Rée (1849–1903)', Oxford:Oxford University Press, 1995, p.752.

Nietzsche and the English Utilitarians

Despite their importance for developing Nietzsche's views on morality, neither Schopenhauer nor Rée are representative figures within a major ethical tradition.[37] In the remainder of this chapter, I will examine Nietzsche's relation to the seminal figures within the three main traditions in moral philosophy: utilitarianism (Bentham and Mill), deontology (Kant), and virtue ethics (Aristotle). Beginning with English utilitarianism, I will outline its basic ideas and principles, examine Nietzsche's critical remarks including those directed against its leading proponents, and note certain similarities.

Utilitarianism judges an action to be right if it is useful for promoting happiness, where happiness is understood as the sum of pleasures. In this way, the value of an action is determined exclusively by its consequences. According to this view, pleasure is good and pain (displeasure) is bad. To claim that we ought to do an action means that if we do not do it, we shall suffer. A desire to obtain happiness and to avoid pain is the only possible motive to action. The reason why we should seek the good of others, is that on the whole such a course will result in the greatest amount of happiness. This doctrine, translated into practical terms, means that in deciding what to do we ought to perform those actions that will likely result in the greatest possible happiness where each person's happiness is to count equally. There are various versions of Utilitarianism, but its 'classical' formulations are found in the writings of Jeremy Bentham (1748–1832) and John Stuart Mill (1806–1873).

In Bentham's *An Introduction to the Principles of Morals and Legislation* (1789), the 'principle of utility' is based on the view that "Nature has placed mankind under the governance of two sovereign masters, *pain* and *pleasure*."[38] Quite simply, 'the principle of utility' is an ethical principle which tells us to approve or disapprove of actions according to a pleasure-pain balance of actions. 'Utility' refers to those properties of an object which result in benefit, advantage, pleasure, good or happiness, or prevent certain harms such as mischief, pain, evil, or unhappiness to the interested party. The principle of utility may apply to the happiness of the individual or to the happiness of the community depending on whose interest is under consideration. Since Bentham regards the community as a 'fictitious body' (i.e. its existence is owed to its members, individual persons), the interests of the community mean nothing else than the

---

37 Schopenhauer, however, has proven influential to contemporary philosophers such as Richard Taylor and David Cartwright, both of whom recognize his contributions to virtue ethics. Yet, rarely is Schopenhauer treated as a major moral philosopher.

38 Jeremy Bentham. *An Introduction to the Principles of Morals and Legislation*, Wilfrid Harrison (ed.), Oxford: Basil Blackwell, 1960, p.125.

sum of the interest of its members. Bentham's famous formula for the measure of right and wrong is "the greatest happiness for the greatest number."[39]

Because there are different pleasures, Bentham goes on to discuss how we are to measure their value. He notes that the degree of pleasure and pain will vary according to certain factors such as its *intensity*, *duration*, *certainty* or *uncertainty*, *propinquity* or *remoteness*. These considerations are important when estimating the value of a pleasure or pain with reference to the individual person, and by itself. Note, that these four factors are properties of the pleasure or pain itself. However, there are two other factors to take into account when it comes to evaluating the tendency of an *act* to produce pleasure or pain: its *fecundity* (i.e. the likelihood that the act will produce more pleasure or pain) and its *purity* (i.e. the likelihood of the act not being followed by sensations of the opposite kind). These last two examples are properties of the act itself, not properties of the pleasure or pain. The final factor comes into play when there are numerous persons involved such that the pleasure and pain of each is under consideration. In this case, Bentham refers to the *extent* (i.e. the number of persons who are affected) of the pleasure or pain.

To offer a parallel to Bentham's ideas about measuring pleasure, we can think of the idea of temperature. Imagine going about with a thermometer under your tongue all the time, measuring your temperature. Sometimes you would have a fever with a temperature above normal, sometimes it would fall below. The degrees above or below normal would parallel the *intensity* of pleasure/pain that Bentham discusses, and how long the fever lasts would be the *duration*. Now, let's imagine drawing a temperature graph over a period of time; one could integrate over that, taking into account both intensity and duration, and this would give the temperature balance over that period. If, for some reason, we thought that hot was good, this would give us a way of

---

39 Although Bentham is often credited as being the originator of this expression, he was not. The *idea* itself comes from Joseph Priestley's *An Essay on the First Principles of Government* (1768), "It must necessarily be understood, therefore, whether it be expressed or not, that all people live in society for their mutual advantage; *so that the good and the happiness of the members, that is, the majority of the members of any state, is the standard by which everything relating to that state must finally be determined*." More than likely, Bentham got the *formula* from Cesare Beccaria's *An Essay on Crime and Punishment* (1764) which first appeared in English translation in 1767. "If we look into history we shall find that laws which are, or ought to be, conventions between men in a state of freedom, have been, for the most part, the work of the passions of a few, or the consequences of a fortuitous or temporary necessity; not dictated by a cool examiner of human nature, who knew how to collect in one point the action of a multitude, and had this only end in view, *the greatest happiness for the greatest number* ('*la massima felicità divisa nel maggior numero*')." It was Beccaria, then, not Bentham, who was the first to use the expression '*the greatest happiness for the greatest number*'.

measuring the value of the consequences of an action. Bentham's view is parallel to this, but of course, what counts is pleasure, not heat.

Regarding Bentham's addition of two further considerations, there is the *certainty* factor, which is simply the probability of actually getting that balance; in much the same way that modern decision theory brings in the idea of 'expected utility'. Bentham also mentions *propinquity*, or nearness in time, which considers *when* the pleasure or pain takes place. Then, Bentham adds *fecundity* which has us look at still later times, and *purity* which is the mix of pleasure and pain. All of these, taken together and balanced out determine the value for an individual. Lastly, we have to consider the *extent*, by calculating similar values for all the individuals involved, and then adding them all up to get the total. This total is what the principle of utility tells us to look at when assessing actions.

In order to distinguish himself from the crass hedonism to which Benthamism may seem liable, John Stuart Mill introduced the notion of qualitative differences among pleasures. Whereas Bentham would claim that "*Prejudice apart, the game of push-pin*[40] *is of equal value with the arts and sciences of music and poetry*",[41] Mill would respond "It is better to be a human being dissatisfied than a pig satisfied; better to be Socrates dissatisfied than a fool satisfied."[42] Despite certain interpretive differences, some of which even led to his 'mental crisis' at the age of twenty, Mill's *Utilitarianism* (1861) was written to defend a Benthamite understanding of happiness amidst mounting criticisms. The goal of the work was to offer a philosophical defense of the utilitarian standard of morals. In the second chapter of *Utilitarianism*, Mill explains that the 'greatest happiness principle', as the foundation of morals, is grounded on a 'theory of life':

> Namely, that pleasure and freedom from pain are the only things desirable as ends; and that all desirable things (which are as numerous in the utilitarian as in any other scheme) are desirable either for pleasure inherent in themselves or as means to the promotion of pleasure and the prevention of pain. (pp.10–11)

Mill's well-known proof of the principle of utility is the subject of the fourth chapter of his essay where he argues that the sole evidence needed to show that anything is desirable, is that 'people do actually desire it' (44). This 'proof' has been criticized by many since Mill's argument shows that happiness is desirable in the sense of *capable* of being desired; the conclusion he wants is that it is

40 According to the *Oxford English Dictionary*, push-pin is "A child's game in which each player pushes or fillips his pin with the object of crossing that of another player."

41 Jeremy Bentham, *The Rationale of Reward*, in *Works*, ed. John Bowring (1838–43), Vol.2, p.253.

42 J.S. Mill, *Utilitarianism*, Oskar Piest (ed.), NewYork: Liberal Arts Press, 1957, p.14.

desirable in the sense of *worthy* of being desired. So, switching between these senses involves an equivocation. This is a maneuver that can be carried out in English, where the 'able' ending can cover both 'capable of' and 'worthy of', but not in German where you have the distinct endings '*bar*' for the one and '*wert*' for the other, a point noticed by Theodor Gomperz, the German translator of Mill.[43]

In an effort to reconcile asceticism or the sacrifice of one's own good with the utilitarian morality, Mill claims that the doctrine can accommodate self-sacrifice insofar as it contributes to the happiness of others. Utilitarianism merely denies that self-sacrifice is itself a good (22). He then goes on to reassert that the happiness which informs this utilitarian standard is not the agent's own happiness but that of all concerned. In doing so, Mill notes a certain affinity between utilitarian and Christian morality:

> As between his own happiness and that of others, utilitarianism requires him to be as strictly impartial as a disinterested and benevolent spectator. *In the golden rule of Jesus of Nazareth, we read the complete spirit of the ethics of utility.* 'To do as you would be done by,' and 'to love your neighbor as yourself,' constitute the ideal perfection of utilitarian morality.[44]

Here, Mill presents utilitarianism as consistent with Christian morality's altruistic teaching, the idea of sacrificing oneself for others for the sake of the general welfare, or happiness. Mill claims that "the unselfish part of our nature" is responsible for our moral feelings, in particular, the natural pleasure we receive from the idea of the pleasure of another, and our being naturally pained by the idea of the pain of another.[45] A similar idea had been expressed by Bentham who argued that human beings possess a "sympathetic sensibility" which meant "the propensity that a man has to derive pleasure from the happiness, and pain from the unhappiness, of other sensitive beings."[46]

There is another account of the connection between the sympathetic emotions and utilitarian morals based on the doctrine of association[47] as propounded by John Locke, David Hartley, and John Stuart Mill's father, James

---

43 See *Collected Works of John Stuart Mill*, Vol. 10, Toronto: University of Toronto Press, 1969, 'Textual Introduction' by J.M. Robson, p. cxxvi.

44 Mill, *Utilitarianism*, p.22 (my emphasis).

45 Mill's *Dissertations*, vol. I, quoted in W.E.H. Lecky's *History of European Morals*, p.21.

46 Bentham. *Principles of Morals and Legislation*, ch. vi, p.171.

47 See *Sidgwicks Discourse* (1835), p.62 of vol. X of the *Collected Works of John Stuart Mill.* Associationism refers to the manner in which our ideas are connected (e.g. similarity or resemblance, contrast, contiguity in space and time, causality, etc.). In this way, psychology (as the basis of moral science) employs methods of observation and experimentation to determine the laws of the mind.

Mill. This doctrine was appropriated by John Stuart Mill who went on to outline the three laws of association. The first law, he states, is "that similar ideas tend to excite one another," the second is "that when two impressions have been frequently experienced (or even thought of)...then whenever one of these impressions or the idea of it, recurs, it tends to excite the idea of the other", and the third law is "that greater intensity in either or both of its impressions is equivalent, in rendering them excitable by one another, to a greater frequency of conjunction."[48] For instance, from birth we tend to be governed solely by self-interest, but the infant learns to associate its pleasures with the idea of its mother, the child with the idea of his family, the adult with his or her class, his or her nation, and finally of all humankind, and in each case a distinct affection is formed.[49] In this way, Mill is able to account for the pain one feels at the sight of suffering in others. If it makes sense then to speak of Mill's view of the *origin* of morality, it will consist of his psychological account of our moral judgements and sentiments, and his claim that human beings are naturally governed by pleasure and pain. It seems to make little difference whether utilitarianism attributes the sympathetic affections to an association of ideas or to the natural constitution of our nature since in both cases their existence is admitted, and their cultivation is an important ingredient of utilitarian morality.

To what extent was Nietzsche familiar with the writings of Bentham and Mill? Nietzsche's library contained a copy of Mill's collected works in German translation with markings throughout, but there is no evidence to suggest that he read Bentham first-hand.[50] It is reasonable to suggest that Nietzsche's understanding of Bentham can be attributed to numerous secondary literature (e.g. Friedrich Lange, Hippolyte Taine, W.E.H. Lecky, Friedrich Ueberweg, etc.), while his knowledge of Mill was based on both primary and secondary sources. There are twenty-one references to Mill, four in the published writings and seventeen in the notebooks (over one third of which are from 1880). Yet, there are only seven references to Bentham, one in the published writings and six in the notebooks. In addition, there are references to utilitarian morals without specifying its proponents. Collectively, there is sufficient material to establish Nietzsche's *evaluation* of utilitarian morality (including his views on Mill and Bentham) even though there is little analysis of their ideas.

---

48 John Stuart Mill, *On the Logic of the Moral Sciences*, Henry M. Magid (ed.), New York: Liberal Arts Press, 1965, p.28.

49 Mill's *Analysis of the Human Mind* quoted in Lecky, p.26. The idea of human beings possessing an innate emotion is expressed elsewhere in Mill's writings. See Friedrich Ueberweg's *History of Philosophy*, Vol. II, trans. Geo. S. Morris, New York: Charles Scribner's Sons, 1873, p.429–30.

50 Thomas Brobjer, *Nietzsche's Ethics of Character*, 1995, pp.135–37.

Nietzsche would have been aware of the distinction between Bentham and Mill's quantitative versus qualitative measure of pleasure through his close reading of W.E.H. Lecky's *History of European Morals* (1869) which alludes to this variation.[51] However, since Nietzsche dismissed pleasure and pain as a standard of moral evaluation, he saw no reason to mark this distinction. In fact, he would likely group together Bentham, Mill, and Spencer[52] as committed to essentially the same view. In terms of Nietzsche's identification or discussion of utilitarianism, he tends to highlight its basic features, that it is a doctrine which judges the value of an action according to its consequences for everyone (KSA 13:372), whether it is useful for promoting happiness where happiness is understood as pleasure and the absence of pain (BGE 225, KSA 5:160). On many occasions, Nietzsche will refer to utilitarianism according to its expressed goal contained in the popular formula: 'the greatest happiness for the greatest number' (SE 6, KSA 1:384).

While Nietzsche grants to utilitarianism its widespread appeal and dominance (BGE 228, KSA 5:164), he rejects the notion that the fundamental goal of humankind is happiness defined as pleasure and the exemption from pain. "Man does *not* strive for pleasure, only the Englishman does" (TI, 1:12, KSA 6:61). This often quoted remark refers, of course, to utilitarianism, that "erroneous moral doctrine that is celebrated especially in England." (GS 4, KSA 3:376). And, in *Beyond Good and Evil*, he notes that "All these ways of thinking that measure the value of things in accordance with *pleasure* and *pain*...are ways of thinking that stay in the foreground and naivetes on which everyone conscious of *creative* powers and an artistic conscience will look down not without derision" (BGE 225, KSA 5:160). The error lies in utilitarianism's falsification of *psychologica* insofar as it treats pleasure and pain as opposites in value (EH III:5, KSA 6:305). For Nietzsche, pain and suffering are responsible for all enhancements of human beings to date, and are often entwined so that whoever desired a high degree of pleasure must be prepared to accept the same amount of pain (GS 12, KSA 3:383).[53]

In terms of their utility, the 'evil instincts', Nietzsche claims, are just as expedient and species-preserving as the benevolent feelings (GS 4, KSA 3:376). Consider for instance, his counterargument to Mill's defense of the Golden Rule. In a section entitled "Marginal note on a *niaserie anglaise*", Nietzsche writes:

---

51 See the long note from pp.89–90 of Lecky's *History of European Morals*.

52 Regrettably, I have abandoned my original plan to include Herbert Spencer in this section due simply to excessive volume.

53 I discuss the value that Nietzsche attributes to suffering in Chapter Two in the section entitled: "The 'Unegoistic Drives'—Pity, Altruism, and Selflessness".

'Do not unto others what you would not have them do unto you.' That counts as wisdom; that counts as prudence; that counts as the basis of morality—as the 'golden rule'. John Stuart Mill believes in it (and what Englishman does not?) But this rule does not brook the slightest attack. The calculation, 'do nothing that ought not be done to you,' prohibits actions on account of their harmful consequences: the concealed premise is that an action will always be requited. But what if someone holding the *Principe* [by Machiavelli] in his hand were to say: 'It is precisely such actions that one must perform to prevent others from performing them first—to deprive others of the chance to perform them on *us*'? On the other hand: let us consider a Corsican whose honor demands a vendetta. He does not want a bullet in his body either; but this prospect, the probability of getting shot, does not deter him from vindicating his honor—And in all decent actions, are we not deliberately indifferent to the prospect of what may happen to us? (WP 925, KSA 13:583)

In presupposing that actions are requited, Mill's utilitarianism may prove to be a dangerous doctrine depending on one's social circumstances, or at least one that is not well-suited to the conditions of life belonging to Machiavelli's era. The 'evil instincts' unleashed from Machiavelli's 'utilitarianism' may prove more effective for self-preservation. In Lecky's critique of utilitarianism, one finds a similar objection. "Gratitude has no doubt done much to soften and sweeten the intercourse of life, but the corresponding feeling of revenge was for centuries the one bulwark against social anarchy" and history has established, as in the case of Rome, "that a career of consistent rapacity, ambition, selfishness, and fraud may be eminently conducive to national prosperity."[54] Although Nietzsche was an admirer of Machiavelli, I do not think that we need to read too much into this passage. It seems that Nietzsche's intent was to use Machiavelli as an example to undermine utilitarianism's pretentious and ahistorical claim to know the interests and goals of everyone. In regarding itself as unconditional (i.e. addressing itself to everyone), utilitarianism displays a lack of historical acumen, and would do well to consider the words of Zarathustra: "A tablet of the good hangs over every people...A thousand goals have there been so far, for there have been a thousand peoples" (Z I:15, KSA 4:74,76).

Utilitarianism, for Nietzsche, is harmful in yet another way. Insofar as its principle of 'the general utility' or 'happiness of the greatest number' addresses itself to 'all', it reduces the individual to a function of the whole. Recall, for instance, Mill's attempt to reconcile the Golden Rule ('To do as you would be done by') with utilitarian morality insofar as utility would enjoin:

that laws and social arrangements should place the happiness or interest of every individual as nearly as possible in harmony with the interest of the whole...and, secondly, that education and opinion, which have so vast a power over human

54 Lecky, *History of European Morals*, p.40 and p.58.

> character, should so use that power as to establish in the mind of every individual an indissoluble association between his own happiness and the good of the whole...[55]

For Nietzsche, the above passage illustrates utilitarianism's view that the well-being of the individual is defined in terms of the collective interests of humankind. In other words, Nietzsche is critical of the idea that the value of a person is measured by her self-sacrifice in the service of society, and that this idea is reinforced through education. It is for this reason, he writes: "The 'love of mankind' with the help of a rational education—Stuart Mill, one laughs to death" (KSA 9:392). Rather than assessing an individual according to her *instrumental* value, Nietzsche claims that attention to one's development and preservation demands the foremost consideration. Otherwise, "When each man finds his own goal in someone else, then *nobody has any purpose of his own in existing.* And this '*existing for others*' is the most comical of comedies" (KSA 8:32–3). Although Mill recognizes and preaches the importance of developing one's individuality (in the private sphere), this is not an essential component of his morality of utility which instead promotes the cultivation of 'fellow-feelings' and even regards self-sacrifice for others as the 'highest virtue'.[56]

Nietzsche's point is that the virtues preached today (e.g. selflessness, self-sacrifice, obedience, chastity, etc.) reinforce the individual's role as a 'public utility', but prove to be a 'private disadvantage' especially for those who "apply their whole strength and reason to their own preservation, development, elevation, promotion, and the expansion of power" (GS 21, KSA 3:393). In order to counter the deprivation of our noblest instincts, Nietzsche proposes the following:

> mankind ought to seek out and create the favorable conditions under which those great redemptive men can come into existence. But everything resists this conclusion: here the ultimate goal is seen to lie in the happiness of all or the greatest number, there in the development of great communities...It seems to be an absurd demand that one man should exist for the sake of another man; 'for the sake of all others, rather, or at least as many as possible!' O worthy man! As though it were less absurd to let number decide when value and significance is at issue" (SE 6, KSA 1:384)!

In this passage, Nietzsche rejects the notion that 'numbers' should determine *value*—a point which becomes evident, he thinks, once we distinguish between the 'man of utility' and what humankind can aspire to: the 'great redemptive men'. It is always a question then of 'useful *for what*', and this will vary depending on the interests of a people or community. According to

---

55 Mill, *Utilitarianism*, p.22.

56 Ibid, p.18, 21.

utilitarianism, 'utility' refers specifically to the 'utility of the herd' by which is meant the 'preservation of the community' or what 'preserves the species'. However, since 'utility' depends on the *intention*, the wherefore (WP 724, KSA 12:372), it makes a difference if it is a morality intended to 'preserve the greatest number' or a morality whose goal is to 'produce a stronger type' (GM I:17n, KSA 5:289). For Mill, Nietzsche's talk of various human 'types' based on physiological differences would be a 'whimsical supposition' since it conflicts with the theory of life underlying the principle of utility which holds that all human beings are governed by pleasure and pain. Hence, Mill's response to Nietzsche would be '*all* men strive for pleasure and the avoidance of pain, *not* simply the Englishman'.[57]

When utilitarianism's presuppositions (e.g. equality of consideration, what is fair for one is also fair for the other), including its endorsement of the Golden Rule, form the core belief system of a society, its judgements of expediency will relate to the preservation of the species, and so the virtues which receive moral honours are such things as "pity, the complaisant and obliging hand, the warm heart, patience, industry, humility, and friendliness are honored—for here these are the most useful qualities and almost the only means for enduring the pressure of existence" and "Slave morality is essentially a morality of utility" (BGE 260, KSA 5:211). Nietzsche asserts that these virtues may contribute well to "*English* happiness", that is, to "comfort and fashion" (BGE, 228, KSA 5:164), but "utilitarians have not considered the conditions under which the perfect man will be the majority" (WP 339, KSA 5:88). This emphasis on the 'perfect man' or higher type is, I believe, the central motivation underlying his critique of utilitarianism,[58] as I had argued was the case for his general critique of morality. Nietzsche often contrasts the 'man of utility' with the 'exemplary

57 Interestingly, Mill was aware of the criticism that his views were distinctively 'English' brought against him by his one-time associate, Hippolyte Taine (See Taine's *History of English Literature*). Nietzsche and Taine corresponded frequently in the late 1880's and were familiar with each other's work. It is also interesting to compare Nietzsche's remark about the Englishman striving for 'pleasure and comfort' with Taine's comment: "Such is our Englishman, with his laws and his administration. Now that he has private comfort and public security, what will he do…?" (*History of English Literature*, New York: Colonial Press, 1900, p.175, vol. 3)

58 Elsewhere Nietzsche objects to the coherence of the utilitarian ideal. He writes: "The value of an action must be judged according to its consequences—say the Utilitarians…But does one know its consequences? For five steps ahead, perhaps. Who can say what an action will stimulate, excite, provoke? As a stimulus?…The Utilitarians are naïve—And in any case we must first *know what* is useful: here too they look only five steps ahead" (WP 291, KSA 13:372). Interestingly, however, the remainder of the section goes on to refer value to physiology as opposed to the consequences of an action.

individual', which, as we have seen, is a familiar move owing to his doctrine of an order of rank among human beings.

The utilitarians are described as 'mediocre types' who, in defending the Golden Rule (i.e. 'Do as you would be done by'), are simply offering a secularized version of Christian morality (D 132, KSA 3:123).[59] In doing so, they fall prey to the same sort of *ad hominem* attacks that Nietzsche levied against their Christian 'cousins', and other philosophical co-conspirators (e.g. Schopenhauer).[60] Such personal attacks, however, even if supported by his appeals to physiology (i.e. that there are different 'types' of individuals), become redundant and in any case, are no worthy substitute for an analysis of the *ideas* of utilitarianism. Had Nietzsche paid more attention to Mill's *views*, he might have realized certain parallels in their thinking. For instance, just as Nietzsche spoke of an order of rank or hierarchy of human beings, so too did Mill. In *Utilitarianism*, Mill's higher type was described as a 'being of higher faculties', 'superior being', and 'highly endowed being' in contrast to the 'inferior', the 'lower grade of existence'.[61] A distinguishing feature of this 'superior being' is his capacity for more suffering, and being more prone to it[62]—a view that Nietzsche espoused on numerous occasions.

There are, of course, important and obvious differences in their conception of human greatness. Although Mill discusses the favourable qualities of a person, he insists that "certainly no known ethical standard decides an action to be good or bad because it is done by a good or bad man…"[63] For Nietzsche, this remark shows a lack of an historical sense on Mill's part as is evidenced by Nietzsche's genealogy of morals which traces the concepts of 'good' and 'evil', not to actions, but to *individuals*. Moreover, Nietzsche claims that "an action in itself is perfectly devoid of value: it all depends on *who* performs it" (WP 292, KSA 12:477). Mill may not have anticipated Nietzsche's genealogical insights, but he did concede value to certain non-virtuous possessions and qualities of a

---

59 Mill would likely agree with Nietzsche's assessment of his ethics as intimately related to Christian ethics. See for instance, *On Liberty*, ch. ii, p.114: "I believe that other ethics than any which can be evolved from exclusively Christian sources must exist side by side with Christian ethics to produce the moral regeneration of mankind."

60 An exception can be found in the *Nachlaß*, where Bentham is praised as a "law-giver" over Rée who is "ruled over" (KSA 10:289). Although Nietzsche would certainly reject the content of Bentham's legislations, he admires his task as a 'philosophical-legislator' (i.e. a commander of values).

61 Mill, *Utilitarianism*, p.13.

62 Ibid, p.13. "A being of higher faculties requires more to make him happy, is capable probably of more acute suffering, and certainly accessible to it at more points, than one of an inferior type."

63 Ibid, p.26.

person such as 'beauties of character'. Yet, for Mill, it would appear that these qualities fall outside the scope of morality since an admirable character is not necessarily a public utility.[64] Whereas Mill makes room for such additional (non-moral) qualities through his 'private/public' distinction, Nietzsche expands the moral realm to include various 'beauties of character'. But, even with this expansion, both thinkers would disagree on what character traits are admirable. For example, Nietzsche would not accept Mill's claim that education should see to it that "the feeling of unity with our fellow creatures shall be…rooted in our character."[65] To claim that human excellence, moral or otherwise, includes feelings of comradery with our fellow men, or that the good of others becomes to the individual "a thing naturally and necessarily to be attended to, like any of the physical conditions of our existence,"[66] is opposed to Nietzsche's conception of well-being which is 'self'-regarding (i.e. relating to his view of higher types), rather than 'other-regarding'.

Thus far, it would appear that Nietzsche's understanding of Mill as a moral philosopher was based on the views and concerns expressed in *Utilitarianism* where Nietzsche challenges the fundamental tenets of utilitarian morality, that 'utility' is the foundation of morals, its 'greatest happiness principle' including the role of pleasure and pain, its praise of the social feelings, and its claim to be a 'science of morals'. But, what about the Mill of *On Liberty* (1859)? Was Nietzsche unaware of the striking similarities between his views and those expressed by Mill? While it is true that Mill reiterates, in *On Liberty*, that he views utility "as the ultimate appeal on all ethical questions", he is careful to add that "it must be utility in the largest sense, grounded on the permanent interests of man as a progressive being."[67] For Mill, the emphasis here is on the claims or interests of each individual.

As Mill goes on to promote individuality and the value of 'different experiments of living', he also warns against certain threats to this individuality. One such threat is the 'tyranny of custom', where the dominance of traditions and customs become impediments to self-assertion, and individual spontaneity. This critique of custom and conventionality parallels Nietzsche's remark in *Daybreak* that "Under the dominion of the morality of custom, originality of every kind has acquired a bad conscience" (D 9, KSA 3:24). And, even earlier Nietzsche had warned against the 'chains of convention' and the 'domination of

---

64 Hilliard Aronovitch has pointed out to me that Mill does, however, think that models for others are important, and that exposure to a proliferation of lifestyles is also important for individuals.

65 Mill, *Utilitarianism*, p.35.

66 Ibid, p.41.

67 Mill, *On Liberty*, p.70.

public opinion' (SE 1, KSA 1:338). Mill is perhaps even more critical than Nietzsche of the individual who possesses a customary character. "Customs", he claims, "are made for customary characters...to conform to custom merely *as* custom does not educate or develop in him any of the qualities which are the distinctive endowment of a human being."[68] Choices proceeding from custom—believing a thing only because others believe it, is nothing more than 'ape-like imitation'. The tendency towards conformity is becoming more and more the norm as "society today has got the better of individuality". And, Mill adds:

> in our times...the individual or family do not ask themselves, what do I prefer? Or what would suit my character and disposition? Or what would allow the best and highest in me to have fair play and enable it to grow and thrive? They ask themselves, what is suitable to my position? What is usually done by persons of my station and pecuniary circumstances?...I do not mean that they choose what is customary in preference to what suits their own inclination. It does not occur to them to have any inclination except for what is customary...conformity is the first thing they think of...[69]

Mill's critique of conformity, like Nietzsche's, stems from his belief in a hierarchy of human beings. For Mill, 'eccentricity of conduct' is the defining characteristic of human greatness. Only the rare few as 'the salt of the earth', have been responsible for the improvement of mankind. These 'persons of genius' represent a 'small minority' but to have them it is necessary to preserve the soil in which they grow, and this requires an atmosphere of freedom. Notice, however, that even though Nietzsche's higher type grows out of a different soil, they both defend an order of rank of human beings which privilege personal development, and recognize that unconditional obedience to custom is an obstacle to human flourishing. Mill even goes so far as to claim that the greatness of England has not been the result of its moral and religious philanthropists, but rather owing to its nonconformist, eccentric types. Both thinkers share a distaste for mediocrity, and fear that human beings are becoming all too similar to each other owing to the 'tyranny of the majority'. There are certain differences in their views which are worth mentioning. For instance, Nietzsche would reject the egalitarianism that Mill combines with his elitism, including the idea that each person counts for one and no one for more than one, and the endorsement of disciplined restraint (i.e. the social principle) since these conflict with Nietzsche's commitment to human inequality and with

---

68 Ibid, p.122.

69 Ibid, pp.125–26.

his notion of Dionysian excess. In addition, Nietzsche accuses customary morality (which could include the morality of utility) of posing a threat to individual flourishing, whereas Mill would view utilitarian ethics as consistent with one's private interests, and never as something injurious to personal development. Mill wanted opportunities for flourishing and experimentation (and hence education, etc.) made available to all. For Mill, then, individuality operates within the context of a morality of utility.

It is important not to confuse Nietzsche's and Mill's praise of 'individuality' with an endorsement of the same brand of individualism. For instance, Nietzsche was an opponent of liberal individualism which he viewed as a license for selfishness, the rather ignoble pursuit of one's personal ends. Nietzsche's concern was that the preoccupation with material desires would undermine the importance of culture. The point is that when left to themselves, people tend to equate nobility with the satisfaction of their self-interests as if the epitome of human achievement was the all-too-human ideal of a mundane and safe 'bourgeois' existence. Nietzsche's conception of 'individuality', or the 'exemplary individual' extends beyond the narrow egoism and material pursuits which he thought were characteristic of modern societies.

In terms of their objectives, Nietzsche would take issue with Mill's attempt in *Utilitarianism* to construct a moral system. Nietzsche denies, for instance, that there are 'moral laws' and sets out to question morality itself. Even the expression 'science of morals' is one that he finds offensive to his taste since it precludes any historical treatment of morality, and hence fails to treat morality as a problem. Mill was much more of a systematic thinker, whereas Nietzsche expressed a distrust of all systematizers (TI 1:26, KSA 6:63). Ultimately, Nietzsche's ethics amounts to an evaluation of [types of] *persons* whereas Mill's utilitarianism is *act-oriented* (yet, nevertheless, consistent with an ideal of self-realization as a rational, fully developed person).

Kant as 'Moral Fanatic'

A dominant feature of German moral philosophy in the nineteenth century is its engagement with Kant's account of morality. Given the numerous references to Kant's ethics in the published writings, notebooks, and letters, it would appear that Nietzsche was no exception. Still it is rather surprising that no work by Kant can be found in Nietzsche's library. Nevertheless, it is almost certain that Nietzsche had read Kant both first-hand and through many secondary sources.[70]

---

70 See Thomas Brobjer, *Nietzsche's Ethics of Character*, 1995, p.198, 196. Brobjer claims that an extensive reading of Kant can certainly be *implied* by the following pieces of evidence—Nietzsche had quoted from Kant in his notebooks, and in a letter to

Despite his references to Kant as a 'moral fanatic' (*Moral-Fanatiker*) (WP 101, KSA 12:340), 'a *cunning* Christian' (TI 3:6, KSA 6:79), 'catastrophic spider' (A 11, KSA 6:177), the 'most deformed conceptual cripple there has ever been' (TI 8:7, KSA 6:110) and 'the great Chinaman from Königsberg' (BGE 210, KSA 5:144), Nietzsche was able to muster some slight praise. In a *Nachlaß* entry from 1887 entitled "Among moralists" (*Unter Moralisten*), Kant is listed as one of the "great moral philosophers" (*Die großen Moral-Philosophen*) (KSA 12:344) even though there was very little about Kant's moral philosophy that Nietzsche considered 'great'.[71] Instead, Kant's greatness, for Nietzsche, can be attributed to his tremendous *influence* as a moral philosopher. In fact, for many philosophers after Kant, the subject of 'morality' is defined in distinctly Kantian terms. Indeed, *moral* philosophy is, arguably, a footnote to Kant. And, among those individuals without a background in philosophy, morality generally conforms to a Kantian picture—the view that moral requirements are unconditional or 'categorical', that is, independent of one's particular desires and inclinations, and for that reason, acquire a special authority. In this way, people are in basic agreement that 'doing the right thing' is distinct from the satisfaction of one's personal interests and desires.

This convergence between a *popular* and *philosophical* understanding of morality was no coincidence since Kant's moral theory begins with the unquestioned acceptance of the moral beliefs of ordinary human beings. Everyone is equipped, he claims, with a reliable pre-philosophical understanding of morality even if, at times, its expression lacks clarity. Or, as he states in *The Critique of Practical Reason*, a ten year old child is capable of using his reason to solve moral problems as effectively as the philosopher. The role of the philosopher is to present the detailed system of morals which conforms to the 'common human understanding', and whose instruction will reinforce our ordinary moral consciousness.

Turning now to Kant's moral theory, we find him announcing in his *Grundlegung zur Metaphysik der Sitten* (1785) that moral philosophy must be cleansed of the empirical and anything pertaining to anthropology. The foundation of morals then "must not be sought in the nature of the human being or in the circumstances of the world in which he is placed, but *a priori* simply in concepts of pure reason."[72] Indeed, the human being is defined by his

---

Herman Mushacke, written in November 1866, Nietzsche proclaimed: "Kant, Schopenhauer, and this book by Lange—I do not need anything else." There is also a letter to Vischer-Bilfinger of January 1871: "I have studied Kant and Schopenhauer with especial predilection" quoted in Middleton, p.77.

71 On occasion, Nietzsche praises Kant for recognizing the moral worthlessness of pity, but this point by no means speaks to Kant's greatness (D 132, KSA 3:125).

72 Ibid, p.45.

or her faculty of reason. Reason, itself, is transcendental insofar as it belongs to the *noumenal* world (i.e. the world of 'things-in-themselves') but also makes an 'appearance' in the *phenomenal* world (i.e. the world of appearances). Thus, human beings in virtue of their faculty of reason inhabit two worlds, dwelling both in the phenomenal world (as subject to the causal laws of nature) and the noumenal world (as subject to the laws of freedom). This move was significant in that it left space for morality, allowing Kant to overcome the challenge to morality presented in his day by the New Science[73] which could not accommodate the moral notions of 'freedom' and 'responsibility' within a world causally determined. Kant goes on to identify the 'good will' (the only thing in the world that is good without limitation) with the rational will, the pure *a priori* practical reason.

An individual with a rational, and hence, good will, must act out of a purely moral motive. Of the three motives behind our actions (i.e. inclination, self-interest, and duty), only duty is properly termed the 'moral' motive. Yet, Kant is adamant that it is not enough to act in accordance with duty, that the truly moral act is done *for the sake of* duty. Duty is often contrasted with the non-moral motives of desire and inclination, the latter pertaining exclusively to our empirical nature. Duty, on the other hand, includes a constraining element whereby we forego our desires and inclinations, and submit to the Moral Law itself, expressed by means of the 'Categorical Imperative'.[74] The categorical imperative passes the test of a genuine moral imperative in its acknowledgement of universal applicability, equal consideration for everyone, and free acceptance by everyone. In contrast with hypothetical imperatives which take the form 'if you want *x* then do *y*', the categorical imperative is unconditional in its command: 'do *x*'. The individual who is capable of recognizing the demands of morality, and hence, free from any empirical contaminants, is said to be 'autonomous'. In his obedience to the Moral Law, the autonomous moral agent is both self-legislative (i.e. he commands and obeys no one but himself) and universally legislative. Because the autonomous individual is his own moral authority, no external authority (e.g. divine commands, tradition) can serve as a criterion for morality.

In its rejection of all empirical intrusions within the domain of morality, Kant's ethics has exerted a decisive influence on moral philosophy. What Kant's moral theory offers is a quite specific and monolithic understanding of morality.

---

73 The New Science, developed by Galileo, Kepler, Newton, Descartes, and others, argued that the universe is governed by physical laws knowable through observation and experimentation.

74 Ibid, p.73."Act only in accordance with that maxim through which you can at the same time will that it become a universal law."

As a set of universal, categorical principles of practical reason, Kant's *Moralität*, as Hegel[75] protested, is abstract, completely detached from *Sittlichkeit* or ethical life (the values embedded in a culture). In place of a morality of practice, Kant provides a rule-driven morality of universal rational principles. His theory basically eliminates any differences among human beings and assumes that we all belong to what he calls 'humanity' and share the moral faculty of reason.

Moral philosophy since Kant centres on the *justification* of moral principles which would allow philosophical debates to be resolved once and for all. Theories might disagree over the fundamental principle of morality, whether it is compassion, the greatest happiness for the greatest number, reason or God, but the task of 'justification' remains firmly entrenched. Nietzsche's dispute with Kant's moral philosophy, however, does *not* involve a clash over the 'correct' justification of morality. Instead, Nietzsche is challenging Kant's specific *conception* of Morality. In regarding morality as an *a priori* principle, Kant is not merely informing us of *a* morality, but *the* Morality (hence, the capitalized 'M') which, as a fact of reason, is the only authentic morality. For Nietzsche, philosophers advocating atemporal moral requirements disregard the history of moral concepts, and simply accept morality as given. He explains:

> Just because our moral philosophers knew the facts of morality only very approximately in arbitrary extracts or in accidental epitomes—for example, as the morality of their environment, their class, their church, the spirit of their time, their climate and part of the world--...they never laid eyes on the real problems of morality; for these emerge only when we compare *many* moralities. In all 'science of morals' so far one thing was *lacking*, strange as it may sound: the problem of morality itself; what was lacking was any suspicion that there was something problematic here. What the philosophers called 'a rational foundation for morality' and tried to supply was, seen in the right light, merely a scholarly variation of the common *faith* in the prevalent morality; a new means of *expression* for this faith;...indeed, in the last analysis a kind of denial that this morality might ever be considered problematic. (BGE 186, KSA 5:106)

Kant represents a paradigm case of a philosopher indoctrinated by the morality of his environment since the ordinary moral consciousness he sought to defend philosophically was the product of a largely Protestant Königsberg.[76] It is precisely for this reason that Nietzsche argues that an historical sense is indispensable for understanding morality, the moral differences among cultures being so great at times, that it defies the notion of an 'ordinary moral

---

75 See Hegel, *Philosophy of Right*, paragraph 33. See also, Charles Taylor in *Hegel and Modern Society*, Cambridge: Cambridge University Press, 1979, pp.76–8. Note, Nietzsche's use of the term *Moralität* does not conform to this Hegelian usage (see my Chapter One).

76 For a discussion of Kant's debt to Pietism, see Roger J. Sullivan, *Immanuel Kant's Moral Theory*, Cambridge: Cambridge University Press, 1989, pp.6–7.

consciousness'. Lacking any historical acumen, Kant failed to treat morality as a problem, and hence, he was in no position to question its *value*. As a reply to Kant, Nietzsche attempts to *de*-monopolize Morality through his typology or genealogy of morals which shows that there exists more than one morality (hence the distinction between 'master/noble morality' and 'slave morality').[77] Kant's failings as a moral philosopher owe much to his lack of an historical sense.

Nietzsche's criticisms of Kant's ethics are not limited to the objection that he ignores the genealogy of morals. As well, Nietzsche opposes the Königsbergean's dualisms, that is, the division of reason into theoretical and practical, and the division of the world into phenomena and noumena. Still, the much more pronounced attack focuses on Kant's moral principle, the categorical imperative, which in turn, leads to further objections, some of which can be traced to Nietzsche's appropriation of Schopenhauer's critique of Kant's ethics from *On the Basis of Morality*.

When Nietzsche remarked that Kant's philosophy was built on the "seduction of morality", that instead of aiming at 'truth' he was really consumed by 'majestic moral structures' having been "bitten by the moral tarantula Rousseau" (D P:3, KSA 3:14), his assertion was that Kant had merely invented a fictitious 'Beyond' for the purpose of accommodating the laws of freedom, and thus morality. In positing an indemonstrable world, a logical 'Beyond', Nietzsche thought that Kant went to extraordinary and unjustifiable lengths to create room for a 'moral realm' (P:3). Although Nietzsche agreed with Kant that moral actions are indemonstrable, he denied the 'real' (noumenal) versus 'apparent' (phenomenal) world dichotomy essential to Kant's system. For Nietzsche, there is but *one* world—the apparent world and it constitutes 'reality' itself. As a result, he repudiates all attempts to ground morality in a transcendent source (God, Reason). To divide the world up into 'real' and 'apparent' as Christianity and Kant had done meant de-valuing 'this world' for the metaphysical comforts located in the world of 'Being', the 'real' world. And, in regard to Kant's other crucial dichotomy, the division of reason into theoretical and practical, Nietzsche was no more sympathetic having claimed that Kant merely "invented a reason (practical reason) for those cases when one

---

77 Kant needed to show that the ordinary moral consciousness was not only common to Königsbergeans, but belonged to all human beings for all times. His riposte to Nietzsche would likely be that the Moral Law is not threatened by the illustration of historical examples. If one wanted to argue that community *x* lived according to values which conflicted with the 'common understanding', then Kant would presumably claim that these people (e.g. Nietzsche's noble type) are irrational.

need not bother with reason, that is, when the needs of the heart speaks, when 'duty' speaks, when morality speaks" (WP 414, KSA 13:422).

It is a short step from Nietzsche's denial of Kant's moral realm to his objection to the unconditional and universal aspect of the categorical imperative. In one of his earliest references to the categorical imperative, Nietzsche undermines its universality by noting that the needs of mankind will vary, and so it does not make sense to "demand from the individual those actions that one desires from all men—a nice, naïve idea, as if everyone without further ado would know which manner of action would benefit the whole of mankind, that is, which actions were desirable at all" (HH 25, KSA 2:46).[78] In fact, it is a "sign of nobility", according to Nietzsche, "never to think of degrading our duties into duties for everybody; not wanting to delegate, to share one's own responsibility; counting one's privileges and their exercise among one's *duties*" (BGE 272, KSA 5:227). Specifically, Nietzsche counters the categorical imperative with the demand that "everyone invent *his own* virtue, *his own* categorical imperative" (A 11, KSA 6:177). He is careful to draw a distinction between 'duty in general' ('impersonal duty' or 'duties for everybody') and a 'duty' ('our duty') suited to the specific condition of one's life. In regard to 'our duties', Nietzsche owed much more to Stendhal than to Kant. Recall, for instance the words of Julien Sorel in *Le Rouge et le noir*:

> One has duties always towards oneself [and later]…I always had the compelling thought of duty with me. That duty, that rightly or wrongly, I had prescribed for myself…[79]

The personal duty that Nietzsche has in mind relates to "an action compelled by the instinct of life [which] has in the joy of performing it the proof it is a *right* action" (A 11, KSA 6:177). Elsewhere, Nietzsche refers to the unconditional feeling that 'everyone must judge as I do' inherent in the categorical imperative as a form of *selfishness*. "For it is selfish to experience one's own judgment as a

---

78 It is interesting to note that a similar objection was offered in Nietzsche's critique of utilitarianism. In any case, the more important point is that Kant might reject Nietzsche's choice of language here (e.g. 'desires' ['*wünscht*'] and 'benefit' ['*wohlfahre*']) to describe the categorical imperative. The authority of the moral law is attributed to reason, and not to such interested, empirical notions like 'desires' and 'benefit'. Still, Nietzsche was correct in identifying the universality belonging to the categorical imperative.

79 Stendhal, *Le Rouge et le noir* (Scarlet and Black), trans. M. Shaw. London: Penguin, 1953, pp.94, 502. Nietzsche had read Stendhal's *Le Rouge et le noir* in 1885, and always regarded him with the greatest esteem owing in part to his capacity for artistic passions, and his psychological insights. On at least one occasion Nietzsche contrasts Kant with Stendhal (KSA 13:641).

universal law...because it betrays that you have not yet discovered yourself nor created for yourself an ideal of your own, your very own—for that could never be somebody else's" (GS 335, KSA 3:562). Further, the universality demanded by the categorical imperative would require that actions can be known, especially the same actions, but Nietzsche's point is that every action that has ever been performed is 'unique and irretrievable' (335). Consequently, we are not entitled to make universal demands on how one is to act since all actions are unknowable. It is important to note, here, that in attacking the universality of the categorical imperative, and divesting it of its transcendental authority, Nietzsche's main purpose is to oppose Kant's ethics with his 'noble morality'.

One of the ways to try to legitimize his 'noble morality' is to show that Kant's abstract theory of morals is rooted in decadence, and what better way to accomplish this task than to reveal its association with Christian morality. Specifically, Nietzsche detected in the categorical imperative the values of a 'subterranean Christianity' (WP 101, KSA 12:340). Just as Schopenhauer had construed Kantian ethics as a 'disguised theological ethics' due to its appropriation of the religious notions of 'duty', 'obedience', and 'law', Nietzsche likewise associated Kant's ethics with Christianity. As stated previously, it is not surprising that Kant, immersed in Pietistic Theology, would construct a moral theory that the community of Protestant Christians in Königsberg could take pride in. Of course, Kant would claim that his moral theory is not supported by Christianity, but conversely, that Christianity is a rationalization of moral thinking.[80] Nevertheless, as Robert C. Solomon states, "Nor was Kant deceiving himself when he looked with pride on his moral philosophy as the heart of Christian ethics, interpreting the commandment to love as well as the desire to be happy as nothing more nor less than the instantiations of the categorical imperative..."[81]

A further objection to the categorical imperative is that it is inherently egoistic, that its maxims can be willed universally only insofar as the individual is a beneficiary of the imperative himself. This criticism, expressed by Schopenhauer, is echoed in Nietzsche as he claims that "the categorical imperative is a *desired* instinct" (KSA 11:431). And, elsewhere Nietzsche objects that in commanding that human beings act outside of all interests and desires, the moral imperative involves "impossible demands" (KSA 7:479). Instead,

---

80 I. Kant. *Critique of Practical Reason* in *The Cambridge Edition of the Works of Immanuel Kant: Practical Philosophy*, ed./trans. Mary J. Gregor, Cambridge: Cambridge University Press, 1999, p.243.

81 R. Solomon. "A More Severe Morality: Nietzsche's Affirmative Ethics", in Y. Yovel (ed.), *Nietzsche as Affirmative Thinker*, Dordrecht/Boston/Lancaster: Martinus Nijhoff Publishers, 1986, p.77.

Nietzsche contrasts Goethe with Kant, insofar as he "strove against the separation of reason, sensuality, feeling, will…" (TI 9:49, KSA 6:151).

If Nietzsche is challenging Kant's conception of morality, what entitles him to simply redefine morality and present it as a replacement for the morality that he has condemned? After all, those philosophers well-disposed towards a Kantian understanding of morality may insist that the qualities belonging to Nietzsche's noble-type are not deserving of our moral approval. In fact, this noble individual, they would likely point out, stands *outside* the moral realm. There is another way of understanding this issue which is nicely articulated by John Casey:

> We could instead say that if a philosopher analyses the idea of the moral so that it excludes a priori many of those qualities and achievements in people that call forth admiration, love, and honour, then he is not really giving us the criteria for 'the moral point of view', but rather propounding a particular *morality*. Or, if it be true that in a particular tradition the idea of the moral is indeed understood in the way this philosopher analyses it, then it is still quite possible for those outside this tradition to choose to guide their lives by criteria or rules that might be other than 'moral'. We might call them 'ethical' just to mark a different set of serious rules. In this alternative tradition the notion of 'moral merit' might have a different, and perhaps lesser role. But as soon as we mark this difference between the two traditions, or forms of life, we see that there is no very good reason for calling them different analyses of the idea of the moral, rather than two different systems of values. This was essentially Nietzsche's criticism of Kant, that in attempting to elicit the criteria of any genuine morality, he produced a particular morality of selfless obedience.[82]

Kant would insist that his morality is not merely *particular* but *universal*, the only Morality since morality for him does not admit of a plural. Nietzsche is not debating Kant over the criteria of the moral point of view, but rather claiming that what Kant takes to be the criterion is "merely *one* type of morality beside which, before which, and after which many other types, above all *higher* moralities, are, or ought to be, possible" (BGE 202, KSA 5:124). Nietzsche, on the other hand, quite willingly announces that his morality is fundamentally particular. The important point here is that the difference between Nietzsche's 'particular morality' and Kant's 'universal morality' is not reducible to the difference between something that is 'not a morality' and something that is an 'authentic morality', but rather the difference is between a 'noble morality' and a 'slave morality'.[83] In this respect, we can admit, following Casey, that there are 'different systems of values'.

---

82 John Casey, *Pagan Virtue*, Oxford: Oxford University Press, 1990, p.204.

83 Ibid, p.80.

On the Nietzschean scheme of things, the role of the genealogist extends beyond the recovery of this moral dualism (or different systems of values) to include an *evaluation* and *legislation* of values. For instance, Nietzsche writes that "even apart from the value of such claims as 'there is a categorical imperative in us,' one can still always ask: what does such a claim tell us about the man who makes it?" (BGE 187, KSA 5:107). By appealing to life as a normative concept, Nietzsche submits Kant to the authority of symptomatology (i.e. morality understood as a sign-language of the affects) where it is shown that Kant's moral code belongs to an advanced phase of decadence, a denaturalization of values. So, when Kant speaks of the 'love of humanity', 'respect for the human being', this amounts to a hatred in regard to the strong and an attempt to give meaning to the existence of the weak and sick at the expense of others. As Keith Ansell-Pearson explains: "Kant's attempt to establish the ground for a metaphysic of morals bears testimony to the schizophrenic experiences of the modern ethical consciousness, full of rancour towards itself for failing to live up to the strictures of its severe morality and full of resentment towards forms of otherness which deviate from established rational norms and do not match the lofty moral standards it has established for itself."[84]

The genealogist then is a 'genuine philosopher', a legislator of values, as opposed to Kant who is denounced as a 'philosophical labourer' (*philosophischen Arbeiter*) since his task merely includes formulating the great data of valuations which have become dominant (BGE 211, KSA 5:144). But, isn't philosophical legislation the crowning achievement of Kant's philosophy? Clearly, Nietzsche and Kant are operating under two completely different conceptions of legislation. Gilles Deleuze is sensitive to this distinction when he writes:

> For Kant, what legislates (in a domain) is always one of our faculties: understanding, reason. We are legislators only insofar as we submit to one of our faculties, as it were the whole of ourselves. But to what do we submit in such a faculty, to what forces?[85]

Kantian legislation, in maintaining that one's true value lies in the noumenal world, alienates the individual from his *natural* 'self'. For Nietzsche, the philosophical legislator, having revealed and evaluated the origin of our moral values, stands above the common prejudices of all metaphysicians, and creates values. However, his *legislation* is not based exclusively on the commands of

---

84 Keith Ansell-Pearson, "Nietzsche and the Problem of the Will in Modernity" in K. Ansell-Pearson (ed.), *Nietzsche and Modern German Thought*, London: Routledge, 1991, p.171.

85 Gilles Deleuze, *Nietzsche and Philosophy*, trans. Hugh Tomlinson, NewYork: Columbia University Press, 1983, p.92.

reason, since the commanding force, for Nietzsche, belongs to the individual's drives.

Nietzsche has wielded his genealogical sword against Kant's antihistorical, moral fanaticism in an effort to validate his 'noble morality'. In the end, Kant's 'M'orality is undermined by Nietzsche's dualism of master/noble and slave moralit*ies*. From there, Kant's ethics gets relegated to the category of 'slave morality' owing to its anti-naturalism, and its hatred of life, while Nietzsche goes on to promote the life-affirming, noble mode of valuation as the solution to the problem of morality.

Nietzsche *Pro* or *Contra* Aristotelian Morals?

As residuum of Christian morality, both Utilitarianism and Kantian ethics were relegated by Nietzsche to the class of 'decadent' moralities. It would appear, then, that if there is any hope of situating Nietzsche's affirmative ethics within the moral tradition, then that hope would lie with Aristotle, the most distinguished representative of virtue ethics. However, an examination of Nietzsche's relation to Aristotle's moral philosophy suffers from certain shortcomings. Most notably, there are *few* references to Aristotle's ethics in Nietzsche's writings. Instead, his interest in Aristotle centres on the Philosopher's views on rhetoric[86] and tragedy (the latter, however, not entirely unrelated to ethics). Hence, unlike Mill and Kant, Aristotle was not treated primarily as a *moral* philosopher. And, whereas Nietzsche's attitude towards Mill, Kant, and most other 'preachers of morals' was revealed through *ad hominem* attacks, Aristotle was one of the few thinkers not victimized by Nietzsche's ruthless tongue.

The dearth of references to Aristotle's ethics cannot be attributed to a lack of familiarity with the *Nichomachean Ethics* and the *Politics*, since Nietzsche had read these texts as well as other important works of Aristotle.[87] Even without many explicit references to Aristotle, one might claim that there are certain striking affinities in their moral thinking that could not possibly be ignored. For instance, some commentators[88] have alluded to the similarity between

---

86 At Basel, Nietzsche lectured on "*Aristoteles' Schriften Zur Rhetorik*" published in *Friedrich Nietzsche on Rhetoric and Language*, Gilman/Blair/Parent (eds.), Oxford: Oxford University Press, 1989, p.194.

87 Thomas Brobjer, *Nietzsche's Ethics of Character*, 1995, p.230.

88 Cf. F.A. Lea's *The Tragic Philosopher: A Study of Friedrich Nietzsche*, London, 1957, p.235; Rose Pfeffer's *Nietzsche: Disciple of Dionysus*, Lewisburg, 1972, p.60; L. Lampert, *Nietzsche's Teaching: An Interpretation of 'Thus Spoke Zarathustra'*, New Haven: Yale University Press, 1986, p.78; P. Foot, "Nietzsche: The Revaluation of Values" in R.C. Solomon (ed.), *Nietzsche: A Collection of Critical Essays*, 1973, 1980, p.164; R.C. Solomon, "A More Severe Morality: Nietzsche's Affirmative Ethics," in Y. Yovel (ed.), *Nietzsche*

Nietzsche's master morality and 'noble type', and Aristotle's conception of *megalopsychia*[89] and the 'great-souled man' μεγαλόψυχος.[90] On the basis of this resemblance, Walter Kaufmann has written that "Nietzsche's debt to Aristotle's ethics is considerable."[91] Kaufmann's claim, however, is supported entirely by one passage from the *Nichomachean Ethics* (Book IV:3), where Aristotle describes the 'great-souled man'. In itself, this evidence will not suffice to treat Aristotle and Nietzsche as belonging to the same ethical tradition. The question then is not whether there are similarities between their ethics, but whether the similarities are enough to warrant Nietzsche's inclusion within the virtue ethics tradition. In this section, my preparatory concern is to examine Nietzsche's relation to and evaluation of Aristotle's ethics. Later, I will draw on the results of this comparative study in order to determine whether Nietzsche's ethics should be placed within the aretaic tradition. Towards this end, I will now turn to a brief account of Aristotle's moral theory before moving on to a comparison with Nietzsche's ethics.

Aristotle's ethics is based on the view that human beings have a certain function or aim to fulfill, and it is for this reason that his theory is considered 'teleological'. The *Nichomachean Ethics* begins with the following statement: "Every art and every investigation, and similarly every action and pursuit, is considered to aim at some good. Hence the good has been rightly defined as 'that at which all things aim'" (*NE* I.i). But Aristotle draws a distinction between 'instrumental' (actions done as means for other ends) and 'intrinsic' (actions done for their own sake) ends. The carpenter, for instance, who builds a lodging to house soldiers fulfills his function as a carpenter. The carpenter's end, however, is not an end in itself but merely instrumental in providing shelter for soldiers until the soldiers execute the next stage of their operation. Aristotle's ethics, though, pertains to the 'highest good', (i.e. the highest practical good attainable by man as an active being) whereby "our activities have some end which we want for its own sake, and for the sake of which we want all the other ends" (*NE* I.i). The task of ethics will be to determine what is the good at which human beings aim, or in other words, what is the best life for a person.

---

as Affirmative Thinker, Boston: Nijhoff, 1986; R.C. Solomon, "Nietzsche *ad hominem*: Perspectivism, Personality and *Ressentiment*" in B. Magnus and K. Higgins (eds.), *Cambridge Companion to Nietzsche*, Cambridge: Cambridge University Press, 1996, p.200.

89 Greatness of soul, magnanimity, dignity, proper pride.

90 The 'great-souled man' has also been translated into English as the 'magnanimous man', and I use the expressions interchangeably.

91 Walter Kaufmann, *Nietzsche: Philosopher, Psychologist, Antichrist*, 4th Edition. Princeton, NJ: Princeton University Press, 1974, p.384.

Aristotle accepts the general opinion that the highest of all practical goods is *εὐδαιμονία*[92] often misleadingly translated into English as 'happiness'—whereas 'happiness' designates a feeling, Aristotle is adamant that eudaimonia is a kind of activity. For this reason, the term 'well-being' or 'living well' would be a more suitable translation. After claiming that eudaimonia is the ultimate end or object of human life because we choose it for itself and no other reason, Aristotle considers in what eudaimonia consists. In order to determine what kind of life is eudaimonia, Aristotle reviews the most common forms. The majority of people aim for *pleasure*, but he quickly rejects this end as a 'life fit for cattle'—its selection betrays a slavish mentality. A life of *wealth* is eliminated as the ultimate end for it is only a means to an end. The more refined seem to aim at *honour*, but honour is discounted since it is based on how one is reflected by others, rather than something that is attributed directly to ourselves. Honour is pursued by those individuals who want their goodness validated or confirmed by others. And, although they want to be respected by others for their virtue, even virtue is not eudaimonia. Virtue is a disposition, not an activity and one can be virtuous and still suffer misfortunes. Further, a virtuous person is still considered good even when he is inactive (e.g. while asleep), but Aristotle denies that a life of inactivity would qualify as 'happy'. Hence, pleasure, wealth, honour, and virtue are rejected as candidates for the best life.

Following Plato, Aristotle seeks to understand the good in terms of a person's function. Although a carpenter is said to be 'good' if he fulfills his function as a builder, Aristotle claimed that the distinctive feature of a human being lies outside one's craft or profession. Rather, the 'good' human being is one who fulfills his function as a human being. Aristotle notes that the distinctive function of a human being cannot consist in merely living, for plants also live, nor in being sentient creatures, for sensation is common to both human beings and animals. What remains as the distinguishing characteristic of a human being is his capacity for reason. Aristotle arrives at the following definition of the good or eudaimonia: "If we assume that the function of a man is a kind of life, viz., an activity or series of actions of the soul, implying a rational principle...the good for man is an activity of soul in accordance with virtue..." (*NE* I.vii).

Since eudaimonia or human excellence will involve the proper functioning of one's soul[93] (i.e. the right exercise of reason), Aristotle provides an account of the nature of the soul. For Aristotle, the soul is the form of the body and is composed of two parts, the rational and irrational. The irrational part is

---

92 eudaimonia.

93 According to Aristotle, "human virtue is *not* that of the body but that of the soul" (*NE* I.xiii).

subdivided into the vegetative (the cause of nutrition and growth) and 'appetitive' (desiring) parts. The vegetative part, as a faculty of soul common to all creatures receiving nourishment, is not relevant to moral considerations—it has no association at all with reason. Conversely, the appetitive component is receptive to reason in the sense that it is submissive and obedient to it. The irrational part by nature "fights against and resists that principle [of reason]" (*NE* I.xiii), and so is not always persuaded by reason. Whether the irrational element is obedient to reason depends on the particular circumstance, but their relation is naturally adversarial insofar as the irrational part "resists and opposes it [reason]" (*NE* I.xiii). It is this antagonistic relation between the rational and irrational parts of the soul which gives rise to the problems and subject matter of morality. The good human being will exhibit rational and guiding control over the passions (the irrational element of the soul).

In keeping with this differentiation of the soul, Aristotle divides virtue into two categories: intellectual and moral. Intellectual virtues are exhibited in thinking, where reasoning is the sole activity. Intellectual virtues like 'wisdom', 'understanding', and 'prudence' owe their existence and development to "instruction, and for this very reason needs time and experience" (*NE* II.i). Moral virtues, on the other hand, involve activities other than thinking in which case there is no guarantee that the precepts of reason will rule over the passions. Moral virtues such as 'liberality' and 'temperance' pertain to a person's *character* (*ēthos*), and so one's moral goodness will be the "result of habit (*ethos*)" (*NE* II.i). Aristotle rejects the view that our moral virtues are the product of nature—"we are constituted by nature to receive them, but their full development in us is due to habit" (*NE* II.i). Morality, then, will involve developing habits, the habits of right thinking, right choice, and right behaviour. It is the role of the legislator to make citizens good by habituation since human beings are born neither good nor bad.

The importance of moral training is evident from the negative influence that pleasure and pain may affect on the individual. Aristotle writes: "If the virtues are concerned with actions and feelings, and every feeling and every action is always accompanied by pleasure or pain, on this ground too virtue will be concerned with pleasures and pains" (*NE* II.iii). Morality, then, will be concerned with the virtue which disposes us to act in the right way with regard to pleasures and pains. As with many feelings or actions, one may feel or act in varying degrees, sometimes to the point of excess or deficiency.[94] Aristotle's 'doctrine of the *mean*' relates to the midpoint between a vice of excess and a vice of deficiency. The knowledgeable person avoids excess and deficiency since

---

94 Aristotle claims that not all actions and feelings admit of a 'mean' since some are 'evil in themselves' (e.g. malice, shamelessness, envy, adultery, murder).

"virtue...is a mean condition, inasmuch as it aims at hitting the mean" (*NE* II.vi). Here, reason steps in to identify and choose the mean, and hence arrive at the right measure in both feelings and actions. Virtue, is now defined as "a purposive disposition, lying in a mean that is relative to us and determined by a rational principle, and by that which a prudent man would use to determine it" (*NE* II.vi). For example, the virtue of courage is described as a mean between rashness (a vice of excess), and cowardice (a vice of deficiency). The table of virtues listed in the *Nichomachean Ethics*, although at times appearing *ad hoc*, is not based on Aristotle's arbitrary preferences but reflect the actual virtues of the upper-class in contemporary Greek society.

Prior to his account of the particular virtues, Aristotle discusses the notion of moral responsibility by examining the motivations and qualities an agent must have in order that we may speak intelligibly of virtues and vices. For instance, since only voluntary actions are subject to moral appraisal, an action must be voluntary (i.e. deliberately chosen) if it is to be considered a virtue or vice. In this way, the originating cause lies in the agent himself. A choice, then, is a voluntary action insofar as it is an act that lies within our power. In fact, Aristotle claims that our characters are determined by our choice of what is good and evil, and that choice itself implies a rational principle and thought, and is the result of deliberation. We deliberate about means, not ends, and since the exercise of moral virtue relates to means, Aristotle argues that virtue lies in our power. The good man performs voluntarily all the means towards the end. Non-voluntary actions are those performed out of compulsion or ignorance.

Aristotle proceeds to apply his doctrine of the mean to the list of moral virtues singled out in Books III and IV of the *Nichomachean Ethics*. For my present purposes, it is not necessary to review his account of each virtue. Instead, I will focus on 'greatness of soul', since as mentioned previously, it is this particular virtue which has generated comparisons with Nietzsche's notion of 'nobility'. The importance of 'greatness of soul' in Aristotle's ethics is recognized by Alexander Grant who claims that, "Aristotle's description of the virtue of great-souledness...throws light upon the whole bearing of his moral system."[95] Similarly, the focal point of Nietzsche's ethics is his conception of human flourishing. While it is evident that both Aristotle's and Nietzsche's ethics are concerned primarily with human excellence, we need to question whether they share the same understanding of what constitutes greatness. Let us turn our attention then to the crucial passage in the *Nichomachean Ethics* on *megalopsychia* and the 'great-souled man' (*NE* IV.3; *ed. cit.*) which prompted Kaufmann to remark that "Aristotle's conception [of *megalopsychia*] apparently

---

95 A. Grant, *The Ethics of Aristotle*, two volumes, London, 1885, Vol. II, p.72.

made a tremendous impression on Nietzsche."[96] Due to its significance, I will cite this passage at length as it appears in Kaufmann's text:

> A person is thought to be great-souled if he claims much and deserves much...He that claims less than he deserves is small-souled...the truly great-souled man must be a good man...Greatness of soul seems...a crowning ornament of all the virtues...Great honours accorded by persons of worth will afford [the great-souled man] pleasure in a moderate degree: he will feel he is receiving only what belongs to him, or even less, for no honour can be adequate to the merits of perfect virtue, yet all the same he will deign to accept their honours, because they have no greater tribute to offer him. Honour rendered by common people and on trivial grounds he will utterly despise, for this is not what he merits....He therefore to whom even honour is a small thing will be indifferent to other things as well. Hence great-souled men are thought to be haughty...The great-souled man is justified in despising other people—his estimates are correct; but most proud men have no good ground for their pride...He is fond of conferring benefits but ashamed to receive them, because the former is a mark of superiority and the latter of inferiority. He returns a service done to him with interest, since this will put the original benefactor into his debt in turn, and make him the party benefited. The great-souled are said to have a good memory for any benefit they have conferred, but a bad memory for any benefit for those which they have received (since the recipient of a benefit is the inferior of his benefactor, whereas they desire to be superior)...It is also characteristic of the great-souled man never to ask help from others, or only with reluctance, but to render aid willingly; and to be haughty towards men of position and fortune, but courteous towards those of moderate station...and to adopt a high manner with the former is not ill-bread, but it is vulgar to lord it over humble people...He must be open both in love and in hate, since concealment shows timidity; and care more for the truth than for what people will think;...he is outspoken and frank, except when speaking with ironical self-deprecation, as he does to common people. He will be incapable of living at the will of another, unless a friend, since to do so is slavish...He does not bear a grudge, for it is not a mark of greatness of soul to recall things against people, especially the wrongs they have done you, but rather to overlook them. He is...not given to speaking evil himself, even of his enemies, except when he deliberately intends to give offence...Such then being the great-souled man, the corresponding character on the side of deficiency is the small-souled man, and on that of excess the vain man. (*NE* IV.iii; *ed. cit.*)

After insisting on a strong 'indebtedness' to Aristotle, Kaufmann provides no argument to support this rather bold claim. The absence of argumentation, however, does not prove Kaufmann wrong for there is certainly some overlap in Aristotle's and Nietzsche's 'higher type'. To begin with, the opening comments of this passage reveal Aristotle's agent- or character-oriented approach to ethics. In addition, Nietzsche's 'gift-giving virtue' (i.e. a sort of insatiable generosity owing to the overflowing nature of the bestower, rather than to the other's needs) has been compared to the great-souled man's

96 Walter Kaufmann, *Nietzsche*, 1974, p.382.

fondness for 'conferring benefits'. Another necessary ingredient of greatness for Nietzsche is the avoidance of feelings of *ressentiment*, and this, too, is reminiscent of the great-souled man's reluctance to 'bear a grudge'.

It is important, however, to examine carefully these examples since they mask certain dissimilarities. For instance, while I agree that Aristotle's and Nietzsche's ethics are both person-oriented, there is an important difference between their agent- or person-orientations which serves to distinguish Nietzsche's position from Aristotle and others who emphasize the agent's inner states or character. Nietzsche's agent-oriented approach is more extreme than Aristotle's insofar as Nietzsche's conception of human excellence depends more on the greatness of the agent's inner constitution than one encounters in Aristotle. As Michael Slote explains: "When Aristotle says that the virtuous individual is the measure of rightness or nobility in actions, he certainly seems to be saying something that might be interpreted as agent-based. But he also says that the virtuous individual perceives or sees what is right or noble to do in any given situation, and the perceptual order is best interpreted, I think, as telling us that actions or acts have a somewhat agent-independent moral status."[97] For Nietzsche, on the other hand, there is no agent-independent moral status because the nobility of an act is traced exclusively to its agent. In contrast with Aristotle's view that possessing the virtues leads to human greatness, Nietzsche's position is that the 'noble' type *determines* virtue. In other words, one's greatness is not based on having these virtues, but it is one's greatness which decides virtue. Given Nietzsche's greater emphasis on the agent's inner constitution, I will later discuss the implications associated with this more extreme agent-centred approach.

In *Thus Spoke Zarathustra* (I:22), the 'gift-giving virtue' is praised as the 'highest virtue'. Notice, however, the manner in which Nietzsche describes this virtue: "This is your thirst: to become sacrifices and gifts yourselves; and that is why you thirst to pile up all the riches in your soul...because your virtue is insatiable in wanting to give. You force all things to and into yourself that they may flow back out of your well as the gifts of your love" (Z I:22, KSA 4:98). Traditionally, generosity is admired on account of its other-directedness, and praised for the salutary effects bestowed on the recipient. But, Nietzsche offers a very different understanding of 'generosity' construed as a form of 'selfishness', as the squandering of one's overflowing and instinctive energies. He also describes the gift-giving virtue as flowing out of the 'riches of your soul', adding that this is the virtue of the body. What is important here is the vitalistic expression that Nietzsche gives to virtue, as it emerges from a sense of

---

97 M. Slote, "Nietzsche and Virtue Ethics", *International Studies in Philosophy*, XXX:3, 1998, p.24.

abundance or fullness. Lacking this instinctive element, Aristotle's notion of 'bestowing' requires calculation where reason (not instinct) will play an integral role. Hence, Aristotle would reject Nietzsche's claim that "The true good, nobility (*Vornehmheit*), greatness of soul (*Größe der Seele*), proceed from abundance…" (WP 935, KSA 13:605). For Aristotle, abundance or excess is an attribute of vice, not virtue.

The idea that magnanimity entails no feelings of resentment is a quality shared by Nietzsche's noble type and Aristotle's great-souled man. As well, 'self-sufficiency' (with an allowance for external goods[98]) would be an attribute common to both. Moreover, I do not deny that there are other noteworthy similarities in their ethics of human flourishing. For instance, both philosophers are elitist, recognizing an order of rank among human beings whereby nobility is privileged, and they reject egalitarianism. Still, it is my view that there are serious differences that become apparent when we consider Nietzsche's description of human excellence. In *Twilight of the Idols* (*Götzen-Dämmerung*, 1888), Nietzsche describes a concrete exemplar of human greatness:

> *Goethe*—not a German event, but a European one:…What he wanted was *totality*; he fought the mutual extraneousness of reason, senses, feeling and will (preached with the most abhorrent scholasticism by *Kant*, the antipode of Goethe); he disciplined himself to wholeness, he *created* himself. In the middle of an age with an unreal outlook, Goethe was a convinced realist: he said Yes to everything that was related to him in this respect—and he had no greater experience than that *ens realissimum* called Napoleon. Goethe conceived of a human being who would be strong, highly educated, skillful in all bodily matters, self-controlled, reverent toward himself, and who might dare to afford the whole range and wealth of being natural, being strong enough for such freedom; the man of tolerance, not from weakness but from strength, because he knows how to use to his advantage, even that from which the average nature would perish; the man for whom there is no longer anything that is forbidden—unless it be *weakness*, whether called vice or virtue. Such a spirit who has *become free* stands amid the cosmos with a joyous and trusting fatalism, in the *faith* that only the particular is loathsome, and that all is redeemed and affirmed in the whole—*he does not negate any more.* Such a faith, however is the highest of all possible faiths: I have baptized it with the name of *Dionysus.* (TI 9:49, KSA 6:151–52)

If Goethe fought against the separation of reason and the passions, then he was certainly at war with Aristotle (among others) for, as I alluded to earlier, Aristotle's ethics treats reason and passion as necessarily adversarial, and

98 In contrast with the Stoic sage who requires no external goods, both Nietzsche and Aristotle acknowledge their value. For Aristotle, the great-souled man's position of superiority depends in part to being moderately disposed towards such external goods as wealth and power (*NE* IV:iii). In *Ecce Homo*, Nietzsche states the importance of such things as diet, place, and climate for well-being (EH II:1–3).

belonging to different faculties of the soul. As well, the notion of '*creating* oneself' is foreign to Aristotle's great-souled man since 'creativity' is not a recognized trait of human excellence. Even the emphasis on 'self-control', which appears *prima facie* to be an obvious similarity, is actually dissimilar insofar as, for Nietzsche, it is a 'master drive' and *not* 'reason' which is the 'controlling' element. Aristotle's account of voluntary action, deliberation, and moral responsibility is at odds with Nietzsche's anti-voluntarism. But, the most crucial difference, or so I will argue, is the Dionysian *attitude* belonging to Nietzsche's 'higher type' described in terms of a complete embrace of everything that befalls a person. Indeed, Goethe is the incarnation of *amor fati.*

The important point is not simply that Aristotle's great-souled man does *not* exude this quality of greatness, but that Nietzsche explicitly *contrasts* Dionysus' tragic wisdom with Aristotle's *lack* of wisdom. He writes:

> Saying Yes to life even in its strangest and hardest problems; the will to life rejoicing over its own inexhaustibility...*that* is what I called Dionysian, *that* is what I understood as the bridge to the psychology of the *tragic* poet. *Not* in order to get rid of terror and pity, and not in order to purge oneself of a dangerous affect by its vehement discharge—Aristotle misunderstood it that way—but in order to be oneself the eternal joy of becoming, beyond all terror and pity—that joy which includes even destroying. (TI 10:5, KSA 6:160)

In attributing to Aristotle a 'misunderstanding' of the experience of tragic art, Nietzsche has dissociated his Dionysian affirmation of life[99] from Aristotle's 'psychology of the tragic poet'. This distancing between himself and Aristotle has ethical implications since Nietzsche's Dionysian affirmation of life *cannot* be severed from his morality. In a letter to Peter Gast dated October 30, 1888, Nietzsche refers specifically to the passage quoted above. He writes: "Are you satisfied by my concluding with the *Dionysus morality* (*der Dionysos-Moral*)? It occurred to me that this group of ideas should not at any price be absent from this *vade mecum* of my philosophy."[100] Since Nietzsche regards Aristotle's philosophy as anti-Dionysian, and labels his own morality as '*der Dionysos-Moral*', one can conclude that Nietzsche did not feel a moral kinship with Aristotelian ethics despite the fact that both emphasize 'human excellence'.

---

99 The idea is that a 'saying-yes to life' involves a 'Dionysian' transcendence of individuality, rather than, as Aristotle claimed, identifying with those individuals susceptible to pain and suffering. For Nietzsche, one loses one's identity as an individual and identifies instead with the 'will to life rejoicing over its own exhaustibility'.

100 Letter to Peter Gast, 30 October 1888 in C. Middleton (ed./trans), *Selected Letters of Friedrich Nietzsche*, 1969, p.319.

Nietzsche's relation to Aristotle's moral philosophy can be gleaned from additional sources. Section 198 of *Beyond Good and Evil*, for example, contains one of the few references to Aristotle's ethics in the published writings. Here, Nietzsche criticizes various moralities as "recipes against the passions" including, among others, "that tuning down of the affects to a harmless mean according to which they may be satisfied, the Aristotelianism of morals" (BGE 198, KSA 5:118). Nietzsche's repudiation of Aristotle's doctrine of the mean relates to their competing views on 'virtue'. For Aristotle, virtue is a midpoint between excess and deficiency, determined by reason, but Nietzsche continually affirms excess over the more traditional emphasis on moderation. In fact, for Nietzsche, virtues do just fine without 'reason'. But, by divorcing reason from virtue, isn't Nietzsche taking issue with not only Aristotle, but also the classical Greek tradition with its 'Reason = Virtue = Happiness' equation?

It would appear that Nietzsche is attempting to usurp this conventional account of virtue, since he aims to replace the ancient conception of virtue (e.g. Ariston of Chios[101]), "virtue is the health of the soul" with "*your* virtue is the health of *your* soul" (GS 120, KSA 3:477) adding that "what is healthy for your body depends on your goal, your horizon, your energies, your impulses..." (120). These comments reflect Nietzsche's opposition to 'abstract' virtue (KSA 12:517). He states: "'Virtue' (*Tugend*) made completely abstract was the greatest seduction to make oneself abstract: i.e. to detach oneself" (WP 428, KSA 13:292). "A virtue" he explains, "must be *our own* invention, *our* most necessary self-defense: any other kind of virtue is merely a danger" (A 11, KSA 6:177). Nietzsche asks: "Is there anything more beautiful than looking for one's own virtues" (BGE 214, KSA 5:151)? Virtues vary depending on the individual or class of individuals insofar as "the virtues of the common man might perhaps signify vices and weaknesses in a philosopher" (BGE 30, KSA 5:48).

The fact that Nietzsche 'personalizes' virtue still does not explain his understanding or conception of 'virtue'. In various places, he defines virtue as "physiological conditions" or "will to power" (WP 255, KSA 10:662) by which an individual or group preserves and enhances itself (WP 175, KSA 12:564). Since the conditions of existence or preservation will vary depending on the 'type' of person(s), Nietzsche does not offer a list of *the* virtues, as one finds in Aristotle. At times, however, he comes close to offering a list of *noble* virtues, or he, at least, names specific virtues that a 'noble type' could perhaps not possibly do without. For instance, Nietzsche refers to 'truthfulness as the highest virtue' (EH XIV:3, KSA 6:367), the 'overcoming of pity' as a noble virtue (EH I:4, KSA 6:270), and he lauds such virtues as "living dangerously" (GS 283, KSA 3:526), "forcefulness", "slavery" (BGE 44, KSA 5:61), "strength of the will",

---

101 Stoic Philosopher of 250 B.C.

"hardness" (BGE 212, KSA 5:146), "*great* suffering" (BGE 225, KSA 5:161), "exploitation" (BGE 259, KSA 5:207), and "egoism" (BGE 265, KSA 5:219), among others. In the *Antichrist*, Nietzsche even aligns himself with Aristotle, who likewise treated pity as a danger (A 7, KSA 6:174).

One could, I suppose, take the time to list the virtues which Nietzsche repeatedly praises, and no doubt, after having done this, will realize additional similarities and differences with Aristotle. But, what I think is deserving of more attention is how Nietzsche positioned himself with respect to the virtue ethics tradition. Just as Aristotle had questioned 'in what does eudaimonia consist?', similarly, Nietzsche had asked: 'what is happiness?' (A 2, KSA 6, p.170), but his answer leads *not* to Aristotle but to Machiavelli. Happiness, he writes, is "the feeling that power is *growing*, that resistance is overcome. Not contentedness but more power; not peace but war; not virtue but fitness (Renaissance virtue, *virtù*, virtue that is moraline-free)" (2). Nietzsche's 'good' man is beyond good and evil, and would likely find Aristotle's great-souled man too moralistic. It was Machiavelli, not Aristotle, who inspired Nietzsche's views on virtue and nobility. Although the expression 'greatness of soul' can be traced to Aristotle, it was Machiavelli's 'refinement' or 'variation' of Aristotle's *megalopsychia* that appealed to Nietzsche. Interestingly, Machiavelli also employed the expression 'greatness of soul',[102] and is quoted in Hippolyte Taine's *History of English Literature*, which Nietzsche had read. Taine writes:

> If you wish for a more serious thinker, listen to the great patriot, the Thucydides of the age, Machiavelli, who, contrasting Christianity and paganism, says that the first places 'supreme happiness in humility, abjection, contempt for human beings, while the other makes the sovereign good consist in *greatness of soul*, force of body, and all the qualities which make men to be feared'...Whereon he [Machiavelli] boldly concludes that Christianity teaches man 'to support evils, and not to do great deeds'...The ideal to which all efforts were turning, on which all thoughts depended, and which completely raised this civilization, was the strong and happy man, possessing all the powers to accomplish his wishes...[103]

Nietzsche certainly felt more at home with Machiavelli's *virtù*, and the virtues of the 'body', rather than with Aristotle's virtues of the 'soul', and the doctrine of the mean where reason plays a pivotal role. In Nietzsche's writings, Machiavelli

---

102 An Aristotelian influence was quite common in Renaissance Italy. In Jacob Burckhardt's *The Civilization of the Renaissance in Italy*, London: Phaidon Press, 1995, p.159, p.234, he explains that the *Ethics* and *Politics* of Aristotle exerted a tremendous influence on Renaissance Italy, in particular Aristotle's discussion of nobility. It is not surprising then that Machiavelli would borrow an Aristotelian term.

103 H. Taine. *History of English Literature*, vol. I, trans. Henry Van Laun, New York: Colonial Press, 1900, pp.182–83.

is consistently praised and his concept of *virtù* is defended against 'virtue' as understood by the 'preachers of virtue' (WP 317, KSA 12:518–19). Yet, there is no evidence to suggest that Nietzsche viewed Aristotle as his *moral* precursor. In fact, Aristotle is hardly visible in the Nietzsche corpus. How trivial it now appears when we read commentators attempting to establish a link between Nietzsche's claim that "*the noble soul has reverence for itself*" (BGE 287, KSA 5:233) and Aristotle's assertion that "The good man ought to be a lover of self, since he will then act nobly..." (*NE* 1169a). Until now, there has been no attempt in the secondary literature to associate Nietzsche's use of 'greatness of soul' with Machiavelli rather than Aristotle.[104]

If it is still not clear that Nietzsche distinguished his ethics from that of the classical Greek tradition, then we just need to consider his evaluation of this period of moral philosophy. In a *Nachlaß* fragment, he writes: "Characteristic of post-Socratic morals—all eudaimonistic and individual" (KSA 7:417). That this remark was not positive is evident from his expressed distaste for eudaimonism (BGE 225, KSA 5:160). And, in another notebook entry, one finds the following remark: "Fight against Plato and Aristotle" (KSA 11:253). Yet, even without referring specifically to Aristotle, Nietzsche's evaluation of him can be inferred from his critique of the 'rational fanaticism' of the Greek philosophers: "The moralism of the Greek philosophers from Plato on is pathologically conditioned; so is their esteem of dialectics. Reason-virtue-happiness, that means merely that one must imitate Socrates and counter the dark appetites with a permanent daylight—the daylight of reason" (TI 2:10, KSA 6:72). Socratic ethics marked a decisive turning point in Western philosophy with this "most bizarre equation" of reason-virtue-happiness. In particular, it was rooted in a pathological need to wage war against the instincts and the unconscious. However, Socrates did not give birth to decadence, he was merely its "extreme case", a symptom of the decay that had already spread throughout old Athens. In echoing this Socratic equation, Aristotle, too, counts "among men of fatigued instincts, among the conservatives of ancient Athens who let themselves go—'toward happiness,' as they said" (BGE 212, KSA 5:146). In the end, Aristotle is regarded as merely another decadent, taking his place alongside numerous others, including Socrates, Plato, Mill and Kant. Clearly, then, Nietzsche does not belong to the classical Greek tradition of virtue ethics with its emphasis on reason and moderation. Instead, his critique of the aretaic

---

104 Each time Kaufmann translates Nietzsche's expression 'greatness of soul', he adds a footnote referring the reader to Aristotle's *megalopsychia*. Machiavelli is never mentioned as a possible source. It is not my claim, however, that each occurrence of 'greatness of soul' in Nietzsche is based on Machiavelli's appropriation of the expression (cf. BGE 212, KSA 5:146).

tradition is meant to stand virtue ethics on its head, rather than to show that he and Aristotle are of one mind. Nevertheless, if virtue ethics is defined exclusively as pertaining to human excellence or personal distinction, then one may be inclined to situate Nietzsche within this tradition while still acknowledging certain differences among its contributors. But, this is *not* my position. In Chapter Five, I will provide a more detailed examination of Nietzsche's ethics and argue that his positive morality is best understood as an *ethics of human flourishing* rather than a radical (or non-conventional) virtue ethics. In particular, it will be shown that Nietzsche appeals to the name of *Dionysus* (and not Aristotle) to understand the best Greek instincts.

*

It was the aim of this chapter to examine Nietzsche's contribution to ethics in an effort to determine his moral legacy. It is evident from the following remark that Nietzsche viewed himself as a *unique* contributor to moral philosophy: "To see and to demonstrate the problem of morality (*Moral*)—that seems to me the new principal task. I deny that it has been done in previous moral philosophy" (WP 263, KSA 11:522). Indeed, Nietzsche's critique of Mill, Kant, and Aristotle (and their respective moral traditions) shows quite clearly Nietzsche's desire to distance himself from all moral philosophy to date. But, he also thought that demonstrating the 'problem of morality' meant more than simply chastizing philosophers for their lack of an historical sense, or for their erroneous presumptions.

A solution to the problem of morality required coming to terms with its 'value'. In this regard, Nietzsche never completely detached himself from his earlier 'moral educators', Schopenhauer and Rée. For instance, Nietzsche was continually preoccupied with the Schopenhauerian question of the 'value of existence', although he despised Schopenhauer's morality of compassion. Rée was influential, not just for inspiring Nietzsche's interest in ethics, but in inspiring Nietzsche's genealogical method. After all, it was precisely Nietzsche's *valuative* history of morals which gave birth to an ethics of human flourishing. The conclusion to this chapter can be summarized in the following way: although Nietzsche is clearly a *critic* of the fundamental aspects of the three main ethical traditions, it would be mistaken to conclude on those grounds that he has no positive morality, or that his moral legacy is restricted solely to undermining the moral tradition. Nietzsche's (affirmative) ethics of human flourishing stands *outside* any tradition, and it will be the task of Chapter Five to present and evaluate Nietzsche's positive morality.

4

Perfectionism and the Revaluation of All Values

So that he may one day become my companion and a fellow creator and celebrant of Zarathustra—one who writes my will on my tablets to contribute to the greater perfection of all things. And for his sake and the sake of those like him I must perfect myself.

—Z III:3, KSA 4:204

'Mankind must work continually at the production of individual great men—that and nothing else is its task'.

—SE 6, KSA 1:383–84

Let us not undervalue this: *we ourselves*, we free spirits, are already a 'revaluation of all values' (*Umwerthung aller Werthe*).

—A 13, KSA 6:179

The inability to situate Nietzsche's ethics within the moral tradition has not prevented commentators from acknowledging his positive contributions to moral philosophy. In recent years, there has been a steady stream of philosophers associating Nietzsche's preoccupation with the production of exemplary human beings with 'perfectionism'. In this chapter, I will examine these perfectionist readings and discuss how Nietzsche's 'perfectionism' relates to his demand for a 'revaluation of all values'. After identifying two forms of perfectionism operative in his writings, *moral* and *political* perfectionism,[1] that is, attending to the perfection of oneself versus a social policy involving the institutionally designed production of human excellence, I argue that there is a *temporal* distinction between the two perfectionisms which correspond roughly to the *early* and *later* stages of the 'revaluation'. Specifically, I show that

1 I am indebted to Daniel Conway's *Nietzsche and the Political*, 1997, p.54 for this distinction between moral and political perfectionism.

Nietzsche's *moral* perfectionism and the rudimentary stage of the revaluation are events designed for the *present* (late modernity), whereas his *political* perfectionism and the completed revaluation belong to the future. Since my study focuses on Nietzsche's *moral* thought (and not the *political*), I utilize this distinction to question whether his affirmative ethics can find a home in late modernity.

Nietzsche and Moral Perfectionism

Although "moral perfectionism has not found a secure home in modern philosophy,"[2] strands of perfectionist thinking are a commonplace within the history of moral thought.[3] The term 'perfectionism' has been defined in various ways. In the late nineteenth century, Sir William Hamilton defined "perfection" as "the full and harmonious development of all our faculties, corporeal and mental, intellectual and moral."[4] In *The Methods of Ethics*, Sidgwick defines "perfection" as "Excellence of Human Nature."[5] However, it has been John Rawls' treatment of perfectionism in *A Theory of Justice* (1971), (where he singles out Aristotle and Nietzsche as its main representatives) which has been the focal point of recent discussion on the topic. On Rawls' account, perfectionism is a "teleological doctrine" with a conception of the good entailing "the realization of human excellence in the various forms of culture."[6] Rawls argues that perfectionism is inimical to the liberal democratic theory of justice he seeks to defend since its claims of excellence would override the claims of justice. Consequently, Nietzsche's form of perfectionism is rejected due to its anti-democratic principles.

The recent influx of moral perfectionist readings[7] of Nietzsche is owed largely to Stanley Cavell's work[8] which offers an explicit challenge to Rawls'

---

2 Stanley Cavell, "Aversive Thinking: Emersonian Representations in Heidegger and Nietzsche," in *Conditions Handsome and Unhandsome: The Constitution of Emersonian Perfectionism*, Chicago: University of Chicago Press, 1990, p.46.

3 Thomas Hurka identifies numerous philosophers belonging to a perfectionist tradition including: Plato, Aristotle, Aquinas, Spinoza, Leibniz, Kant, Hegel, Marx, Nietzsche, H. Rashdall, T.H.Green, etcetera. (Thomas Hurka, *Perfectionism*, Oxford: Oxford University Press, 1993)

4 William Hamilton, *Lectures on Metaphysics*. Vol. 1 of 2, Mansel and John Veitch (eds.), New York: Sheldon and Company, 1880, p.14.

5 Henry Sidgwick, *The Methods of Ethics*, 7th Edition, London: Macmillan, 1907, p.9.

6 John Rawls, *A Theory of Justice*, Cambridge, MA: Harvard University Press, 1971, p.25.

7 Daniel Conway, *Nietzsche and the Political*, 1997; James Lippitt in *Nietzsche's Futures*, 1999; and James Conant in *Nietzsche's Post-Moralism*, 2001 interpret Nietzsche as a perfectionist, and all acknowledge their indebtedness to Cavell's essay (1990).

version of Nietzschean perfectionism. In order to appreciate Cavell's riposte, I shall turn now to Rawls' exposition of Nietzsche's perfectionism from *A Theory of Justice.* In section 50, Rawls describes two forms of perfectionism; 1. '*moderate perfectionism*' (whose principle is one among others and "[directs] society to arrange institutions and to define the duties and obligations of individuals so as to maximize the achievement of human excellence, in art, in science, and culture"), and 2. '*strong perfectionism*' (the maximization of excellence is the sole principle of institutions and obligations). It is the 'strong' version of perfectionism which Rawls attributes to Nietzsche on the basis of the following passage from *Schopenhauer as Eduator*:

> Mankind must work continually to produce individual great human beings—this and nothing else is the task...[F]or the question is this, how can your life, the individual life, retain the highest value, the deepest significance?...Only by your living for the good of the rarest and most valuable specimens [as cited in Rawls, p.325n].

For Rawls, this ominous passage conveys Nietzsche's elitist sensibilities, that the common or mediocre human being shall devote his or her life to the production of those rare few who epitomize human excellence. As we shall later see, the interpretation of this passage will prove to be a decisive factor in determining the nature of Nietzsche's perfectionism. For now, the important point is that Rawls interprets Nietzsche's call for the production of great individuals as an aspect of *social policy*. On this reading, Nietzsche demands the implementation of those conditions necessary to maximize the achievement of excellence in the arts and sciences, and the goodness of an action will be judged by its success in maximizing these forms of excellence. Rawls then draws attention to some of the unsavoury consequences associated with Nietzsche's effort to advance a conception of the good which maximizes the good of the few at the expense of the majority. In particular, Rawls opposes perfectionism's attempt to privilege "a higher life" since this principle legitimizes the unequal treatment of human beings. It is Nietzsche's anti-egalitarian brand of perfectionism which conflicts with the interests of 'liberty' and 'justice' Rawls aims to promote. Given Rawls' prior commitment to liberal democratic ideals, he is certainly justified in dismissing perfectionism as a viable option in the 'original position'.

In regard to the passage quoted above from *Schopenhauer as Educator*, Cavell concedes that Rawls is correct to reject Nietzsche's view (i.e. to promote the production of individual great human beings) as a principle of justice crucial to

---

8 Stanley Cavell, 1990. While it is true that John Rawls (1971) had already pegged Nietzsche a perfectionist, it was Cavell's more detailed treatment which subsequently influenced Nietzsche scholarship.

the life of democracy. But, Cavell claims that Rawls has read this passage too literally as implying that "there is a separate class of great men (to be) for whose good, and conception of the good, the rest of society is to live."[9] In an interesting interpretive twist, Cavell insists that Nietzsche's disdain for official culture "is itself an expression of democracy and commitment to it" since "only within the possibility of democracy is one committed to *living* with or against, such culture."[10] In rejecting perfectionism as a viable option in the 'original position', Cavell contends that Rawls has abandoned certain merits of perfectionism, one of which is a programme of moral education valuable for the development of citizens in a democratic society. He writes: "I understand the training and character Emerson [and Nietzsche] require for democracy as preparation to withstand not its rigors but its failures, character to keep the democratic hope alive in the face of disappointment with it."[11]

To a large extent, the disagreement between Cavell and Rawls rests on their conflicting interpretation of the passage from *Schopenhauer as Educator*. In failing to observe the sentences immediately following the 'focal passage'[12], Rawls has taken Nietzsche's quote out of context to mean that one should live 'for the good of the rarest and most valuable specimens'. Cavell cites the important sentences omitted from Rawls' truncated quotation where Nietzsche goes on to explain:

> The young person should be taught to regard himself as a failed work of nature but at the same time as a witness to the grandiose and marvellous intention of this artist...By coming to this resolve he places himself within the circle of *culture*; for culture is the child of each individual's self-knowledge and dissatisfaction with himself. Anyone who believes in culture is thereby saying: 'I see above me something higher and more human than I am; let everyone help me to attain it, as I will help everyone who knows and suffers as I do.'[13]

On Cavell's reading, the individual is not concerned with the maximization of culture, but with 'something higher', and this is what Nietzsche, in the next sentence, refers to as "a higher self" which has yet to be attained. Cavell shifts the emphasis away from the maximization of a given state of culture to the discovery of one's *own* reality. The 'something higher and more human' is not "that of someone *else*, but a further or eventual position of the self now

---

9 Cavell, p.49.

10 Ibid, p.50.

11 Ibid, p.56.

12 Following James Conant, I will hereafter refer to this passage from *SE* as the "focal passage."

13 *Schopenhauer as Educator*, cited in Cavell, 1990, p.51.

dissatisfied with itself."[14] On this reading, Nietzsche's perfectionism amounts to perfecting 'one's own nature' rather than the promotion of an elitist social policy. Of course, this narrow reading of Nietzsche's perfectionism conflicts, as I will later show, with his numerous anti-egalitarian remarks. It is no doubt a shortcoming on the part of Cavell to assess Nietzsche's perfectionism on the basis of an early essay. To treat *Schopenhauer as Educator* (1874) as Nietzsche's *vade mecum* is to ignore the perfectionist strand in his thought which runs through his entire corpus.

Another difficulty with Rawls' interpretation relates to the final sentence that he quotes regarding the living for rare specimens and not for the majority. In the English translation of *Schopenhauer as Educator* from which Rawls quotes, the word *Exemplare* had been unfaithfully translated as 'specimens' (it has since been translated more accurately as 'exemplars'). According to Cavell, the term 'specimens' misleadingly connotes a biological association where one's value can be specified independently of its effect on the individual. Specimens, he explains, are samples belonging to a class or genus so that "one either is or is not a specimen."[15] As a result, Rawls' account is rejected since a specimen could not serve as an exemplar unless everyone possessed common traits. If Nietzsche's *gröſse Mensch* is a specimen of a genus from which we (mediocre types) are necessarily excluded due to a lack of noble traits, then this higher type cannot serve as an exemplar. This objection is echoed by James Conant who proceeds to clarify the distinction between a specimen and an exemplar. "A specimen," he writes, "exhibits what is essential in order to count as a member of a genus. An exemplar exemplifies one way of excelling *qua* member of a genus."[16] So, the exemplary individual can influence members of its *own* genus. By reading Nietzsche's *gröſse Mensch* as a specimen, rather than an exemplar, Rawls misreads Nietzsche as advocating a social policy aimed at promoting the interests of the biologically privileged. But, the issue of semantics may not be as costly as Cavell and Conant seem to think, for there is an alternative account which neither consider. It could be that what Nietzsche meant by *Exemplare* was an exemplar of what the highest possibility is for human beings *as* a species, which the majority are incapable of attaining. For instance, he explains: "What concerns me is the problem of the order of rank within the species man [*der Gattung Mensch*], in whose progress I by and large do not believe, the problem of the order of rank between human types [*menschlichen Typens*] which have always

14 Cavell, p.52.

15 Ibid, p.50.

16 James Conant, "Nietzsche's Perfectionism: A Reading of *Schopenhauer as Educator*", 2001, p.195.

existed and always will exist" (KSA 13:481). Perhaps, Cavell's concern with democratizing Nietzsche was responsible for this oversight.

As part of his campaign to 'democratize' Nietzsche, Cavell transfers the sphere of perfectionism from the *social-political* to the *moral*, focusing on the individual's struggle to attain perfection within democratic life. In this way, there is no preaching of a new political order since human flourishing is viewed as a legitimate project within contemporary society. Hence, Nietzsche's actual aim involves:

> Calling for the further or higher self of each, each consecrating himself/herself to self-transformation, accepting one's own genius, which is precisely not, it is the negation of, accepting one's present state and its present consecrations to something and culture.[17]

But, which account of perfectionism, Rawls' or Cavell's, is most faithful to Nietzsche's text(s)? Both philosophers rely almost exclusively on Nietzsche's *Schopenhauer as Educator*, and offer conflicting readings. While this early essay provides a clear expression of perfectionist thinking, it is by no means the only source nor the best source of Nietzsche's perfectionism. When Nietzsche writes: "Mankind must work continually to produce individual great human beings—this and nothing else is the task...Only by your living for the good of the rarest and most valuable specimens" (SE 6, KSA 1:383–85), I believe that Rawls is *correct* in reading these remarks as an elitist social policy (an exclusionary *political perfectionism*) where the sacrifice of the majority is necessary for the promotion of individual excellences. This anti-democratic, political perfectionist reading is confirmed elsewhere in Nietzsche's writings. For instance, consider these elitist statements: "Slavery and the division of labor: the higher type (*der höhere Typus*) possible only through the subjugation of the lower, so that it becomes a function" (WP 660, KSA 12:96). Even more telling is the following passage expressing Nietzsche's social attitudes:

> we are by no means 'liberal'; we do not work for 'progress'; we do not need to plug up our ears against the sirens who in the market place sing of the future: their song about 'equal rights,' 'a free society,' 'no more masters and no more servants' has no allure for us. We simply do not consider it desirable that a realm of justice and concord should be established on earth (because it would certainly be the realm of the deepest leveling and *chinoiserie*)...we think about the necessity for new orders, also for a new *slavery*—for every strengthening and enhancement of the human type also involves a new kind of enslavement... (GS 377, KSA 3:629)

---

17 Rawls, *A Theory of Justice*, section 50, quoted in Cavell, p.53.

Cavell's reading of Nietzsche as celebrating the perfection of one's *own* nature within a democratic society entirely neglects Nietzsche's strongly illiberal political perfectionism. Nietzsche consistently argues that the "democratic movement" is "a form of the decay of political organization" *and* "the decay of man, making him mediocre and lowering his value" (BGE 203, KSA 5:126). Finally, Nietzsche offers his unequivocal support for "aristocratic society" since only its work has brought about "every enhancement of the type 'man'...a society that believes in the long order of rank and differences in value between man and man, and that needs slavery..." (BGE 257, KSA 5:205).

While the advantage of Rawls' reading is that it captures Nietzsche's anti-democratic and elitist sensibilities, it does not always describe accurately the nature of his political perfectionism. Recall, for instance, Rawls' definition of perfectionism as "the realization of human excellence in the various forms of culture."[18] As Cavell notes correctly, Rawls fails to recognize that Nietzsche has become sceptical of the ability of these cultural institutions (e.g. universities and religions) to serve as a vehicle to human excellence. In fact, Nietzsche laments that "our institutions are no good anymore..." (TI 9:39, KSA 6:140). In other words, our liberal institutions as they stand *today* (i.e. in decadent modernity) are incapable of producing, let alone, 'maximizing' the achievement of human excellence. Cavell expresses the objection in this way: "It makes no obvious sense to ask for some given thing to be maximized in what this [Rawls'] perfectionism craves as the realm of culture, the realm to which, as Nietzsche puts it, we are to consecrate ourselves..."[19]

Despite their respective shortcomings, the interpretations of Rawls and Cavell pave the way to certain key interpretive issues relating to Nietzsche's perfectionism. For instance, after pronouncing a verdict of 'decadence' on modernity, how can Nietzsche fulfill his political aim of producing great human beings as a matter of institutional design? Throughout his writings, he makes sporadic reference to such living exemplars of human greatness as Goethe, Napoleon, Caesar, Borgia, Thucydides, Bizet, etcetera. Note, however, that Nietzsche's inclusion of Napoleon and Bizet suggests that human greatness is not confined to vitalistic ages although he believes that the opportunities for the emergence of exemplary individuals is increased greatly if they are products of a *healthy* period, especially, *aristocratic* societies. For example, in referring to the social conditions responsible for producing Julius Caesar, and other higher types, Nietzsche writes: "Those large hothouses for the strongest kind of human being that has so far been known—the aristocratic commonwealths of the type of Rome or Venice..." (TI 9:38, KSA 6:140). While aristocratic

---

18 Rawls, *A Theory of Justice*, 1971, p.25.

19 Cavell, 1990, pp.48–9.

societies provide the soil from which these higher types usually grow, Nietzsche, himself, is not afforded the same luxury of existing in a vitalistic age. However, the fact that he admits to being a child of decadent modernity does not cause him to renounce his exemplary status. On the contrary, Nietzsche views himself as a 'lucky strike'. Late modernity may not be conducive to the mass-production of great human beings, but it is false to claim that human greatness is unattainable in this period. Nietzsche's moral perfectionism, as I see it, relates to the capacity for greatness within late modernity, and his own era serves as a stage on which he can strive to resuscitate depleted resources. His *political* perfectionism (i.e. the political task of breeding or willing great human beings) belongs to the "philosophers of the *future*" who will be responsible for the legislation of values. In his own day, Nietzsche bides his time traveling, attending to his well-being, and producing philosophical works aimed at facilitating a revaluation of values.

The task of perfectionism commences in the *present* as Nietzsche turns his attention to the possibility of human flourishing in late modernity. During this 'interim', Nietzsche anticipates that *moral* perfectionism will serve as an eventual catalyst for the *political* perfectionism he envisions for the future. Daniel Conway explains Nietzsche's project of moral perfectionism as "the conviction that one's primary, overriding—and perhaps sole—ethical 'obligation' is to attend to the perfection of one's ownmost self" and this "involves cultivating one's native endowment of powers and faculties; eliciting from within oneself the perfections that lie dormant, undiscovered, or incomplete; and so fortifying one's soul with the virtues constitutive of a sterling character."[20] Clearly, Nietzsche thinks that this is a viable project within his own crepuscular age, one that can sustain an 'ideal' of human flourishing. In fact, he specifically took up this issue in his unpublished notes from the Spring–Summer of 1874. There he questioned how Schopenhauer's 'genius' was compatible with the decadent age to which he belonged. Nietzsche asks: "How was it possible for Schopenhauer to endure living in his age without attempting in some way or other to become its reformer? And didn't the weakness of the modern age weaken his image of life" (CWFN 11:361, KSA 7:806–7)? Nietzsche's response was that Schopenhauer could endure to live in his age because he is "the liberating destroyer. The free thinker" (361). It was Schopenhauer's genius that allowed him to take action against the 'weakness of his age'. The question now is: how is this project of moral perfectionism to be realized in light of the two thousand years of Christian-moral domination?

---

20 Daniel Conway, *Nietzsche and the Political*, 1997, p.54.

Self-Overcoming

The tenability of human flourishing in late modernity will depend, *inter alia*, on one's success at resisting and counteracting the decadent values and perspectives belonging to one's age. In fact, Nietzsche regards such aversive endeavours as a requirement for the philosopher:

> What does a philosopher demand of himself first and last? To overcome his time in himself, to become 'timeless'. With what must he therefore engage in the hardest combat? With whatever marks him as the child of his time. Well then! I am, no less than Wagner, a child of this time; that is, a decadent: but I comprehended this, I *resisted* it. (CW P, KSA 6:11, my emphasis)

Although these remarks fall short of outlining what is needed to enact an overcoming of one's time, they illustrate nicely Nietzsche's recognition of the feasibility of such a task. Specifically, Nietzsche not only proclaims his own decadence, but insists that he 'resisted' it. As a 'child of his time', he cannot denounce its values and perspectives through a *discursive* dismissal alone, since the task of self-overcoming (*Selbstüberwindung*) attends to the tensions and struggles that emerge within one's own soul. In other words, he aims to participate in everything that he will ultimately overcome.[21]

How does a 'decadent', then, overcome or resist his 'decadence'? In Nietzsche's case, he not only diagnoses his 'sickness' (with modernity), but prescribes a regimen of 'self-discipline' as a palliative (CW P, KSA 6:12). The importance that he attributes to self-control is evident from the following passage:

> The most spiritual men, as the *strongest*, find their happiness where others would find their destruction: in the labyrinth, in hardness against themselves and others, in experiments; their joy is self-conquest; asceticism becomes in them nature, need, and instinct. Difficult tasks are a privilege to them; to play with burdens that crush others, a recreation. Knowledge—a form of asceticism. They are the most venerable kind of man; that does not preclude their being the most cheerful and the kindliest. (A 57, KSA 6:243)

---

21 Daniel Conway overemphasizes Nietzsche's self-avowed decadence while underscoring his efforts to *exempt* himself from his own diagnosis of decadence. Conway offers a pessimistic reading of the resources available in modernity to produce great human beings, claiming that, at best, modernity's higher types are only a different type of decadent. This reading, I think, is contradicted by Nietzsche's claims that 'lucky strikes' can appear in any historical period. Further, when Nietzsche describes himself as a 'decadent', it is not for the purpose of conceding his lowly status, but conversely, to announce his (supposed) superiority in being a child of a decadent period but *overcoming* it (cf. EH I:2, KSA 6:266). So, overcoming decadence becomes a *measure* (*not* the defining feature) of his greatness.

In the absence of *a priori* rules or principles for advancing to this 'venerable' or elevated state, Nietzsche appeals to 'self-experimentation', understood in terms of various regimens of ascetic practices. The ascetic nature attributed here to the 'strongest' type is consistent with Nietzsche's general description of the 'higher type' as possessing "the greatest multiplicity of drives, in the relatively greatest strength that can be endured," but under the "control" of a "master" or "chief" drive which overcomes the "weakened" or decadent drives (WP 966, KSA 11:289). Note, however, that the 'philosophical' asceticism practised by the 'most spiritual men' must not be confused with Christian asceticism. The latter involves a "hatred of the senses" whereas the former implies a "severe and cheerful continence" as "the will of one's dominating instinct" (GM III:9,8, KSA 5:356,355). Unfortunately, Nietzsche is rather elusive when it comes to a detailed explanation of the behavioural consequences of this form of asceticism. As I shall discuss in Chapter Five, this elusiveness attests to his performative justification of his ideal of human flourishing, and his lack of concern for morality understood as the promotion of what one 'ought' to do. Instead, Nietzsche's ethical concern lies with the character traits of exemplary human beings.

In fashioning the 'higher type' (e.g. himself) with an ascetic character, Nietzsche is drawing attention to the various tensions within the soul. Insofar as he views himself as a battlefield of opposing values, self-overcoming is meant to capture his capacity to extricate himself from the prevailing values of his age, in order to realize his 'higher', more vitalistic, affective existence. Of course, what Nietzsche is so eager to overcome is the Christian world-view, especially its commitment to the 'ascetic ideal' and its '*ressentiment* morality' which impede human excellence. But, in this declaration of war on Christianity, the real battle commences in the soul, where the individual's capacity to endure the most diverse drives will determine the range of his affective existence. The important point is not so much the victory (over the impoverished drives) secured by the 'higher type's' disciplining nature, but the need for the active engagement of the 'higher' with the 'lower' in order to fulfil the task of transforming or overturning decadent values. Although decadence is *overcome*, it also functions as a condition for human flourishing. Together, both are invaluable to the task of self-overcoming since "negating *and destroying* are conditions for saying Yes" (EH XIV:4, KSA 6:368).

An *agonal* impulse is certainly characteristic of the 'higher type'. Once the 'soul' has experienced the great tension of having been exposed to a host of opposing values, it realizes a more heightened affective existence. Nietzsche seems to think that there is something truly life-affirming about the 'soul' experiencing a full range of diverse values and perspectives. The individual capable of enduring the sharpest contrast among antithetical values will display a greater level of self-overcoming, and enjoy a more life-affirming existence. After experiencing a wide array of values, it will be necessary to protect the 'distances' within the soul from such enemies as Christian morality and egalitarianism. Towards this end, Nietzsche appeals to the 'pathos of distance' (*Pathos der Distanz*) as a protective measure. Out of this "*pathos of distance*", he observes, comes "the craving for an ever-new widening of distances within the soul itself, the development of ever higher, rarer, more remote, further-stretching, more comprehensive states...the continual 'self-overcoming of man'" (BGE 257, KSA 5:205). In order to stave off the threat of humanitarian impulses (with the potential to infect even the 'healthy'), the 'pathos of distance' will reflect the natural rank ordering of values (drives) within the soul based on "the ingrained difference between strata" (257). In adhering to the natural hierarchy of value distinctions, the 'pathos of distance' eliminates the threat of a disordered soul—one whose values are the expression of decadent drives. The 'pathos of distance' is essential to Nietzsche's task of self-overcoming insofar as it immunizes the individual from decadent values, and hence, authenticates the philosopher's overcoming of the morality of his time. The preservation of a natural hierarchy of values is a preliminary step toward the development of Nietzsche's positive morality.

Revaluation of All Values

The overcoming of Christian morality receives its penultimate expression in Nietzsche's demand for a 'revaluation of all values' (*Umwerthung aller Werthe*). The first reference to a 'revaluation' in the published writings occurs in *Beyond Good and Evil* (1886) to describe an *Umwerthung* that had already taken place—"the paradoxical formula 'god on the cross'...promised a revaluation of all the values of antiquity" (BGE 46, KSA 5:67). This reference to an historical 'revaluation' parallels Nietzsche's account of the 'slave revolt in morals' discussed in greater detail (and with greater derision) in the First Essay of the *Genealogy* where resentful Christians are accused of inverting noble values. While Nietzsche is intensely critical of this initial revaluation of values, he proudly announces a second attempt at revaluation. In the *Antichrist*, he locates the Renaissance as the seat of this attempted revaluation, this time it is "the *revaluation of Christian values*" (A 61, KSA 6:250), the effort "to bring the *counter*-values, the *noble values* to victory" (61). These two historical events, the one negative (slave morality) and the other positive (noble morality) inform Nietzsche's demand for a revaluation of all values. In short, the revaluation involves a critique of the prevailing, Christian values and an affirmation of an alternative, life-affirming mode of valuation.[22] The demand for a revaluation of values bears a striking resemblance to the motto of Diogenes the Cynic, '*paracharattein to nomisma*', translated literally as 'restamp the coinage' which is a metaphorical expression for starting over again with new values in society.[23]

In his demand for 'revaluation', Nietzsche often emphasizes its destructive aspect, describing it as the "liberation from all moral values" which will then offer hope for a "new morning" (EH VII:1, KSA 6:330). In its earliest phase, the revaluation can be viewed as a declaration of war on the anti-naturalism of Christian morality which has resulted in the diminution of man. Although he places his trust in "*new philosophers*...toward spirits strong enough and original enough to provide the stimuli for opposite valuations and to revalue and invert 'eternal values'" (BGE 203, KSA 5:126), it is clear that Nietzsche identifies himself as a 'new philosopher', and assigns *himself* the task of revaluation. For instance, in *Ecce Homo*, the "revaluation of all values" is defined as "my formula for an act of supreme self-examination (*Selbstbesinnung*) on the part of humanity become flesh and genius in me" (EH XIV:1, KSA 6:365).

What reasons could Nietzsche have for maintaining that "a 'revaluation of all values' is perhaps possible for me alone" (EH I:1, KSA 6:266)? First of all, he realizes that before our current values can be revalued, they must first be *understood*, and he credits his *Genealogy* as offering the best insights into the 'optics of value'. In his review of that work, Nietzsche acknowledges its contribution towards the revaluation: "Three decisive preliminary studies by a psychologist for a revaluation of all values" (EH XI, KSA 6:353). Elsewhere, he reinforces the importance of an historical sense for the task of 'revaluation': "I sought in history the beginning of the construction of reverse ideals" (WP 1041, KSA 13:493). In addition to his self-professed genealogical 'expertise', Nietzsche claims to possess the 'know-how' to '*reverse perspectives*' due to his personal experiences with, and ultimate mastery over the instincts of decadence, which itself, required that he occupy the dual perspectives of the 'sick' and 'healthy' (EH I:1, KSA 6:266). The mastery over the decadent instincts requires a capacity for 'self-overcoming' (and a 'pathos of distance') which is a '*precondition*' (*Vorbedingung*) of the revaluation. Nietzsche explains:

> For the task of a *revaluation of all values* more capacities may have been needed than have ever dwelt together in a single individual—above all, even contrary capacities that had to be kept from disturbing, destroying one another. An order of rank among these

---

22 Later, I will discuss Nietzsche's affirmative ethics.

23 See Horst Hutter, "With the 'Nightwatchman of Greek Philosophy': Nietzsche's Way to Cynicism" in *Nietzsche and the Rhetoric of Nihilism*, 1989. Hutter writes: "The phrase '*Umwerthung aller Werthe*' may even be considered a fairly complete rendition of the kynic phrase 'paracharattein to nomisma,' both denotatively and connotatively." (p.117)

> capacities; distance; the art of separating without setting against one another; to mix nothing, to 'reconcile' nothing; a tremendous variety that is nevertheless the opposite of chaos. (EH II:9, KSA 6:294)

In acknowledging 'self-overcoming' and a 'pathos of distance' as an essential preliminary step toward the goal of revaluation, Nietzsche is maintaining that only a 'healthy' type of person can instigate or inspire a revaluation of all values. It would seem then that the individual capable of uncovering Christian morality, overcoming the instincts of decadence, and establishing an order of rank of his drives, all prerequisites for a revaluation, must himself, be a model of human flourishing of some sort. Of course, Nietzsche privileges his own 'genius' and talent for exposing the 'mendaciousness of millennia', and serving as a catalyst for a revaluation. Is it not the case then that human flourishing is not only a consequence of the revaluation, but also a precondition of it? I will return to this point later.

How is Nietzsche's perfectionism related to the task of revaluation? It is worth noting that while the expression 'revaluation of all values' is a signature *leitmotif* from the writings of 1888,[24] 'perfectionism' is a term that Nietzsche never used to describe his project. Yet, *if* perfectionism is to serve as an adequate characterization of Nietzsche's affirmative thinking, then it is important to consider how it relates to his project of a revaluation of all values. Insofar as their main objective is the production of great human beings, it would seem that Nietzsche's *political* perfectionism is a statement of the revaluation. For instance, the revaluation of Christian values (and the democratic movement he associates with them), would give rise to a 'new morning', a radical aristocratic society leading to the fulfillment of his fundamental political aim of producing, by institutional design, exemplary human beings. The expressed intent of a revaluation of values is "to prepare a *reversal of values* for a certain strong kind of man of the highest spirituality and strength of will…" (WP 957, KSA 11:582).

While *political* perfectionism fits nicely with Nietzsche's understanding of a (completed or successful) revaluation of all values insofar as they represent the political task of producing exemplary individuals in a post-Christian epoch, there seems to be a difficulty in equating his *moral* perfectionism with the *early* stage of the revaluation. Viewed from a temporal standpoint, both the *initial* phase of the revaluation and Nietzsche's *moral* perfectionism are projects undertaken in the *present*, in late modernity. But, when we consider the agenda for this early stage of the revaluation (i.e. the task to be performed in the

---

24 Although introduced in the published writings in 1886, the 'revaluation' becomes a serious *leitmotif* in *Ecce Homo*, *Twilight of the Idols*, and the *Antichrist*.

present), it would seem that it is restricted to a *repudiation* of the reigning values. In other words, the *Umwerthung* commences in Nietzsche's own age with a critique of the current values, what he describes as "the No-saying, No-*doing* part [of my task]...the great war" (EH X:1, KSA 6:350). Consequently, one might infer that Nietzsche's *moral* perfectionism is synonymous with this rudimentary stage of the revaluation where the emphasis is placed on a critique of moral values. On this reading, the most that one could offer under the *present* circumstances is an *attack* on the reigning values. As a result, Nietzsche's *moral* perfectionism would be reduced to a *critique of, or resistance to Christian morality, rather than to the creation of new values since value-creation is a task reserved for the future.*

Several commentators have discussed the difficulty in reconciling Nietzsche's *present* demand for the creation of new values with the *future-oriented* task of the revaluation of all values. The problem is that Nietzsche will often speak of value-creation as a legitimate endeavour *today* in decadent, late modernity, but as Robert C. Solomon objects, "There is no context...within which the new virtues we are to 'create' are to be virtues, for a virtue without a practice is of no more value than a word without a language, a gesture without a context."[25] In pronouncing his own age 'decadent', Nietzsche is denied a context for value-creation—there is no '*ethos* of the *Iliad*', or anything like the great cultural harvest of the world of antiquity, the *imperium Roman* or the *Renaissance.* Any attempt to advance new values without a practice leads to "the somewhat pretentious and sometimes absurd self-glorification of nineteenth century German romanticism."[26]

In his interpretation of Nietzsche's *Umwerthung*, Daniel Conway states that the revaluation "does not (and could not) involve the creation *ex nihilo* of new values, which might directly contribute to the founding of a post-Christian epoch."[27] Conway claims that the construction of 'new' values is an option "only to healthy peoples and ages," and that in late modernity Nietzsche "can do no more than challenge and perhaps reverse the reigning values of his age."[28] One reason that both Conway and Solomon deny the plausibility of value-creation in late modernity is that they interpret the act of value-creation as applying exclusively to the *collective* values operating within society (as opposed to the values betraying who one is). From there, they conclude that since Nietzsche brands modernity 'decadent', there is no practice available in which it makes sense to speak of creating new values. Hence, the legislation of new

---

25 Robert C. Solomon, "A More Severe Morality: Nietzsche's Affirmative Ethics", 1986, p.76.

26 Ibid, p.76.

27 Daniel Conway, *Nietzsche's Dangerous Game*, 1997, p.182.

28 Ibid, p.183.

values belongs to a healthy, future age while the inhabitants of modernity must wallow in their own decadence. While I agree that Nietzsche's major preoccupation is the human flourishing resulting from the creation of new values for *society* (or perhaps a return to the old) expressed by means of his *political* perfectionism, there is also room for an understanding of value-creation for the *individual* in late modernity, however 'pretentious' and 'self-glorifying' this may prove to be. A practice is only required when the creation of new values is intended for society in general.

Further consideration of the readings of Conway and Solomon suggests that their interpretation is, in one respect, seriously flawed. For instance, if we construe Nietzsche's initial efforts of revaluation as involving simply a campaign against the prevailing values, then that would mean that Nietzsche would be left with *no* values. Solomon and Conway have ruled out the possibility that Nietzsche is advancing *new* values on the grounds that values can only be created in a future, post-Christian epoch. The consequence of their interpretation is that Nietzsche is living in modernity without any values. Yet, the notion of a value-*less* individual is entirely untenable since it is impossible for any human being to live without values. Even the nihilist, one should note, values himself as one who negates! And, one of Nietzsche's cardinal tenets is that life demands that we posit values of some sort. Indeed, it could be said that human beings are condemned to evaluate. Perhaps a third alternative would be that Nietzsche lived in accordance with the decadent values of his day, but this account must be quickly dismissed, since it would imply that Nietzsche was a 'closet' Christian who dedicated himself to its expulsion or overcoming.

It should be recalled from my discussion from Chapter One that Nietzsche distinguishes between morality understood as the conditions for the life and growth of a *people* (A 25, KSA, 6:194), and a 'private' morality described as "the sum of the conditions of *my* existence which prescribe an *ought* only if I *want myself*."[29] It is this latter conception of morality which commentators have all too often ignored which forms the basis, or so I will argue in the next chapter, of Nietzsche's ethic of human flourishing within modernity.

---

29 Letter to Paul Rée quoted in Kaufmann's introduction to Nietzsche's *Gay Science*, p.20.

5

Nietzsche's Positive *Morality*

Are you satisfied by my concluding [*Twilight of the Idols*] with the Dionysus morality (*Dionysos-Moral*)?

—Letter to Peter Gast, October 30, 1888

Zuerst das Nöthige—und dies so schön und vollkommen als du kannst! 'Liebe das, was nothwendig ist'—amor fati dies wäre meine Moral…

—KSA 9:643

In this chapter, I argue that Nietzsche has a positive morality, an ethic of human flourishing that is applicable to the 'moral interim', the preparatory period leading to his forecasted political perfectionism. Having already discussed Nietzsche's application of the term 'my morality' as an expression of the life-affirming morality belonging to this (self-anointed) exemplar of human excellence in modernity, I turn to a discussion of the specific affirmative ideals he advances: '*amor fati*', 'eternal return', 'give *style* to one's character' and 'become what one is'. In doing so, I challenge the widespread view that Nietzsche is a champion of *self-creation* or *self-fashioning* whose affirmative ideals entail the promotion of human flourishing through an act of free will.[1] Instead, I contend that Nietzsche offers an *anti-voluntaristic* model of human flourishing consistent with both his 'fatalism' and his project of a revaluation of all values.

Before we can proceed with an explication of Nietzsche's positive morality, it will be necessary to clarify his notion of 'fatalism' since it differs from its classical formulation where the individual is understood as the product of predeterministic forces operating in the universe. Classical fatalism is "the belief that all events are necessitated (determined) to happen the way they do in fact happen no matter what we do to try to avoid them or prevent them."[2]

---

1 I discuss Nietzsche's critique of free will in Chapter Two.

2 Peter A. Angeles, *Dictionary of Philosophy*, 1981, p.225.

Nietzsche explicitly rejects this view of fatalism, what he refers to as *Türkenfatalismus*. He writes:

> Mohammedan fatalism (*Türkenfatalismus*) embodies the fundamental error of setting man and fate (*Fatum*) over against one another as two separate things: man, it says, can resist fate and seek to frustrate it, but in the end it always carries off the victory; so that the most reasonable thing to do is to resign oneself or to live just as one pleases. In reality every man is himself a piece of fate; when he thinks to resist fate in the way suggested, it is precisely fate that is here fulfilling itself; the struggle is imaginary, but so is the proposed resignation to fate; all these imaginings are enclosed within fate.—The fear that most people feel in face of the theory of the unfreedom of the will is fear in face of Mohammedan fatalism: they think that man will stand before the future feeble, resigned and with hands clasped because he is incapable of effecting any change in it...The follies of mankind are just as much a piece of fate as are its acts of intelligence: that fear in face of a belief in fate is also fate. You yourself, poor fearful man, are the implacable *moira* enthroned even above the gods that governs all that happens...in you the whole future of the world of man is predetermined: it is of no use for you to shudder when you look upon yourself. (WS 61, KSA 2:580).

In declaring that 'man himself is a piece of fate', Nietzsche is hoping to remove the fears associated with Mohammedan fatalism, fears which give rise to feelings of 'resignation' or 'doing as one pleases' and originate with the false belief in the distinction between man and fate. We can expect, then, that Nietzsche's brand of fatalism will *exclude* its popular construal as 'what will be, will be'. In the above passage, however, there is no definitive statement of Nietzsche's fatalism, just simply a repudiation of a particular form of fatalism.

What is needed now is an explanation of Nietzsche's 'fatalism', his view that "The single human being is a piece of *fatum* from the front and from the rear, one law more, one necessity more for all that is yet to come and to be" (TI 5:6, KSA 6:87). To begin with, this claim was prompted by Nietzsche's response to the naïve demand of moralists who say: "Man *ought* to be such and such!" For Nietzsche, it makes no sense to speak of an 'ought' when "reality shows us an enchanting *wealth of types*..." (6). These remarks suggest that Nietzsche's fatalism emerges from his opposition to the *voluntaristic-based* principles promoted by moral philosophers, principles which conflict with Nietzsche's physiological views, specifically the anti-egalitarian belief that nature has bequeathed different 'types' of human beings, all of whom are immune to moralistic prattle. It is of no use then, according to Nietzsche, to offer moral formulas or principles (what amounts to a *discursive* justification) to convince people of what they *ought* to do. An understanding of Nietzsche's fatalism will require an appreciation of his views on physiology.

Brian Leiter offers the most insightful account of Nietzsche's fatalism, one which recognizes the importance of physiology in Nietzsche's thought.

According to Leiter, Nietzsche's fatalism can be described best as 'causal essentialism', "the doctrine that for any individual substance (e.g. a person or some other living organism) that substance has 'essential' properties that are causally primary with respect to the future history of that substance, i.e. they non-trivially determine the space of possible trajectories for that substance."[3] Leiter distinguishes this position from classical fatalism insofar as causal essentialism does not claim that the particular outcome of a person's life is *necessary*, since it only *circumscribes* trajectories, rather than necessitate any particular one. Taking into account Nietzsche's physiological perspectives, Leiter reiterates Nietzsche's position as the view that "natural facts about a person circumscribe what that person becomes, though, within the limits set by the natural facts, the precise details of what a person becomes depend (causally) upon other factors" and "*that factors other than natural facts about the person may still play a causal role in the trajectory of a person's life—within the limits circumscribed of course, by the natural facts.*"[4]

Nietzsche may not articulate his account of fatalism with the theoretical precision described by Leiter, but he certainly does believe that what a person is (e.g. character, personality, anatomy, values) is determined to a great extent by one's physiological constitution. These facts fix the trajectory of one's life while still allowing for external causal factors (e.g. environment, education). However, these external factors must yield to the limits set by the physiological facts—the latter always being causally primary with respect to a person's life. In the case of the acorn and the oak tree, the acorn determines the specific trajectory to be realized—an oak tree rather than a peach tree. Yet, there are other contributing factors responsible for the 'flourishing' of the oak tree. Nature has determined that the acorn will become an oak tree, not a peach tree, but even still, it makes a difference whether the acorn has been planted in soil or the desert sand. The point here, of course, is that the environment is a significant factor in influencing the possible range of trajectories, whether the oak tree flourishes or wilts, but it cannot alter the fact that the acorn is destined to become an oak tree, rather than a peach tree. Similarly, in the case of a human being, one's physiological facts circumscribe the possible trajectories of his life, but the environment to which one belongs is not predetermined by these facts.

Although he credits '*values*' as being an example of an 'external causal factor', Leiter is not concerned with explaining the importance of moral values or ideals for understanding Nietzsche's affirmative ethics. So, my task in this chapter is to pick up from where Leiter left off. In acknowledging that 'values'

---

3 Brian Leiter, "The Paradox of Fatalism and Self-Creation in Nietzsche", 1998, p.225, my emphasis.

4 Ibid, pp.223–24.

('environment') can influence what we become within the limits set by our natural facts, we can question, as Nietzsche does, how our reigning values have influenced what we have become and to what extent these values (external causes) are conducive to the flourishing of human beings, either collectively, as a particular group, or for certain individuals. The crucial point that needs to be recognized is that *values* matter even in light of Nietzsche's fatalism (i.e. causal essentialism)! Hence, his affirmative ethics will involve promoting those ideals conducive to human flourishing even though Nietzsche realizes that this promotion will be constrained by the natural facts about the person. To clarify then, Nietzsche's promotion of moral ideals will matter, but he will only be able to influence a select group of individuals, the fortunate few who possess the 'right' natural facts (physiological constitution) but whose capacity for greatness has been hitherto thwarted by their exposure to the 'wrong' social values.[5] Nietzsche's positive morality, then, involves his effort to orchestrate the flourishing of these potential 'higher types'. In this chapter, I argue that Nietzsche seeks to influence his select readership through a *performative* justification where he presents the character of Zarathustra (*Thus Spoke Zarathustra*, 1883–1885), and later, his own heroic self from *Ecce Homo* (1888) as exemplars of greatness whose influence will depend on their capacity to impart to his readers a *pathos* for the ideal that they promote.

My reading of Nietzsche as an *anti-voluntarist* has been a theme expressed throughout this study, but is perhaps most forceful when it is contrasted with the popular portrayal of Nietzsche as a prototypical philosopher of self-creation. To begin then, I turn my attention to his affirmative ideals, and discuss how they have been misinterpreted in the secondary literature. From there, I focus on Nietzsche's fatalism and the manner in which he hopes to convey his positive morality.

Nietzsche's Ethic of Human Flourishing

Despite his contempt for modernity, Nietzsche refused to succumb to its decadent mode of valuation. In a letter to Paul Rée,[6] Nietzsche not only confesses to having a 'private morality', but reveals where it can be found—Book IV of *The Gay Science* entitled "Sanctus Januarius". Indeed, within the fifty pages comprising Book IV, one finds the clearest expressions of his affirmative ideals including: '*amor fati*', 'eternal return', 'become what one is', and 'give *style* to one's character', many of which centre on the theme of *self-creation* or *self-fashioning*.

---

5 'Wrong' in the sense of 'not conducive to their flourishing'.

6 See my discussion on Nietzsche's reference to "*meine Moral*" from Chapter One.

Crucial for an understanding of Nietzsche's positive morality is section 335 of *The Gay Science* which, although receiving considerable attention, has been frequently misunderstood. In this passage, Nietzsche encourages his readers to stop dwelling on the "moral value of our actions" and instead "*limit* ourselves to the purification of our opinions and valuations and to the *creation of our own new tables of what is good*" (GS 335, KSA 3:563). Moreover, Nietzsche is adamant that the creation of these new values is reserved for those who "live in the *present*" (335) indicating, contra Conway, that Nietzsche's affirmative ethic is advanced within modernity. As we read on, Nietzsche describes this contemporary ethical task as follows: "We, however, *want to become those we are*—human beings who are new, unique, incomparable, who give themselves laws, who create themselves" (335). It is a commonplace within Nietzsche scholarship to interpret these remarks as the rallying-cry of the prototypical philosopher of self-creation,[7] as one who preaches the creation of one's own self through an act of free will.

Karl Jaspers' important study from 1936 provides one of the earliest readings of Nietzsche as a champion of self-creation. According to Jaspers, "Nietzsche…never doubts that man is free and that he develops himself" and that "man's freedom has its own specific meaning: the freedom of self-realization is simply creation."[8] Nietzsche continues to be heralded within contemporary circles as *the* philosopher of self-creation. For instance, if we consider Alexander Nehamas' influential and 'creative' study, *Nietzsche: Life as Literature*, the author claims that Nietzsche's 'maxim' to "become those we are…human beings who create themselves" (GS 335) is the central theme of *Thus Spoke Zarathustra* which is "constructed around the idea of creating one's own self."[9] This alleged voluntarism is essential to Nehamas' aesthetic model of interpretation which maintains that Nietzsche viewed life itself from the perspective of the artist. According to Nehamas, this aesthetic ideal is captured in our voluntary efforts to give 'style' to our lives. In place of a descriptive ideal of human flourishing, Nehamas proposes that Nietzsche wrote his autobiography, *Ecce Homo*, in an "effort to create an artwork out of himself…His great innovation was to accomplish this end by saying that to create oneself is the most important goal in life…"[10]

---

7 E.g. Karl Jaspers (1965), Alexander Nehamas (1985), Richard Rorty (1989), Peter Berkowitz (1995), J.P. Hattingh (1996), Derek Collins (1997). Two exceptions are Brian Leiter (1998) and Daniel Conway (1997).

8 Karl Jaspers, *Nietzsche: An Introduction to the Understanding of his Philosophical Activity*, trans. C.F. Wallraff and F.J. Schmitz, Baltimore: John Hopkins University Press, 1997, p.154. Originally published as *Nietzsche: Einführung in das Verständnis seines Philosophierens*, Walter de Gruyter and Company, 1936.

9 Alexander Nehamas, *Nietzsche: Life as Literature*, 1985, p.174.

10 Ibid, pp.8, 233–34.

Let us now return to section 335 of *The Gay Science* to determine whether value-creation is an inherently voluntaristic project. To begin with, it should be noted that in his reference to this passage, Nehamas had simply quoted a few sentences which made it appear that those "who give themselves laws, who create themselves" (335) do so by dint of an act of will. We can see, however, from the remainder of the passage that there is reason to reject this reading. Nietzsche goes on to explain:

> To that end [self-creation] we must become the best learners and discoverers of everything that is lawful and necessary in the world: we must become *physicists* in order to be able to be *creators* in this sense—while hitherto all valuations and ideals have been based on *ignorance* of physics or were constructed so as to *contradict* it. Therefore: long live physics! (GS 335, KSA 3:563–64)

What Nietzsche means by 'creation' is a specific reliance on science to determine what is 'lawful and necessary in the world'. If this sounds odd, then it is only because the passage has not been considered in its entirety. After asserting earlier that "every action is unknowable", Nietzsche admits that "our opinions, valuations, and tables of what is good certainly belong among the most powerful levers in the involved mechanism of our actions, but that in any particular case the law of their mechanism is indemonstrable" (335). If we can utilize science to establish the effects of these 'powerful levers' on our actions, then we can with relative certainty identify a 'lawful' pattern between the actions effected by certain values. So, when Nietzsche exhorts us to create 'our own new tables of what is good', he wants us to draw on these scientific results, in order to identify those values which will causally determine actions in a new and life-enhancing manner. The creation of new values then does not occur from within a voluntaristic standpoint. Science cannot reveal the laws behind the mechanisms of our actions for these are indemonstrable, but since values can be causal determinants of our actions, we can ascertain which values prove salutary for the notion of human flourishing that Nietzsche advances. The 'type' of individual who one is may be a fact of nature, but this does not rule out certain environmental determinants such as social values.[11] Since Nehamas refuses to take seriously Nietzsche's comments on physiology, he fails to appreciate Nietzsche's fatalism.[12]

Another passage frequently cited to support the view that Nietzsche is a proponent of self-creation is section 290 of *The Gay Science*. Nietzsche writes:

---

11 It should be pointed out that even the 'choice' to create the values which will causally determine one's life trajectories is, itself, determined by the 'type' of person one is.

12 Nehamas, *Nietzsche: Life as Literature*, 1985, p.120.

> *One thing is needful.*—To 'give style' to one's character—a great and rare art! It is practiced by those who survey all the strengths and weaknesses of their nature and then fit them into an artistic plan until every one of them appears as art and reason and even weaknesses delight the eye. Here a large mass of second nature has been added; there a piece of original nature has been removed—both times through long practice and daily work at it. Here the ugly that could not be removed is concealed; there it has been reinterpreted and made sublime. Much that is vague and resisted shaping has been saved and exploited for distant views…In the end, when the work is finished, it becomes evident how the constraint of a single taste governed and formed everything large and small. Whether this taste was good or bad is less important than one might suppose, if only it was a single taste! (GS 290, KSA 3:530)

Unlike section 335 with its various injunctions, this passage provides a *descriptive* account of the individual who 'gives style' to his character. But, there is nothing in this passage which necessitates a voluntaristic reading. In fact, one finds just the opposite since the 'practice' of 'surveying one's strengths and weaknesses and fitting them into an artistic plan' is ultimately the result of "the constraint of a single taste" which has "*governed* everything large and small" (290). This 'single taste' has nothing to do with an individual's free choice over who he becomes, but rather, is an expression of who one is. Therefore, the 'single taste' is a reflection of a particular human 'type'. In this case, it is only Nietzsche's 'higher types' who fit the description of 'giving style' to their character. The fact that Nietzsche relies on aesthetic expressions (e.g. fitting one's strengths and weaknesses into an *artistic plan*) in his description of styling one's life should not be construed as an endorsement of free will, since Nietzsche does not hold that human freedom is a prerequisite for artistic expression. Conversely, he claims that the artist's realization that everything he does is of *necessity* is responsible for his *creativity* (BGE 213, KSA 5:148).[13] Similarly, when he praises Goethe in *Twilight of the Idols* (1888) for having "*created* himself" (TI 9:49, KSA 6:151), this remark must be read within the context of that work which is decisively fatalistic.[14] Hence, Nietzsche's references to self-creation or creativity should not be read as requiring free will, even though these notions include a *feeling* of freedom.

---

13 "Artists seem to have more sensitive noses in these matters, knowing only too well that precisely when they no longer do anything 'voluntarily' but do everything of necessity, their feeling of freedom, subtlety, full power, of creative placing, disposing, and forming reaches its peak—in short, that necessity and 'freedom of the will' then become one in them" (BGE 213, KSA 5:148).

14 Responding to the moralist's demand that "you ought to be such and such!", Nietzsche writes: "The single human being is a piece of *fatum* from the front and from the rear, one law more, one necessity more for all that is yet to come and to be" (TI 5:6, KSA 6:87). And, presumably, he does not wish to *exclude* Goethe!

That Nietzsche's affirmative ideals are intertwined with his fatalism is evident from his imperative to 'become what one is'. Borrowed from Pindar's *Pythian* 2, 73,[15] the capacity to 'become what you are' (*γένοί οῖος ἐσσί)* is, for Nietzsche, the most distinctive quality of human flourishing. Although there are only five references[16] to the expression in the published writings, the injunction to 'become what one is' figures prominently in Nietzsche's affirmative ethics. In particular, the notion of 'becoming what one is' is so significant for Nietzsche's *Ecce Homo* that he decided to subtitle the work: "How One Becomes What One Is" (*Wie man wird, was man ist*). It is this text, and not *The Gay Science* (where the expression is introduced), which offers the best insights into the meaning of this expression. Written as a sort of philosophical autobiography, Nietzsche begins by announcing his need "to say *who I am*" (EH P:1, KSA 6:257). What is interesting is that throughout *Ecce Homo*, Nietzsche continually discusses his life in *fatalistic* terms. For instance, he begins the first section claiming that "The good fortune of my existence, its uniqueness perhaps, lies in its fatality" (EH I:1, KSA 6:264). Later in the text, he attributes his stay in Rome to "some sort of fatality...at work" (EH IX:4, KSA 6:340). And, in the final chapter, Nietzsche remarks, "It is my fate that I have to be the first *decent* human being" (EH XIV:1, KSA 6:365).

Nietzsche's description of his life as 'fated' is confirmed by the lone passage in *Ecce Homo* where he discusses the meaning of 'becoming what one is'. He writes:

> At this point the real answer to the question, *how one becomes what one is*, can no longer be avoided. And thus I touch on the masterpiece of the art of self-preservation—*of selfishness*...To become what one is, one must not have the faintest notion *what* one is...Morally speaking: neighbor love, living for others, and other things *can* be a protective measure for preserving the hardest self-concern. This is the exception where against my wont and conviction, I side with the 'selfless' drives: here they work in the

15 The original text reads: *genoi' hoios essi mathôn.* Nietzsche leaves out the participle '*mathôn*', but this is not an uncommon practice. During the early editorial process, even some Alexandrian scholars omitted the participle. The inclusion of the participle would render the following English expression: "since you have learned what you are, become that person" or "become such a person as you have learned to be." I owe this point to Derek Collins, "On the Aesthetics of the Deceiving Self in Nietzsche, Pindar, and Theognis", *Nietzsche-Studien*, 1997, p.294.

16 I was able to locate the following references: GS 270, 335; Z IV:1; EH 'Subtitle'; EH II:9. The phrase also appears in letters. For example, in a letter to Lou Salomé dated end of August, 1882: "Lastly, my dear Lou, the old, deep, heartfelt plea: *become the being you are*!", in Middleton, p.191. And, in a letter to Carl von Gersdorff dated November 24 and December 1, 1867, Nietzsche explains that he included the expression 'become what you are' as an epigram for an essay he had just completed entitled: *De fontibus Laertii Diogenis.* See Middleton, p.29.

> service of *self-love, of self-discipline.* The whole surface of consciousness—consciousness *is* a surface—must be kept clear from all great imperatives. Beware even of every great word, every great pose! So many dangers that the instinct comes too soon to 'understand itself'—.Meanwhile the organizing 'idea' that is destined to rule keeps growing deep down—it begins to command; slowly it leads us *back* from side roads and wrong roads; it prepares *single* qualities before giving any hint of the dominant task, 'goal' (*Ziel*), 'aim' (*Zweck*), 'meaning' (*Sinn*). (EH II:9, KSA 6:293–94)

For Nietzsche, 'becoming what one is' requires that 'one not have the faintest notion *what* one is', and accompanying this state of ignorance is 'selfishness' or egoism (e.g. self-love, self-discipline). The emphasis on selfishness reinforces the idea that human excellence is a matter of one's personal well-being. Nietzsche denies, however, that personal well-being is attainable through our volitional efforts. In particular, he claims that consciousness is not a contributing factor to one's self-development: it must "be kept clear of all great imperatives" (9). There is no conscious effort involved, then, in becoming what one is. Instead, it is *drives* which work in the service of self-love and self-discipline. To 'become what one is' requires "the organizing 'idea'" which grows "deep down—it begins to command" (9). The reference to "deep down" can be traced to *Beyond Good and Evil* where Nietzsche explains that although "learning changes us…at the bottom of us, really 'deep down,' there is something unteachable, some granite of spiritual *fatum*, of predetermined decision and answer to predetermined selected questions" (BGE 231, KSA 5:170). Therefore, the creativity spoken of in section 335 of *The Gay Science* is not the product of one's free will, but is a product of one's *fated* physiological constitution. Nietzsche may speak of creativity, self-mastery, self-discipline but the mastery or disciplining of oneself is merely the product of another drive (i.e. a ruling or commanding drive).[17] In the end, "our values…grow out of us with the necessity with which a tree bears fruit" (GM P:2, KSA 5:248). Hence, one 'becomes what one is' without any concerted effort (i.e. no goal-directed self-fashioning), because what one becomes is out of 'necessity', the result of unconscious instinctual operations.[18]

---

17 See Nietzsche's discussion of the six means of combating the vehemence of a drive in *Daybreak* 109. He writes: "*that* one *desires* to combat the vehemence of a drive at all, however, does not stand within our power; nor does the choice of any particular method; nor does the success or failure of this method. What is clearly the case is that…our intellect is only the blind instrument of *another drive* which is a *rival* of the drive whose vehemence is tormenting us" (D 109, KSA 3:98). See also WP 481, KSA 12:315; WP 966, KSA 11:289.

18 See Claudia Crawford, "Nietzsche's Physiology of Ideological Criticism", in Clayton Koelb (ed.), *Nietzsche as Post-Modernist: Essays Pro and Contra*, Albany: State University of New York Press, 1990, p.165.

In his reading of this passage from *Ecce Homo* and section 290 of *The Gay Science*, Derek Collins identifies a conflict between Nietzsche's view of agency, and the imperatives of creating and giving style to oneself. In particular, he explains that the goal of self-creation is compromised by Nietzsche's problematized notion of agency citing a "tension between Nietzsche's goal-directed aesthetics of the self and his resistance to an overt systematization of those aesthetics."[19] Yet, the closest that Collins comes to appreciating the fatalistic element in Nietzsche's thought is the admission that what drives self-creation must be located outside of agency, adding that, "the actual source for this impetus is not named" but that it is "somewhere in the depths."[20] But, Nietzsche is *not* silent about what lies hidden 'in the depths', and so it is the failure to treat seriously his views on physiology (especially his reconceptualized 'subject') which perpetuates the voluntaristic readings in the secondary literature. This oversight led Collins to (mis)interpret the notion of 'becoming what one is' as being identical to the creation of new tables of the good whereby "we will be actively involved in our own self-fashioning, in destroying and at the same time creating normative values."[21] Following Nehamas, Collins claims that "self-creation" and "giving style to one's character" are "both organically related to the process of becoming what one is."[22]

Leslie P. Thiele offers a more plausible reading of 'become what one is' (although he mistakenly writes 'become *who* one is'),[23] one which takes account of the significance of *drives* in determining the nature of the individual. He writes: "Without doubt Nietzsche believed the individual to be a product of nature…the bearer of innate drives and valuations that can be neither created nor destroyed."[24] These drives cannot be created since human greatness is decided at birth, it is a matter of inheritance. According to Thiele's interpretation, external influences (e.g. education and environment) are merely the means of nurturing the greatness that in rare individuals has been predetermined, in the same way that "to produce an oak tree one must start with an acorn, not a mustard seed."[25] Only the noble individual will be preoccupied with the development of his potential which, as Thiele notes, is a never-ending process of self-overcomings. Despite his sensitivity to the higher type's *fated* existence, Thiele denies any sort of tension:

---

19 Collins, 1997, p.299.

20 Ibid, p.299.

21 Ibid, p.277.

22 Ibid, p.294.

23 Nietzsche does not write "*wer*" (who), but "*was*" (what).

24 Leslie P. Thiele, 1990, p.207.

25 Ibid, p.208.

> This imperative of self-development does not contradict Nietzsche's tenet of innate determination. Growth is nothing but the rearrangement of drives...The players remain the same, but they are reorganized...Great style, for Nietzsche, is not something everyone can achieve. Organized mediocrity is still mediocrity. Just as the caliber of society's highest exemplars determines the value of that society, so too the caliber of the inner drives, assuming they are correctly ordered, determines the greatness of the individual.[26]

There is much to admire in Thiele's discussion of Nietzsche's maxim 'become what one is', but like the previous commentators to whom I have referred, Thiele claims that the heroic disposition is active in the cultivation of one's excellence. But, for Nietzsche, the only hero (if it even makes sense to call the 'self' a hero) is the master or ruling drive, for only it is responsible for the 'ordering'; it alone accounts for individual greatness. In the end, Thiele associates Nietzsche's dictum "Become who you are" with "living one's life as a work of art."[27] Yet, he departs from traditional voluntaristic readings in claiming that "the self is not so much created as unfolded."[28]

Daniel Conway, on the other hand, has contributed significantly to debunking the traditional reading of Nietzsche as a 'radical voluntarist'. In his examination of Nietzsche's critique of voluntarism, Conway mentions Nietzsche's opposition to the 'traditional' view of human agency as "linked to the causal efficacy of the will" and he correctly identifies Nietzsche's notion of human flourishing as an "expression of one's physiological destiny."[29] Despite his concern to undermine voluntaristic readings of Nietzsche, Conway argues on the basis of section 360 of *The Gay Science* that Nietzsche makes an allowance for the limited volitional expression of one's native vitality.[30] In this passage, Nietzsche draws a distinction between 'two kinds of causes':

> I have learned to distinguish the cause of acting from the cause of acting in a particular way, in a particular direction, with a particular goal. The first kind of cause is a quantum of dammed up energy that is waiting to be used up somehow, for something, while the second kind is, compared to this energy, something quite insignificant, for the most part a little accident in accordance with which this quantum 'discharges' itself in one particular way—a match versus a ton of powder. Among these little accidents and 'matches' I include 'purposes'...They are relatively random, arbitrary, almost indifferent in relation to the tremendous quantum of energy that presses...to be used up somehow. People are accustomed to consider the goal (purposes, vocations, etc.) as the *driving force*, in keeping with a very ancient error; but it is merely the *directing* force—one

26 Ibid, pp.209–10.

27 Ibid, p.215.

28 Ibid, p.215.

29 Daniel Conway, *Nietzsche's Dangerous Game*, 1997, p.52–3.

30 Ibid, p.55.

> has mistaken the helmsman for the steam. And not even always the helmsman, the directing force. Is the 'goal' (*Ziel*), the 'purpose' (*Zweck*) not often enough a beautifying pretext, a self-deception of vanity after the event that does not want to acknowledge that the ship is *following* the current into which it has entered accidentally? that it 'wills' to go that way *because it—must?* that is has a direction, to be sure, but—no helmsman at all? (GS 360, KSA 3:607-8)

Conway argues that human volition (however limited) enters the picture in Nietzsche's account of the second cause, the cause of acting in a particular way, where Nietzsche likens agency to a 'directing force'. "The humble helmsman", Conway observes, "cannot possibly generate sufficient energy to propel the vessel he steers, but he can nevertheless influence the ship's initial course and ultimate destination."[31] But, Conway does not explain how such an 'influence' is possible given that Nietzsche considers the directing force (i.e. the volitional resources of the helmsman) as "quite insignificant", as a "little accident" compared to the driving force.[32]

According to Nietzsche, it is a common prejudice to regard intentions or purposes as the 'driving force', since in actuality they are merely the '*directing* force', hence "one has mistaken the helmsman for the steam" (360). Conway mistakenly claims, however, that the reference to the helmsman as the 'directing force' implies some level of volition. But, for Nietzsche, the volitional activity traditionally attributed to the helmsman is "a self-deception of vanity" suggesting instead that the helmsman's course is predetermined, the ship goes that way because it "*must*", and that in the final analysis there is "no helmsman at all". Recall for instance, Nietzsche's description of the higher type: "a well-turned out human being...*must* perform certain actions...he carries the order, which he represents physiologically" (TI 6:2, KSA 6:89). Nietzsche even describes his own overcoming of decadence as outside the sphere of volition: "I took myself in hand, I made myself healthy again: the condition for this—every physiologist would admit that—is *that one be healthy at bottom*" (EH I:2, KSA 6:266).

The preceding remarks suffice to discredit the view that Nietzsche is a 'radical voluntarist'. At the same time, I have shown that human flourishing is essentially the product of one's physiological constitution. I would like to return now to a discussion of Nietzsche's affirmative 'ideals' from the fourth book of *The Gay Science* which centre on the *attitude* to life exemplified by the 'higher type'. In the opening section of Book IV Nietzsche announces: "I want to learn more and more to see as beautiful what is necessary in things; then I shall be

---

31 Ibid, p.55.

32 By 'driving force', Nietzsche presumably means the subconscious network of drives and impulses.

one of those who make things beautiful. *Amor fati*: let that be my love henceforth!" (GS 276, KSA 3:521). The same sentiment is conveyed by Nietzsche's 'doctrine' of the eternal return[33] from section 341 of *The Gay Science*. In that famous passage, the thought of eternal return is presented as a 'test' of some sort. Nietzsche asks us to imagine being approached by a demon who proposes the idea of eternal return, and then questions our response to the thought: "how well disposed would you have to become to yourself and to life *to crave nothing more fervently* than this ultimate confirmation and seal" (GS 341, KSA 3:570)? And, in *Ecce Homo*, Nietzsche refers to the thought of eternal return as "a formula of the highest affirmation" (EH IV:2, KSA 6:311). The twin teachings of '*amor fati*' and 'eternal return' are intended to capture the exemplary individual's attitude towards life in contrast to Christianity's hostility towards life.

But, why does Nietzsche think that human flourishing rests on one's capacity to affirm, embrace, and to love life in its totality? One might admire his motivation to erase *ressentiment* and the ascetic ideal from the world's stage without agreeing with him that '*amor fati*' and 'eternal return' are adequate replacements for the ascetic ideal. It seems to me that a true 'test' of character or greatness does not involve an affirmation of life in all its colours[34] for clearly there are objectionable and disastrous features of existence which we should acknowledge as such, instead of calling "good…even the most terrible and questionable qualities of life" (WP 1050, KSA 13:224). A nobler attitude would be to affirm life *in spite of* its objectionable elements, to prefer that certain events not happen, but in case they do, to face them with strength and courage. My suggestion implies the recognition and overcoming of mishaps, whereas Nietzsche's ideal does not even regard them as mishaps. In fact, Nietzsche has no grounds for conceiving them as 'mishaps'. Instead, his ideal amounts to the beautification and glorification of even the most hideous aspects of existence, an ideal which may be based on his view of the inter-relatedness of events.[35]

---

33 The idea that whatever happens, has happened an infinite number of times in the past, and will continue to happen infinitely, precisely in the same way as it is happening now. There is a voluminous amount of secondary literature on the 'eternal return' and I have no interest in adding to it. My discussion of eternal return is limited to how the 'doctrine' relates to Nietzsche's positive morality.

34 One could presumably affirm eternal return out of weak motives (e.g. fear of death). So, it doesn't appear that eternal return is a reliable indicator of the attitude to life of exemplary individuals.

35 See *Zarathustra*, "Have you ever said Yes to a single joy? O my friends, then you said Yes too to *all* woe. All things are entangled, ensnared, enamored; if ever you wanted one thing twice, if ever you said, 'You please me, happiness! Abide moment!' then you

Finally, one may question why such a proud atheist as Nietzsche would choose the capacity to affirm the continual turning upside down of 'the eternal hourglass of existence' as a measure of greatness. It is rather odd, as Simon May observes, that "Nietzsche does not make the affirmation of a *finite* existence, his test of strength…"[36] especially given his remarks from the opening section of *Schopenhauer as Educator*: "In his heart every man knows quite well that, being unique, he will be in the world only once and that no imaginable chance will for a second time gather together into a unity so strangely variegated an assortment as he is: he knows it but he hides it like a bad conscience" (SE 1, KSA 1:337).[37]

Nietzsche never expressed any concern or doubt over the legitimacy of his formula for the affirmation of life. He confidently and repeatedly expressed his ideal in terms of an affirmation of the world as it is, without subtraction or exception, and desiring its eternal repetition—and baptized it with the name 'Dionysus'. The doctrine of '*amor fati*' was the accepted formula (the highest state a philosopher can attain) underlying Nietzsche's Dionysianism. For Nietzsche, the Dionysian was emblematic of the overflowing Hellenic instinct, whose excess of energy generated a 'Saying-Yes' to life. But lest we forget, Nietzsche insists that he *is* the philosopher embodying the doctrine of "*amor fati*"—"that one wants nothing to be different, not forward, not backward, not in all eternity" (EH II:10, KSA 6:297). Indeed, he states that "*amor fati* is my inmost nature" (EH XIII:4, KSA 6:363). Surely, one might claim, he has fooled no one in maintaining the posture of an exemplary human being. In fact, reading Nietzsche's self-portrait from *Ecce Homo* gives the impression that he suffered from delusions of grandeur in addition to his illness-related sufferings. While it is undeniable that he embellished his life story, the capacity to influence others does not depend on his *own* success at attaining greatness.

In *Ecce Homo*, Nietzsche's 'noble lie' did not extend to all facets of his life, as there is no evidence to suggest that he was insincere in his description of his life as fated, even if he grossly exaggerated the precise details of his life. The crucial question now is what is the relation between Nietzsche's affirmative ideals ('*amor fati*', 'eternal return', 'become what one is') against the backdrop of his fatalism. How can we even extract an ethic rooted in fatalism?

---

wanted *all* back. All anew, all eternally, all entangled, ensnared, enamored—oh then you loved the world" (Z IV:19,10, KSA 4:402).

36 Simon May, *Nietzsche's Ethics and his War on 'Morality'*, Oxford: Oxford University Press, 1999, p.121.

37 By this time, Nietzsche was already familiar with the idea of eternal return but had not yet appropriated it as his own. See, for instance, the preceding meditation, *On the Uses and Disadvantages of History for Life*, (KSA 1:261), where Nietzsche attributed (a form of) the doctrine to the Pythagoreans.

Performative Justification: *Zarathustra* and *Ecce Homo*

In ruling out individual autonomy, one wonders how an ethic can be derived from Nietzsche's view of the unaccountability for one's actions. In the end, we seem to be left with the following (non-ethical) consequence:

> One may no longer praise, no longer censure, for it is absurd to praise and censure nature and necessity. As he [the man of knowledge] loves a work of art but does not praise it since it can do nothing for itself, so must he stand before the actions of men and before his own. He can admire their strength, beauty, fullness, but he may not find any merit in them. (HH 107, KSA 2:103)

Moral qualities do not apply to objects of nature, including human beings. "We do not accuse nature of immorality when it sends us a thunderstorm and makes us wet: why do we call the harmful man immoral? Because in the latter case we assume a voluntarily commanding free will, in the former necessity" (HH 102, KSA 2:99).

In *Ecce Homo*, Nietzsche presents himself as an object of nature deserving admiration—as if to say: 'look at me, I am a gift of nature, a physiological success, a healthy, exuberant, life-affirming human being who instinctively chooses the ideal means for my flourishing (e.g. the right climate, recreation, diet, etc.)—greatness is my destiny!' Leaving aside the self-aggrandizement, how could 'admiration' (for Nietzsche or anyone else for that matter) be the cornerstone of an ethics? In fact, the *flourishing* of 'herd morality' suggests that the types of individuals that Nietzsche glorifies are precisely those *not* admired by society in general. A more reasonable conclusion given Nietzsche's assertion that human excellence is primarily inherent (inborn) is that his 'ethics' is merely reducible to the *classification* or *categorization* of different 'types' of human beings. In other words, Nietzsche can do no more than 'grade' human beings ('healthy' or 'decadent') according to their physiological success or failure, in the same way that a jeweller 'grades' stones. The only message here, and it certainly does not appear to be an 'ethical' one, is that you, the individual, are fated to be the person you are. The problem with this conclusion, however, is that it undermines Nietzsche's demand for a 'revaluation of all values'. And, it is worthwhile noting that the strongest expression of Nietzsche's fatalism occurs in the writings of 1888, the same year that he emphasizes the task of 'revaluation'.

The difficulty then is to explain how Nietzsche can promote an affirmative ethic, as well as demand intelligibly a revaluation of values when the lives of human beings are scripted according to their physiological destiny. Like most philosophers, Nietzsche's goal to is persuade his readership, *but* in claiming that a human being is a piece of *fatum*,[38] Nietzsche is not entitled to appeal to moral formulas as a means of persuasion. In fact, throughout his writings, he avoids any moral theorizing while still speaking with an authoritative voice. I shall conclude this study by arguing that Nietzsche does promote a positive morality which is consistent with his fatalism, and which can account for his project of a 'revaluation of all values'.

Although couched in fatalistic terms, Nietzsche's ethic of human flourishing can only be justified *performatively* as opposed to the common emphasis on *discursive* justification. The promotion of human excellence is not a matter of providing formulas or principles describing what one 'ought' to do, but by serving as a model to be emulated. Nietzsche's ethic can only succeed if he imparts to the reader a *pathos* for the ideal that he (supposedly) bodies forth.[39] In what follows, I claim that there are two texts responsible for Nietzsche's *performative* promotion of human excellence, *Zarathustra* and *Ecce Homo*.

Having introduced his major ethical ideals in Book IV of *The Gay Science* (1882), Nietzsche devoted his next work, *Thus Spoke Zarathustra* (1883–85), to the advancement of those ideals through the character of Zarathustra. In the Prologue, informed by the death of God, Zarathustra becomes a crusader of human excellence. Zarathustra preaches the ideal of the *Übermensch* in an effort to convince his auditors that salvation is found in man, not God. But, Zarathustra's error lies in the assumption that the announcement of the death of God will automatically lead his auditors to a revaluation of values. At this early stage in the text, Zarathustra relies on a voluntarist standpoint for the promotion of the *Übermensch* ideal. Yet, there is also an *anti*-voluntaristic element at work here. For example, the Prologue documents Zarathustra's failure to convince his auditors to renounce their belief in God even though they 'know' that God is dead. This 'knowledge' does not suffice for them to abandon their belief in God. It is at this point that Zarathustra realizes that a refutation of values is useless if the individuals who live according to these values are *unable* to reject them. When Zarathustra descended from the mountains to speak to the people, he had no idea that he would be preaching to the 'sick and decaying'. From there on in, he resolves to speak only to companions, not to

38 TI 6:2, KSA 6:89.

39 My reading should not be confused with Nehamas' interpretation which claims that in *Ecce Homo*, Nietzsche presented himself as an 'ideal character', that he created himself as a work of art. Nehamas is wrong to view *Ecce Homo* as a voluntaristic expression of Nietzsche's notion of human flourishing. This text, as I have shown, portrays a Nietzsche whose existence is described as fated.

the people, realizing that a discursive critique alone lacks the transformative effect he desires.

At the end of Part II, Zarathustra is in a rather sorry state having failed as an educator. Even worse, Zarathustra himself was forced to abandon the *Übermensch* ideal having been touched by the Soothsayer's[40] nihilistic prophecy: "*All is empty, all is the same, all has been.*" In Part III, however, Zarathustra again promotes the *Übermensch* ideal but realizes that his auditors will not be moved by discourse, but only by his ability to present himself as a concrete example of a flourishing, *übermenschlich* way of life. Still, the problem is that Zarathustra's ambition to become an *Übermensch* is presented in a voluntaristic fashion (as a transformation requiring an act of free will) which perhaps explains his lack of success at promoting human flourishing. At some point in Part III, Zarathustra realized that the promotion of human excellence will require that he become the *Übermensch*, and in Part IV we encounter a Zarathustra personifying Nietzsche's ideal of human flourishing. Although Nietzsche does not reveal what triggered the transformation, it is safe to assume that Zarathustra must have been 'healthy at bottom'. Zarathustra's promotion of human excellence will prove effective if it succeeds in convincing his auditors that the life of Zarathustra is preferable to their own, a form of persuasion that discourse alone could not generate. The success of the 'teaching', then, depends on the text's (Zarathustra's) capacity to influence Nietzsche's readership to an alternative way of life.

In *Ecce Homo*, Nietzsche decides to bring his 'literature' to 'life', presenting *himself* as a living example of human flourishing. Just as Zarathustra served as a model to be emulated, Nietzsche now hopes to convey to his readers a *pathos* for human excellence by announcing who he is. By this time, however, his self-portrait is painted in exclusively fatalistic terms. In order to derive an understanding of how Nietzsche was blessed by nature, we need to consider his (self-professed) *übermenschlich* qualities. He writes:

> What is it, fundamentally, that allows us to recognize *who has turned out well*? That a well-turned-out person (*ein wohlgerathner Mensch*) pleases our senses, that he is carved from wood that is hard, delicate, and at the same time smells good. He has a taste only for what is good for him; his pleasure, his delight cease where the measure of what is good for him is transgressed. He guesses what remedies avail against what is harmful; he exploits bad accidents to his advantage; what does not kill him makes him stronger. Instinctively, he collects from everything he sees, hears, lives through, *his* sum: he is a principle of selection, he discards much. He is always in his own company, whether he associates with books, human beings, or landscapes: he honors by *choosing*, by *admitting*, by *trusting*. He reacts slowly to all kinds of stimuli, with the slowness which long caution

---

40 The Soothsayer is an allusion to Schopenhauer.

> and deliberate pride have bred in him: he examines the stimulus that approaches him, he is far from meeting it halfway. He believes neither in 'misfortune' nor in 'guilt'; he comes to terms with himself, with others; he knows how to *forget*—he is strong enough; hence everything *must* turn out for his best...I have just described *myself*. (EH I:2, KSA 6:267)

Nietzsche credits his greatness to being a 'well-turned-out person' which amounts to being a *physiological* success—'being healthy at bottom'. It should be emphasized though that however contagious this conception of greatness may be, it is powerless against the physiological *failures*.[41] As a transformative doctrine, it has the potential to influence only the few, Nietzsche's higher types. In all likelihood, the majority of people would not be transformed by Nietzsche's self-portrait which he knew quite well. For this reason, his efforts of performative persuasion are directed only to potential candidates for human flourishing whose potential excellence has been thwarted by living within a society whose values are inimical to their flourishing. The reigning, decadent social values are external causal factors which place the higher type's inherent, vitalistic affective existence in a state of remission (without undermining his 'natural' or inborn greatness). Presumably, Nietzsche's powers of persuasion would be reserved for those who possess this vital store of affective energy, but who have thus far lacked the stimulus to ignite it.

My reading of Nietzsche as offering a performative justification of an ethic of human flourishing is consistent with his fatalism, and his demand for a revaluation of all values. In the absence of any volitional resources on the part of humankind, Nietzsche recognized the importance of implementing the right 'conditions of existence' to promote human flourishing. As an exemplar of human flourishing in late modernity, Nietzsche took up the task of influencing performatively those other 'lucky strikes', individuals whom nature endowed with a similar *übermenschlich* physical constitution. The success of the revaluation of values lies in the capacity of these modern-day exemplars of excellence to generate optimism for what humankind can become, until the much sought-after arrival of the 'philosophical legislator'. If Nietzsche fails to impart a *pathos* of excellence to his select readership then their potential for greatness will be in vain, as will any hopes for a revaluation of all values.

---

41 Nietzsche did not think that a discursive justification, say, preaching a biological, physiological teaching of the superiority of certain human beings, would be persuasive since having 'knowledge' is not enough to secure acceptance. Just as Zarathustra failed to convince his auditors to forfeit their belief in God even when they 'knew' that God was dead, so too would Nietzsche if he relied exclusively on discourse. And, so this explains Nietzsche's motivation for offering a *performative* justification.

Conclusion

The aim of this chapter has been to show that Nietzsche has an affirmative ethics. Yet, even his own admission in his letters, notebooks, and published writings to having a 'morality', what he alternately refers to as 'my morality', 'private morality', or 'Dionysian morality' will not prove convincing for many readers. Moral philosophy, they will insist, has to do with 'human activities that are looked upon as good/bad, right/wrong, correct/incorrect', 'conforming to the accepted rules of what is considered right', 'having the capacity to be influenced by an awareness of right and wrong', 'the capacity to influence others according to rules of conduct judged right or wrong' or 'the manner in which one behaves in relationship with others'.[42] The lack of a carefully articulated practical ethics will certainly disappoint many readers. Instead, Nietzsche shifts the emphasis from 'actions' to 'actor', specifically, the 'type' of person whom nature has bequeathed. "It is not actions that prove him [the noble human being]—actions are always open to many interpretations, always unfathomable…*The noble soul has reverence for itself*" (BGE 287, KSA 5:233). As we have seen, Nietzsche's ethics is person-oriented, centering on the type of human being who has 'turned-out-well'. In identifying himself as such a person, Nietzsche has shown that his affirmative ideals are applicable within modernity, even if his fundamental concern lies in the future-oriented (political) task of the institutionalized production of exemplary human beings.

The popular reading of Nietzsche as a philosopher of self-creation was vehemently denounced in favour of an anti-voluntaristic model of human flourishing. In addressing the challenge of providing a positive morality amidst a fatalistic view of human beings, I argued that Nietzsche turns to a *performative* justification where he presents the character of Zarathustra, and later, his own life, as a model of human excellence to be emulated by those similarly constituted. The question as to why we should accept Nietzsche's morality or why we should revalue values is a position that cannot be *argued* for. Commenting on his writings, Nietzsche says that they are addressed to the few, to "those who can breathe the air of my writings…one must be made for it" (EH P:3, KSA 6:258). To readers who share Nietzsche's moral sensibilities and value the flourishing of the higher type, his 'teaching' may prove inspirational and transforming, and for those readers unmoved by his rhetoric, they reveal themselves to be a different type of individual. Having boasted, "I am no man. I am dynamite" (EH XIV:1, KSA 6:365), Nietzsche left it to the reader to determine whether he succeeded in igniting a *pathos* of human flourishing or

---

42 Peter Angeles, *Dictionary of Philosophy*, New York: Barnes and Noble, 1981, pp.178–79.

whether his misplaced confidence in a select readership reduced him to a mere 'firecracker'.

Bibliography

Secondary Sources

Andler, Charles. *Nietzsche, sa vie et sa pensée*, Paris: Éditions Gallimard, 1958.

Andreas-Salomé, Lou. *Ma vie.* Paris: Presses Universitaires de France, 1977.

Angeles, Peter. *Dictionary of Philosophy.* New York: Barnes and Noble, 1981.

Anscombe, G.E.M. "Modern Moral Philosophy." *Philosophy*, vol. XXXIII, January 1958.

Ansell-Pearson, Keith. "Nietzsche and the Problem of the Will in Modernity" in *Nietzsche and Modern German Thought.* K. Ansell-Pearson, ed. London: Routledge, 1991.

———. *Nietzsche Contra Rousseau.* Cambridge: Cambridge University Press, 1991.

———. *An Introduction to Nietzsche as a Political Thinker: The Perfect Nihilist.* Cambridge: Cambridge University Press, 1994.

Aquinas, St. Thomas. *Selected Writings of St. Thomas Aquinas.* Robert Goodwin, trans. New York: MacMillan, 1965.

Aristotle. *Introduction to Aristotle.* Richard McKeon, ed. New York: Modern Library, 1947.

Atwell, John. *Ends and Principles in Kant's Moral Thought.* Boston: Martinus Nijhoff, 1986.

———. *Schopenhauer: The Human Character.* Philadelphia: Temple University Press, 1990.

Beccaria Cesare. *On Crimes and Punishments.* Henry Paolucci, ed. and trans. New York: Bobbs-Merrill, 1963.

Bentham, Jeremy. *An Introduction to the Principles of Morals and Legislation.* Wilfrid Harrison, ed. Oxford: Basil Blackwell, 1960.

Bergmann, Frithjof. "Nietzsche's Critique of Morality" in *Reading Nietzsche.* R.C. Solomon and K.M. Higgins, eds. Oxford: Oxford University Press, 1988, pp.29–45.

Bergmann, Peter. *Nietzsche: "The Last Antipolitical German".* Bloomington: Indiana University Press, 1987.

Berkowitz, Peter. *Nietzsche: The Ethics of an Immoralist.* Cambridge, MA: Harvard University Press, 1995.

Bernstein, John A. *Nietzsche's Moral Philosophy.* London: Associated University Presses, 1987.

Blondel, Eric. *Nietzsche: The Body and Culture.* Seán Hand, trans. Stanford: Stanford University Press, 1991.

Brobjer, Thomas. *Nietzsche's Ethics of Character: A Study of Nietzsche's Ethics and its Place in the History of Moral Thinking.* Uppsala, 1995.

Brown, Richard. "Nihilism: Thus Speaks Physiology" in *Nietzsche and the Rhetoric of Nihilism.* T. Darby, B. Egyed, B. Jones, eds. Ottawa: Carleton University Press, 1989.

Burckhardt, Jacob. *The Civilization of the Renaissance in Italy.* London: Phaidon Press, 1995.

Cameron, Frank. "Beyond Pity and Cruelty: Nietzsche's Stoicism." *De Philosophia*, vol. xiii, No.2, Fall-Winter 1997, pp.191–206.

———. "Dionysos contre le crucifié: Le tournant ésthetique de Nietzsche." in *Préparer l'agrégation et le capes de philosophie*, vol. 2. *Dioti* 4, Ellipses, CRDP Midi-Pyrénées, 1998, pp.53–58.

Cartwright, David. "Kant, Schopenhauer, and Nietzsche on the Morality of Pity." *Journal of the History of Ideas*, Jan.–March, 1984, pp.83–98.

———. "Nietzsche's Use and Abuse of Schopenhauer's Moral Philosophy for Life" in *Willing and Nothingness: Schopenhauer as Nietzsche's Educator.* C. Janaway, ed. Oxford: Oxford University Press, 1998, pp.116–150.

———. "Schopenhauer's Narrower Sense of Morality" in *Cambridge Companion to Schopenhauer*. C. Janaway, ed. Cambridge: Cambridge University Press, 1999.

Casey, John. *Pagan Virtue*. Oxford: Oxford University Press, 1990.

Cavell, Stanley. "Aversive Thinking: Emersonian Representations in Heidegger and Nietzsche" in *Conditions Handsome and Unhandsome: The Constitution of Emersonian Perfectionism*. Chicago: University of Chicago Press, 1990, pp.46–57.

Clark, Maudemarie. "Nietzsche's Immoralism and the Concept of Morality" in *Nietzsche, Genealogy, Morality*. Richard Schacht, ed. Berkeley: University of California Press, 1994.

Collins, Derek. "On the Aesthetics of the Deceiving Self in Nietzsche, Pindar, and Theognis." *Nietzsche-Studien*, 1997, pp.276–299.

Conant, James. "Nietzsche's Perfectionism: A Reading of *Schopenhauer as Educator*" in *Nietzsche's Post-Moralism: Essays on Nietzsche's Prelude Philosophy's Future*. Richard Schacht, ed. Cambridge: Cambridge University Press, 2001, pp.181–257.

Conway, Daniel. "Literature as Life: Nietzsche's Positive Morality." *International Studies in Philosophy*, 1989.

———. "A Moral Ideal for Everyone and No One." *International Studies in Philosophy*, Vol.22, No.2, 1990, pp.17–30.

———. "Returning to Nature: Nietzsche's *Götterdämmerung*" in *Nietzsche: A Critical Reader*. Peter Sedgwick, ed. Oxford: Blackwell, 1995.

———. *Nietzsche and the Political*. New York: Routledge, 1997.

———. *Nietzsche's Dangerous Game: Philosophy in the Twilight of the Idols*. Cambridge: Cambridge University Press, 1997.

Crawford, Claudia. "Nietzsche's Physiology of Ideological Criticism" in *Nietzsche as Postmodernist: Essays Pro and Contra*. Clayton Koelb, ed. Albany: State University of New York Press, 1990.

Danto, Arthur. *Nietzsche as Philosopher*. New York: MacMillan, 1965.

———. "Some Remarks on *The Genealogy of Morals*" in *Reading Nietzsche*. R.C. Solomon and K. Higgins, eds. New York and London: Oxford University Press, 1988.

Darby, Tom, Béla Egyed, and Ben Jones, eds. *Nietzsche and the Rhetoric of Nihilism: Essays on Interpretation, Language, and Politics*. Ottawa: Carleton University Press, 1989.

Deleuze, Gilles. *Nietzsche and Philosophy*. Hugh Tomlinson, trans. New York: Columbia University Press, 1983.

Detwiler, Bruce. *Nietzsche and the Politics of Aristocratic Radicalism*. Chicago: University of Chicago Press, 1990.

———. "Nietzschean Self-Creation and the Critique of Liberal Institutions." *International Studies in Philosophy*, 1995.

Donagan, Alan. *The Theory of Morality*. Chicago and London: University of Chicago Press, 1977.

Donnellan, Brendan. *Nietzsche and the French Moralists*. Bonn: Bouvier, 1982.

———. "Friedrich Nietzsche and Paul Rée: Cooperation and Conflict." *Journal of the History of Ideas*, October, 1982, pp.595–612.

Ferry, Luc and A. Renaut, eds. *Why We are Not Nietzscheans*. Robert de Loaiza, trans. Chicago: University of Chicago Press, 1997.

Foot, Philippa. "Nietzsche: The Revaluation of Values" in *Nietzsche: A Collection of Critical Essays*. R.C. Solomon, ed. New York: Doubleday, 1973.

Foucault, Michel. "Nietzsche, Genealogy, History" in *The Foucault Reader*. P. Rabinow, ed. New York: Pantheon Books, 1984.

Fuss, Peter and H. Shapiro, eds. *Nietzsche: A Self-Portrait from His Letters*. Cambridge, MA: Harvard University Press, 1971.

Gilman, Sander, Carole Blair, David J. Parent. *Friedrich Nietzsche on Rhetoric and Language*. Oxford: Oxford University Press, 1989.

Geuss, Raymond. "Nietzsche and Morality." *European Journal of Philosophy*, April 1997, pp.1–20.

Grant, A. *The Ethics of Aristotle*. Two Volumes. London: 1885.

Haar, Michel. *Nietzsche and Metaphysics*. Michael Gendre, trans. Albany: State University of New York Press, 1996.

———. *Par-delà le nihilisme: Nouveaux essais sur Nietzsche*. Paris: Presses Universitaires de France, 1998.

Hamilton, William. *Lectures on Metaphysics*. Vol. 1 of 2. New York: Sheldon and Company, 1880.

Hattingh, J.P. "Living One's Life as a Work of Art." *South African Journal of Philosophy*, 15 (2), May 1996, pp.60–72.

Heckman, Peter. "The Indictment of Morality in *Daybreak*." *International Studies in Philosophy*, 1996, pp.3–14.

Heidegger, Martin. *Nietzsche*. 4 Vols. David Farrell Krell, trans. New York: Harper Collins, 1991.

Honderich, Ted, ed. *The Oxford Companion to Philosophy*. Oxford: Oxford University Press, 1995.

Hunt, Lester. *Nietzsche and the Origin of Virtue*. New York: Routledge, 1991.

Hurka, Thomas. *Perfectionism*. Oxford: Oxford University Press, 1993.

Hutter, Horst. "With the 'Nightwatchman of Greek Philosophy': Nietzsche's Way to Cynicism" in *Nietzsche and the Rhetoric of Nihilism*. T. Darby, B. Egyed, B. Jones, eds. Ottawa: Carleton University Press, 1989.

Janaway, Christopher, ed. *Willing and Nothingness: Schopenhauer as Nietzsche's Educator*. Oxford: Clarendon Press, 1998.

——— ed. *Cambridge Companion to Schopenhauer*. Cambridge: Cambridge University Press, 1999.

Jaspers, Karl. *Nietzsche: An Introduction to the Understanding of his Philosophical Activity*. Charles F. Wallraff and Frederick J. Schmitz, trans. Baltimore: Johns Hopkins University Press, 1997.

Kant, Immanuel. *The Cambridge Edition of the Works of Immanuel Kant: Practical Philosophy*. Mary J. Gregor, trans. and ed. Cambridge: Cambridge University Press, 1999.

Kaufmann, Walter. *Nietzsche: Philosopher, Psychologist, Antichrist*. Princeton: Princeton University Press, 1974.

Krell, David Ferrell. *Infectious Nietzsche*. Bloomington: Indiana University Press, 1996.

Lampert, Laurence. *Nietzsche's Teaching: An Interpretation of Thus Spoke Zarathustra*. New Haven: Yale University Press, 1986.

Lange, Friedrich. *The History of Materialism*. 3 Vols. Ernest C. Thomas, trans. London: Kegan Paul, 1925.

Langsam, Harold. "How to Combat Nihilism: Reflections on Nietzsche's Critique of Morality." *History of Philosophy Quarterly*, April 1997, pp.235–253.

LaRochefoucauld. *Maximes*. London: Arthur L. Humphreys, 1902.

Lea, F.A. *The Tragic Philosopher: A Study of Friedrich Nietzsche*. London, 1957.

Lecky, W.E.H. *History of European Morals*. New York: George Braziller, 1955.

Leiter, Brian. "Morality in the Pejorative Sense: On the Logic of Nietzsche's Critique of Morality." *British Journal of the History of Philosophy*, Feb. 1995, pp.113–145.

———. "Nietzsche and the Morality Critics." *Ethics*, Jan. 1997, pp.250–85.

———. "The Paradox of Fatalism and Self-Creation in Nietzsche" in *Willing and Nothingness: Schopenhauer as Nietzsche's Educator*. C. Janaway, ed. Oxford, 1998, pp.217–257.

———. "Nietzsche and Aestheticism." *Journal of the History of Philosophy* 30, 1992, pp.275–280.

Lippitt, John, ed. *Nietzsche's Futures*. New York: St. Martin's Press, 1999.

MacIntyre, Alasdair. *After Virtue*. Notre Dame: University of Notre Dame Press, 1981.

Magnus, Bernd and K. Higgins, eds. *Cambridge Companion to Nietzsche.* Cambridge: Cambridge University Press, 1996.

May, Simon. *Nietzsche's Ethics and his War on 'Morality'.* Oxford: Oxford University Press, 1999.

Middleton, Christopher, trans. and ed.. *Selected Letters of Friedrich Nietzsche.* Chicago: University of Chicago Press, 1969.

Mill, J.S. *Utilitarianism.* Oskar Piest, ed. New York: Bobbs-Merrill, 1957.

———. *On the Logic of the Moral Sciences.* Henry M. Magid, ed. New York: Bobbs-Merrill, 1965.

———. *On Liberty.* Gertrude Himmelfarb, ed. New York: Penguin Books, 1988.

Moore, Gregory. "Nietzsche, Degeneration, and the Critique of Christianity." *Journal of Nietzsche Studies,* 19, Spring 2000, pp.1–18.

Morgan, George. *What Nietzsche Means.* New York and London: Harper and Row, 1941.

Müller-Lauter, Wolfgang. *Nietzsche: His Philosophy of Contradictions and the Contradictions of His Philosophy.* David J. Parent, trans. Urbana and Chicago: University of Illinois Press, 1999.

Nehamas, Alexander. *Nietzsche: Life as Literature.* Cambridge, MA: Harvard University Press, 1985.

Nielsen, Kai. "Nietzsche as a Moral Philosopher." *Man and World* 6, 1973, pp.182–205.

Nussbaum, Martha. "Pity and Mercy: Nietzsche's Stoicism" in *Nietzsche, Genealogy, Morality.* Richard Schacht, ed. Berkeley: University of California Press, 1994.

Pfeffer, Rose. *Nietzsche: Disciple of Dionysus.* Lewisburg, 1972.

Platts, Mark. *Moral Realities.* New York: Routledge, 1991.

Poole, Ross. "Nietzsche: The Subject of Morality." *Radical Philosophy,* Spring 1990.

Rawls, John. *A Theory of Justice.* Cambridge, MA: Harvard University Press, 1971.

Reboul. Olivier. *Nietzsche critique de Kant.* Paris, 1974.

Rée, Paul. *De l'origine des sentiments moraux.* Michel-Francois Demet, trad. Paris: Presses Universitaires de France, 1982.

Rorty, Richard. *Contingency, Irony and Solidarity.* Cambridge: Cambridge University Press, 1989.

Ross, W.D. *Aristotle.* New York: Meridian Books, 1959.

Rosset, Clément. *Joyful Cruelty: Toward a Philosophy of the Real.* David F. Bell, trans. Oxford: Oxford University Press, 1993.

Schacht, Richard. *Nietzsche.* London and New York: Routledge, 1983.

——— ed. *Nietzsche, Genealogy, Morality: Essays on Nietzsche's* Genealogy of Morals. Berkeley: University of California Press, 1994.

Schopenhauer, Arthur. *Essay on the Freedom of the Will.* Konstantin Kolenda, trans. New York: Bobbs-Merrill, 1960.

———. *The World as Will and Representation,* vols. 1 and 2. E.F.J. Payne, trans. New York: Dover Publications, 1969.

———. *Manuscript Remains: Early Manuscripts (1804–1818).* E.F.J. Payne, trans. Oxford: Berg, 1988.

———. *On the Basis of Morality.* E.F.J. Payne, trans. Providence, R.I.: Berghahn Books, 1995.

Sidgwick, Henry. *The Methods of Ethics.* London: MacMillan, 1907.

Slote, Michael. "Nietzsche and Virtue Ethics." *International Studies in Philosophy,* XXX:3, 1998.

Small, Robin. "Ressentiment, Revenge, and Punishment: Origins of the Nietzschean Critique." *Utilitas,* 9 (1), March 1997, pp.39–58.

Solomon, Robert C. *Nietzsche: A Collection of Critical Essays.* New York: Doubleday, 1973.

———. "A More Severe Morality: Nietzsche's Affirmative Ethics" in *Nietzsche as Affirmative Thinker.* Y. Yovel, ed. Dordrecht: Nijhoff, 1986, pp.69–89.

——— and K. Higgins. *Reading Nietzsche.* New York and London: Oxford University Press, 1988.

———. "Nietzsche *ad hominem*: Perspectivism, Personality, and *Ressentiment*" in *Cambridge Companion to Nietzsche*. B. Magnus and K. Higgins, eds. Cambridge: Cambridge University Press, 1996, pp.180–222.

———. *The Joy of Philosophy*. Oxford: Oxford University Press, 1999.

——— and Kathleen Higgins, eds. *What Nietzsche* Really *Said*. New York: Schocken Books, 2000.

Stack, George. *Nietzsche and Emerson: An Elective Affinity*. Athens, Ohio: Ohio University Press, 1992.

Stendhal. *Scarlet and Black*. M. Shaw, trans. London: Penguin, 1953.

Strong, Tracy. *Friedrich Nietzsche and the Politics of Transfiguration*. Berkeley: University of California Press, 1975.

Sullivan, Roger J. *Immanuel Kant's Moral Theory*. Cambridge: Cambridge University Press, 1989.

Taine, Hippolyte. *History of English Literature*. Henry Van Laun, trans. New York: Colonial Press, 1900.

Thatcher, David. "*Zur Genealogie der Moral*: Some Textual Annotations." *Nietzsche-Studien*, 1989, vol. 18, pp.587–99.

Thiele, Leslie Paul. *Friedrich Nietzsche and the Politics of the Soul*. Princeton, N.J.: Princeton University Press, 1990.

Ueberweg, Friedrich. *History of Philosophy, from Thales to the Present Time*. Geo. S. Morris, trans. New York: Charles Scribner's Sons, 1871.

Young, Julian. *Nietzsche's Philosophy of Art*. Cambridge: Cambridge University Press, 1992.

Index

H

I

J

K

L

M

N

O

P

STUDIES IN THEORETICAL AND APPLIED ETHICS

Sherwin Klein, *General Editor*

This series invites book manuscripts and proposals in English on either theoretical or applied ethics. Books submitted on traditional moral philosophers or on one or more ethical problems they have considered are welcome. However, authors should demonstrate strong connections between historical and contemporary philosophical concerns in ethics. Preference will be given to works that deal with perennial philosophical issues in ethics in an original, clear, and scholarly manner rather than manuscripts which have historical significance alone. Books that approach applied ethics, for example, business and biomedical ethics, from a philosophical perspective are also welcome. Manuscripts should display expertise in both philosophy and the areas illuminated by the philosophical insights.

Please send manuscripts and proposals with author's vitae to

Sherwin Klein
Edward Williams College
Fairleigh Dickinson University
150 Kotte Place
Hackensack, NJ 07601

To order other books in this series, please contact our Customer Service Department:

(800) 770-LANG (within the U.S.)
(212) 647-7706 (outside the U.S.)
(212) 647-7707 FAX

Or browse online by series:

www.peterlangusa.com